The Food Lover's Guide to the Real New York

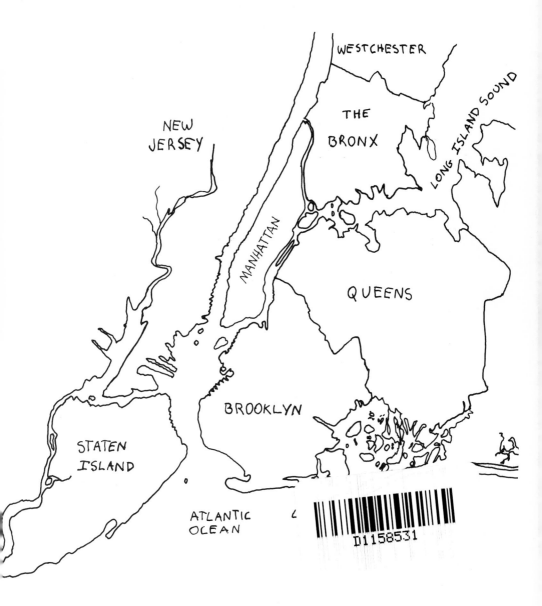

WESTCHESTER

NEW JERSEY

THE BRONX

LONG ISLAND SOUND

MANHATTAN

QUEENS

BROOKLYN

STATEN ISLAND

ATLANTIC OCEAN

The Food Lover's
New
5 Boroughs of
Markets

Myra Alperson   Mark Clifford

Based on the excursions of Hungry Pedalers Gourmet Bicycle Tours, Inc.
Photographs by **Erica Lansner** and **Amalie Rothschild**
Maps by **Sheila McManus** and **Howard Scherzer**
Illustrations by **Sheila McManus**

Guide to the Real York

Ethnic Restaurants, and Shops

Prentice Hall Press • New York

SHEILA McMANUS

Published by Prentice Hall Press
A Division of Simon & Schuster, Inc.
Gulf+Western Building
One Gulf+Western Plaza
New York, NY   10023

PRENTICE HALL PRESS is a trademark of Simon & Schuster, Inc.

Library of Congress Cataloging-in-Publication Data
Alperson, Myra
The food lover's guide to the real New York.

Includes index.
1. Restaurants, lunch rooms, etc.—New York (N.Y.)—
Directories. I. Clifford, Mark, 1957- . II. Title.
TX907.A377 1987   647′.95747′1   86-22718
ISBN 0-13-323189-5

Designed by Joseph E. Baron

Manufactured in the United States of America

10 9 8 7 6 5 4 3 2 1

First Edition

Acknowledgments

Special thanks from the authors to our gifted editor, Gareth Esersky, whose wit, patience, and insights nurtured this book . . . and to our agent, Nancy Trichter, who sold our proposal faster than it takes to bicycle from Manhattan to Flushing; to Howard Scherzer, who has been a constant inspiration to us and who deserves credit for the name Hungry Pedalers; to talented photographers Erica Lansner and Amalie Rothschild, who captured the neighborhood details that help make this book special; to Sheila McManus, designer of the original Hungry Pedalers logo, for her spirited drawings and maps; to designer Joe Baron and production editor Tracy Behar, who put everything together; and to the shopkeepers and restaurant owners throughout New York's five boroughs without whom this book could not exist.

Contents

Introduction

The popular image of New York is one of skyscrapers and pulsing crowds in a maze of steel, glass, and concrete. It is an image of chic museums, arty boutiques, and expensive restaurants. It is the borough of Manhattan and it is a cliché.

We want to show you the city beyond the cliché. The real New York is a cluster of Asian food stores jammed onto Flushing's Main Street; it is sausages and dried fish hanging in Brighton Beach shops where customers speak Russian and Yiddish; it is Hassidic Jews in fur hats and caftans continuing centuries-old customs that they've transplanted from Hungary to Williamsburg. The real New York is homestyle spicy collard greens and sweet potato pie served at a family-run restaurant in Harlem. It's a Polish restaurant in Greenpoint with cold fruit soup; the real New York is smoked mozzarella, fresh lard bread, and zucchini blossoms in an Italian enclave in the Bronx.

This New York, you'll discover, thrives beyond Wall Street's high-finance canyons and midtown's corporate boardrooms in the neighborhoods peopled by immigrants new and old. It's a New York of corner luncheonettes and candy stores, one that is forever the same yet always changing. Where Irish or Germans dominated a generation or two ago today there are Indians, Koreans, Greeks, Russians, and Latin Americans. Where there were cabbage and potatoes, now there are *empanadas* and *bistec a caballo*. Blessed with the greatest variety of food ever baked, boiled, sautéed, or fried in one city, New York's neighborhoods draw pilgrims in search of epicurean adventure. Words like *shashlik, felafel, roti, samosa, polenta,* and *spanakopita* are becoming as much a part of New York's food vocabulary as roast beef and potatoes.

We founded the Hungry Pedalers Gourmet Bicycle Tours in 1983 to explore the kaleidoscope of cultures that lies beyond mid- and downtown Manhattan. Along with Howard Scherzer, our colleague, mapmaker, and geologist, we've shown thousands of people that cycling is one of the most intimate and pleasurable ways to explore the nooks and crannies of this forever fascinating and changing city. Admittedly, the idea of bicycling in New York strikes some people as lunacy, but we hope that you'll use the tours listed in the back of this book to learn that it needn't be. For those of you who don't cycle, we've designed this book to make those neighborhoods accessible to you.

Whether by bike, car, bus, or subway, travel to New York's neighborhoods with the sense of exploration you would take to a foreign country. With that spirit, you'll rediscover that breaking bread and lifting a toast with a stranger plants the roots of intimacy. A shared meal bridges the distance between cultures. New York has a treasure unparalleled in history: its stunning diversity of people. With this book and a sense of adventure you can unearth secrets greater than those locked in any museum.

Remember, when exploring an unfamiliar neighborhood, bring along a good map and a friend.

We hope you enjoy the restaurants and markets we've recommended, but we're sure there are others that you think are terrific. If this is the case, please write to us, in care of the publisher.

Bon voyage and bon appétit!

—Myra Alperson
Mark Clifford

BROOKLYN

Between New York and Brooklyn, there is nothing in common, either in object, interest, or feeling—nothing that even apparently tends to their connexion, unless it be the waters that flow between them. And even those waters, instead of, in fact, uniting them, form a barrier between them which, however frequently passed, still form and must forever continue to form an unsurmountable obstacle to their union."
—General Jeremiah Johnson, 1833

Brooklyn was a sleepy village on the other side of the East River when General Johnson voiced his outrage at its proposed incorporation into New York. Today, Brooklyn is where New York lives in endlessly stretching blocks of houses fronted by thumbnail-size front lawns, where New York plays stickball in the street, ambles to the corner, and lies on the wide beach. Brooklyn is a sprawling tumble of colors, cultures, and classes, but for all that it hasn't changed: It is as much at odds with "the city" as in General Johnson's time. That sense of otherness is as palpable as the spicy smell of pizza and sausages in Bensonhurst, the sound of reggae music in Bedford-Stuyvesant, or the sight of vat upon vat of glistening green and black olives in shops on Atlantic Avenue.

You can eat kosher food in Manhattan, but only in Brooklyn can you eat it at a lunch counter surrounded by bearded, black-suited Hassidim around the corner from their temples. In Brooklyn you can sip vodka in a Russian tearoom on the boardwalk and watch the ebb and flow of the Atlantic tide. It's in Brooklyn that giddy dancers twirl in Russian and Polish nightclubs where tables moan under the weight of food. In Brooklyn you'll find scores of Caribbean *roti* stands serving curried chicken and goat to hundreds of thousands of residents. The Syrians and Yemenis proffer garlic-laced *babaganouj* and *tahini* on Atlantic Avenue and Court Street while a few blocks away the bakers and butchers of Carroll Gardens still make breads and sausages the way their parents and grandparents did in Sicily or Bari.

If the "home borough" were still a separate city, its 2.2 million residents would make it the fourth largest in the United States. In the dense blocks stretching from the rolling glacial hills in the north to sandy southern beaches, still live the Jews, Italians, and Irish whose parents and grandparents made up the flood tide of immigrants at the turn of the century who stamped twentieth-century New York with its character.

Archetypal Brooklynites had harsh voices, abrasive accents, and a fierce loyalty to the Dodgers. The departure of the Dodgers for Los Angeles in 1957 helped erode that caricature, as have new immigrants—from the Caribbean, Russia, Poland, and scores of other countries. Brooklyn's dozens of neighborhoods now include the largest concentration of Caribbean islanders outside the West Indies, the largest Russian settlement outside the Soviet Union, and the largest Jewish community outside Israel. There are surprises: A Syrian-Jewish community thrives here, as does a Christian-Arab one; Brooklyn is also the land of *Saturday Night Fever* disco-delirium, where young Italian Americans in designer jeans stroll beside their black-garbed grandparents. Of course, it is a borough tied to the ocean, so fishing boats still steam out of Sheepshead Bay before dawn for the deep Atlantic waters, and the crowds still flock to Coney Island for the beach, hot dogs, and honky-tonk.

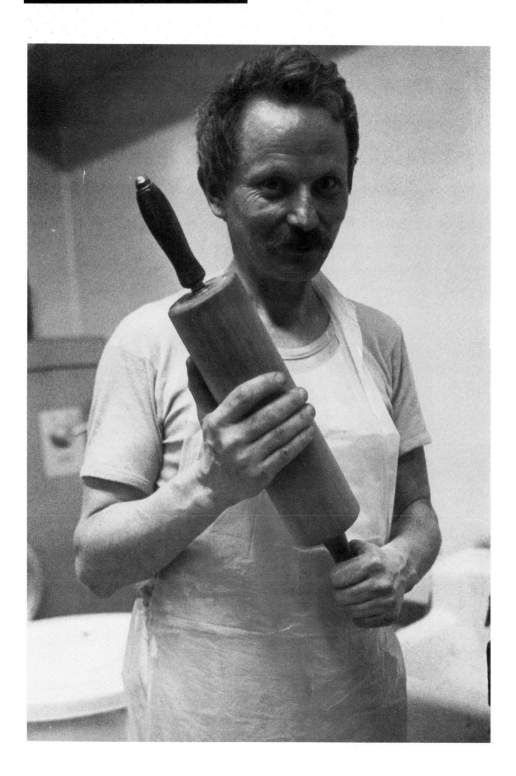

ATLANTIC AVENUE: BABAGANOUJ IN BROOKLYN

To Get There

By subway: Take the A, E, or F train to Jay St./Borough Hall or the 2, 3, 4, 5, R, or J train to Borough Hall/Court St.; walk south on Court St. about six blocks to Atlantic Ave.

By car: Exit the Manhattan or Brooklyn bridges at Adams St., turn right on Tillary St., left on Court St. to Atlantic Ave.

By bike: From Manhattan, cross the Brooklyn Bridge and continue until the bike ramp ends at Adams and Tillary Sts.; turn right at Tillary St. and make a sharp left at Court St.; continue to Atlantic Ave. (Also see Hungry Pedalers directions from Prospect Park area in "Brighton Beach K'nish K'nosh" on page 232.)

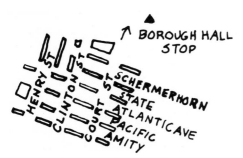

BOROUGH HALL STOP

▲ = A, 2, 3, 4, 5
TRAIN

Belly dancing in Brooklyn? You can buy the pantaloons, the finger cymbals, the bras, the tambourines—in short, everything but the rhythm—right around the corner from Borough Hall. Some of the old-timers still know this area as Little Syria—so dubbed decades ago by the old *Brooklyn Eagle*—but now it's expanded into a polyglot Arab neighborhood. It's a tightly packed stretch of Atlantic Avenue and several blocks of Court Street near Brooklyn Heights, which has been dominated by the Levantine influence since the first Syrian families settled there around the turn of the century. And it's brought a fascinating touch to an area with a rich American literary tradition and some of New York's most exquisite architecture. Once home to Walt Whitman, Hart Crane, Thomas Wolfe, and Truman Capote, Brooklyn Heights today claims Norman Mailer. South of Atlantic Avenue are the historic districts of Cobble Hill and Carroll Gardens. These areas of lovely brownstone homes and converted carriage houses along quiet, narrow, tree-lined streets are relative newcomers to landmarking, and worth a stroll—which you'll probably need after dining on Lebanese *kibbee* (ground lamb flavored with cinnamon and pine nuts) or Moroccan *couscous* (a pasta stew in a meat, fish, or vegetarian base), or cheating with a piece of honey-soaked *baklava* baked in layers of fillo dough and butter for dessert. Don't miss the Brooklyn Heights Promenade, which you can reach by heading north up Clinton Street and turning left on Remsen Street, to the end—a five-minute walk: It affords stunning views of the lower Manhattan skyline any time of day or evening.

Even Atlantic Avenue itself has changed. Once rather bedraggled and neglected—except for the continuous presence of the Middle Eastern stores—new boutiques, antique shops, and fancy restaurants compete for precious space.

MARKETS

By far the best-known market here is **Sahadi Importing Co.** (187 Atlantic Ave., Tel.: 718/624-4550), which in recent years has not only physically expanded to include an importing arm for nonedibles from the Middle East, but has also widened its repertoire of foodstuffs. Co-owner Charles Sahadi, grandnephew of founder Abraham Sahadi, supervises the hectic operation of what remains a family business. On Saturday, the busiest day, we suggest you get there early or be prepared to wait. As a third-generation Lebanese American (Lebanon was part of Syria when the first Christian Arabs emigrated), Mr. Sahadi has reached out to accommodate third-generation Americanized tastes, especially as the area has attracted more young professionals with eclectic palates. So you'll find boxes of tortellini and imported European preserves here, and other non-Mediterranean "gourmet" foods, as well as the usual pistachio nuts, almonds, walnuts, and pine nuts; bins of different kinds of rice; spices—zatar, saffron, oregano, sage, peppers, cumin, and coriander; the rosewater, anise, and orange blossom flavorings; barrels of olives (more than a dozen kinds); jars of coffee beans and tea leaves (like chamomile, fresh mint, rose hips, linden, hibiscus); containers of *tahini* (sesame paste); a half-dozen varieties of fresh *halvah* (a sweet sesame confection), as well as imported halvah from Greece and Lebanon; dried fruits; and honey-soaked pastries. Sahadi's also sells expensive backgammon games; Middle Eastern drums called "durbeks" and the various accoutrements required by belly dancers; rugs; a wide range of cooking utensils, from wooden mortars and pestles to more expensive brass versions; many examples of the "couscousier," the colander-with-double-boiler used to prepare this famous dish; and various ceramic coffee and glass tea sets so that servings of Arabic coffee or steamed mint tea can be savored in just the right way. The store also has a good selection of cookbooks, including some on French, Greek, and Armenian cuisine, as well as Middle Eastern cookery.

The saga of the Sahadis mirrors that of Atlantic Avenue's merchant families. The original A. Sahadi & Co. (which still packages food under that label) was founded in lower Manhattan around 1898, when the intersection of Washington and Rector Streets was the crowded hub of New York's immigrant Syrian colony. Most of the newcomers were Christians from the Levant who fled the oppression of Ottoman occupiers in their homeland. (Sephardic Jews with stores along Kings Highway share a similar history—see "Kosher Brooklyn," page 49.) Although the immigrant families moved on to better housing, mostly in Brooklyn, many merchants remained, and the Sahadis were among the holdouts. They finally left in the late 1940s, when construction of the Brooklyn-Battery Tunnel resulted in the razing of their neighborhood. Their most practical choice then was to join their compatriots on Atlantic Avenue, and here they thrived.

Charles Sahadi and his younger brother Robert close their store on Sundays—unlike many of the other neighborhood shops—because their thriving six-day business, including a substantial mail-order operation, makes up for the lost Sunday revenue. In early 1986, the Sahadis renovated the entire store, taking over the adjacent annex, which formerly served as an office. Even so, if you find Sahadi's too crowded for your taste, or if you come by on a Sunday, you'll still have an excellent choice of markets. **Shammas & Co.** (197 Atlantic Ave., Tel.: 718/855-2455), and **Malko Bros.–Cassatly Co.** grocers (199 Atlantic Ave., Tel.: 718/855-2455), are on the same block. Across the street, a fine selection of cooking essentials is available at **Oriental Pastry & Grocery, Co.** (170 Atlantic Ave., Tel.: 718/875-7687), which also has its own bakery.

We like the way Shammas has its vats of olives, shelves of olive oils, and vast selection of spices, nuts, sweets, and dried beans neatly displayed so that you can get a close look at what is on sale and not feel too crowded. The storekeepers are friendly and eager to bargain with you, especially if you inquire about some of the more elaborate cooking items or furniture,

like the small smoking tables of inlaid wood and mother-of-pearl, which several stores sell. These tables, with hexagonal or octagonal table tops, are imported from Syria and range in price from about $90 to $250.

At Oriental Pastry, a huge inventory is crammed into a smaller space, but the selection and quality are high. Here, in addition to barrels of spices and such specialties as dried okra, you can also find myrrh and frankincense, the biblical incenses, loofah mitts, and other natural household products. In the rear, owner Gary Moustapha, an energetic man with a thick mustache, vends his freshly baked baklava and other pastries, including a new concoction called "carrot delight," which he sells in small cubes for 20 cents. But you absolutely shouldn't miss the cheese-and-honey pastries (*halawa be aljeben* and *koonafa be aljeben; jeben* is Arabic for cheese) that are his specialties and are only available on weekends. The sweet cheese filling is homemade, and Mr. Moustapha declines to part with the recipe. "But you can always buy it if you come early enough," he smiles. Mr. Moustapha also has several cookbooks on hand; we recommend Helen Corey's *Art of Syrian Cookery.*

A new addition to the neighborhood, definitely worth a visit, is **Soueidan Corp.** (155 Atlantic Ave., Tel.: 718/330-0415), a combination butcher, bakery, and grocery open 24 hours. The central aisle is filled with imports from Lebanon—packaged vegetables, sauces, soups, and condiments, as well as vats of olives, nuts, and candies. (A line of American products is also available.) You can also buy *halal*

Bagging almonds at A. Sahadi & Co.

meat, beef acceptable in the Muslim diet, which owner Anis Soueidan also describes as kosher meat because the slaughtering process is virtually the same. A full selection of sweet pastries and breads is also available and one of our favorite purchases was a jar of fig marmalade from Lebanon, sweet, thick, and subtly flavored with anise.

RESTAURANTS

Budget-conscious food lovers have been dining on Atlantic Avenue for years, and with good reason. Restaurants with Middle Eastern cuisine, including several on Court Street, have long offered healthy, substantial meals at reasonable prices. Most prominent among them are **Moroccan Star** (205 Atlantic Ave., Tel.: 718/596-1919), **Dar Lebnan** (151 Atlantic Ave., Tel.: 718/596-9215), **Son of the Sheik** (165 Atlantic Ave., Tel.: 718/625-4023), **Adnan** (129 Atlantic Ave., Tel.: 718/625-2115), and **Almontaser** (218 Court St., Tel.: 718/624-9267). Appetizers like babaganouj (grilled or smoked eggplant with tahini, garlic, lemon juice, and olive oil), *hummus* (spiced, mashed chick-peas with tahini), and the now ubiquitous *felafel* (fried, spiced chick-pea balls) have been staples on menus here long before they were popular in Manhattan's gourmet delis. *Tabouli*, salad made with cracked wheat, scallions, parsley, and fresh mint, or Lebanese cucumber salad is a refreshing prelude to hot entrées. The most popular dishes tend to be beef, chicken, or lamb kebabs, kibbee, *glabas* (spiced lamb with green pepper), and, in some restaurants, curry dishes. You can expect to spend from $5 to $9 for the main dishes; lunch prices are a few dollars less. At restaurants like Moroccan Star and Adnan, French and North African cuisine is also touted, so you will find broiled fish dishes or variations of couscous.

Sido Restaurant (151 Atlantic Ave., Tel.: 718/237-4019) opened here in October 1986, but has a long-established branch in Manhattan's Kips Bay neighborhood. Though the restaurant is relatively luxurious, with wood paneling and fine paintings of the major Muslim capitals of the Middle East, the menu is (for now, anyway) both low-key and low-price. Probably the best deal is the Sido dinner, which includes soup (lentil, bean, or vegetable), an appetizer platter of hummus, babaganouj, and stuffed grape leaves, a shish kebab entrée, dessert (custard or pastry), and coffee, all for less than $14.

BAKERIES

Atlantic Avenue has two main bakeries: **Near East** (183 Atlantic Ave., Tel.: 718/875-0016) is reached by a steep stairway to the basement, where the selling area is small (and often crowded), and the baking goes on in the rear. Specialties are the sweet baklava (you can buy containers of party-size baklava) and meat or spinach pies, which often sell out early in the day. The bakery has been operated by the Kanatous family for about 30 years. **Damascus Bakery** (195 Atlantic Ave., Tel.: 718/855-1456) is one of the metropolitan area's largest suppliers of pita bread, the circular "pocket" bread now popular for sandwich-making as well as for dips. You can choose from five different kinds of pitas: plain (white flour), whole wheat, sesame, onion, and pumpernickel. You can

ABDUL NAJJAR

Abdul Najjar came to New York from Lebanon in 1972 and for many years operated the superb Café Tripoli at 163 Atlantic Avenue, where he served homemade Middle Eastern dips and salads, pastries, and ice cream, including such mouth-watering flavors as cashew, apricot, and cantaloupe. The café closed in late 1985, but Mr. Najjar's recipes survive. Here are a few:

BABAGANOUJ

1 large eggplant
1 or 2 cloves garlic
lemon juice
tahini

olive oil
paprika
chopped parsley

Either charbroil (smoke) the eggplant for 15 minutes or bake it unwrapped for about 1 hour at 400° F. Skin the eggplant and mash it or put it through a meat grinder (as Mr. Najjar does). Mash the garlic and mix it into the eggplant with 1 cup lemon juice, or to taste. Add about ¼ pound tahini and mix well by hand. Just before serving, add olive oil to taste. Garnish with paprika and parsley.

FOOL (FAVA BEANS)

Mr. Najjar uses canned fava beans, adds a small amount of water, and cooks the beans over high heat until just slightly hot. He then adds mashed garlic, salt, olive oil, and lemon juice to taste.

BAKLAVA (In the chef's own words: "The first time, very, very hard—the second time, very easy.")

2 pounds of fillo dough (available in the
   neighborhood, fresh or frozen)
1½ pounds of ground walnuts

butter
sugar
lemon juice

Put five sheets of fillo dough on each side of the baking tray and lightly pour melted butter over them, enough to cover. Mix the walnuts with "a drop" of white sugar and spread over the fillo. Cover the mixture with more fillo dough and add melted butter as follows: 10 sheets of dough; butter; 7 sheets of dough; butter; 7 sheets of dough; butter. Bake for 1½ hours at 350° F. Before serving, cut baklava into portions and pour on more butter. Then pour on a simple syrup coating, which is made with 3 cups of sugar cooked in water with a drop of citric acid or lemon juice. The sugar should cook until it boils. Makes one 9-by-12-inch tray of baklava.

also purchase *marcouk*, a paper-thin folding bread used in Arab cuisine to pick up food in lieu of utensils, and the luscious zatar bread, a flat, circular bread flavored with zatar (thyme), sesame, and olive oil. The popular *lahem jahne*—sometimes nicknamed Lebanese pizza—is a concoction of spicy chopped lamb on round bread, which is best eaten when hot. (Damascus has a microwave oven on the premises.) *Ma'amul* (date pastries), *brazet* (sesame cookies), and *goraybe* (powdery, light, almond-flavored, ring-shaped cookies) are among the not-so-rich specialties you may elect if you find the baklava too buttery and sweet.

Atlantic Avenue is, of course, more than a giant *souk*—its cultural life lives on, too. Although the old-timers may no longer live here, many recent immigrants from the Middle East call this area home, and a new Institute for the Propagation of Islam at 143 State Street, one block north of Atlantic Avenue, serves many new residents. Its Arabic, English, and Islamic school was founded in part so that the many Yemeni children living on and near Court Street could retain their culture, even as they become Americanized. Along Court Street, Yemeni businesses and social clubs—with no women in sight—are the signs of this new Middle Eastern community.

A tour of Atlantic Avenue won't be complete until you've spent time at **Rashid Sales Co.** (191 Atlantic Ave., Tel.: 718/852-3295). Owner Stan Rashid is a former schoolteacher who opened the business to provide Atlantic Avenue's shoppers with Arab-language magazines, audiocassettes and records of music from the entire Middle East (including Armenia and Greece), and videocassettes from Egypt. You'll see Korans and fundamentalist Islamic tracts on one shelf and, nearby, Arab-language magazines—like the Arabic *Elle*, for instance—with attractive blond models on the cover sporting the latest European fashions. Scholarly journals on Palestine studies or related fields are also available, along with current Arab-American and foreign newspapers. There is a fine selection of cookbooks, too, but few are in English. Among the latter are a $4 paperback (with frequently incomplete recipe directions) and a comprehensive hardcover costing more than $20. You can also buy key chains, T-shirts, or decals with the names of countries with ties to Arab culture or the Mediterranean. A first visit to Rashid's can be overwhelming. The Middle East is dense with different traditions, and the store attempts to reach out to all of them. Although you may feel a bit confused and daunted at first, spend time at the store and ask questions. An hour or more at Rashid's can provide the first step to grasping the complexity of the Middle East—and it's only minutes away from the Brooklyn Bridge.

AFRICA IN BROOKLYN

To Get There

 By subway: Take the IRT 2, 3, 4, or 5 to Nevins St., walk back on Flatbush Ave. and bear left on the Fulton Mall, then make a left for 1½ blocks on Bond St.

 By car, bike, and foot: From Middle Eastern Atlantic Ave. (at Court St.): Go west on Atlantic Ave. for 5 blocks to Bond St., then turn left for 2 blocks.

Unless you're familiar with West African cuisine, you may not know what to do with foodstuffs such as stockfish, smoked deer, cassava leaf, plantain flour, palm oil, and spices on sale at the small **West African Business Enterprises** shop in downtown Brooklyn (42 Bond St., Tel.: 718/875-0082). But if you've got the curiosity and the time, it's worth a visit; you can walk there from Middle Eastern Atlantic Avenue in about 10 minutes and, of course, it's quicker by bike or car. Between customers who come in to make purchases and discuss news of home, owners Ivy Zoe Cooper, a Liberian, and Amadou Teré, from the Ivory Coast, will explain what the foods are and how they are used: large cans of palm nut concentrate for soups and stews and large cans of garden eggs (a vegetable), both from Ghana; *kola* nuts, a stimulant; dried shrimp; hot pepper sauces; and more. When you first get there, don't be put off by the wares for sale outside the store, which doubles as a gift shop. Here you can find American standards such as pocketbooks, bookbags, inexpensive jewelry, scarves, sunglasses, earmuffs, hats, gloves, batteries, pens, and toys. Inside, the wares are more interesting. Besides the food, there are shelves of lovely, colorful cotton fabrics, mostly from the Ivory Coast, and some African-style garments that have been assembled in Liberia, Nigeria, and the United States. You'll also find wood carvings; jewelry made of beads, shells, or copper (some African, some American); cloth dolls; and African magazines.

BRIGHTON BEACH K'NISH K'NOSH

The ocean always lures city dwellers, and New Yorkers swarm to the waterside on weekend afternoons. Some may go to the Caribbean, some to the Hamptons, but those who really want to play at the seaside need go no farther than the boardwalk-laced beaches of southern Brooklyn.

Coney Island, Brighton Beach, Sheepshead Bay, and Manhattan Beach make up the city's finest ocean area. You can buy big, cheap bluefish on the sidewalk in Sheepshead Bay from a full-bearded, rubber-booted fisherman who's just stepped off his boat; drink vodka in a teahouse on the Brighton boardwalk as creased Russian women swathed in black stroll past;

sip a lime-cherry rickey and eat knishes at the incomparable Mrs. Stahl's under the el; ride the old wood-frame roller coaster and nosh the original Nathan's frank at Coney Island.

Once a real island, all that separates Coney Island (which also includes Brighton Beach and Manhattan Beach and makes up one edge of Sheepshead Bay) from the mainland today is a fetid creek trickling along the auto-clogged Belt Parkway. Yet the Coney Island area is still a world apart—part honky-tonk, part seaside bathing beach, part immigrant neighborhood, and part fishing port.

Sausage slicer.

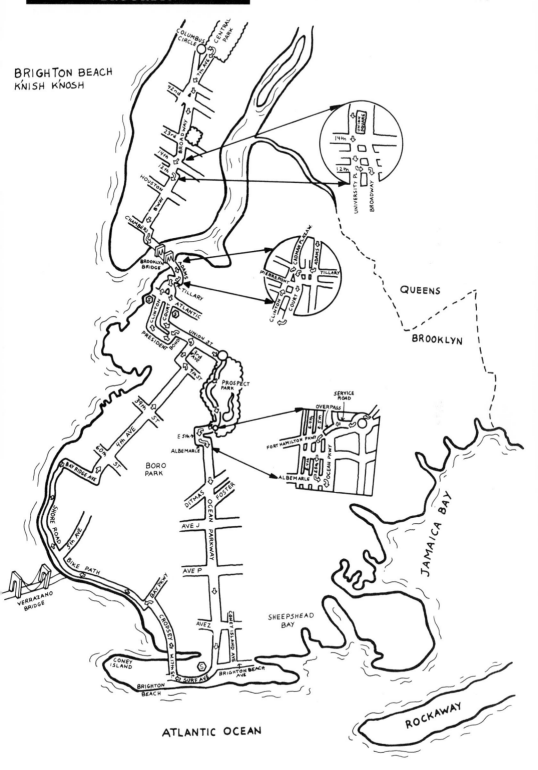

BRIGHTON BEACH
KNISH KNOSH

QUEENS

BROOKLYN

PROSPECT PARK

BORO PARK

JAMAICA BAY

VERRAZANO BRIDGE

SHEEPSHEAD BAY

CONEY ISLAND

BRIGHTON BEACH

ROCKAWAY

ATLANTIC OCEAN

BRIGHTON BEACH

To Get There

By subway: Take the D train and get off at Ocean Pkwy./Brighton Beach Ave. or Brighton Beach/Brighton 6th St. The Brighton 6th St. stop is next to Mrs. Stahl's and is at the eastern end of the Brighton Beach Ave. shopping strip.

By car: Take Shore Parkway to Ocean Parkway. Turn right on Ocean Parkway and drive half a mile to Brighton Beach Avenue, which is under the el. Park here. You are at the western edge of the shopping area.

By bike: See the instructions for "Brighton Beach K'nish K'nosh" on page 232.

BRIGHTON BEACH
▲ = D IND TRAIN

Brighton Beach, once a rather exclusive bathing enclave at the eastern end of the Coney Island boardwalk, is now a thriving Russian neighborhood. A walk under the clattering el, past the fruit stands spilling out into the streets, past kosher butchers and dairy restaurants, past Russian grocers and restaurants, is a walk back in time to the tumult of the Lower East Side a half-century ago.

After the el passes overhead on Brighton Beach Avenue you may hear the tight-throated wail of a Russian singer pouring out of a record store. Old men in dark, shapeless suits shuffle along the street. The neighborhood became known as "Odessa by the Sea" with the arrival of thousands of Russian Jews who emigrated during the U.S.-Soviet détente of the 1970s. Roughly half of the 90,000 Russian Jews who have come to the United States have settled in the New York area. More

Selling pirogen under the el.

than 10,000 of them are in Brighton Beach; the rest are concentrated in Queens (Rego Park and Forest Hills), Manhattan (Washington Heights), the Bronx (Parkchester), and also in the Flatbush and Borough Park sections of Brooklyn.

Most of the new arrivals to Brighton Beach are secular Jews, a fact reflected in the foods—ham and pork sausages—and the Russian gifts, such as painted wooden spoons and wooden dolls. The kosher butchers and dairy restaurants up and down Brighton Beach Avenue are holdovers from the earlier Jewish neighborhood, the one in which Neil Simon grew up and later memorialized in his *Brighton Beach Memoirs*. Although many parents send their children to yeshivas rather than to local public schools, this is a largely nonreligious Russian-Jewish community overlaid on an aging second- and third-generation Jewish-American population.

Brighton Beach bakers take a breather.

That makes for some changes. "Even the Jewish, they don't eat kosher anymore," complains Sam Taub at **Feldman & Taub**, a kosher butcher on Brighton Beach Avenue. Yet Brighton Beach still manages to support three kosher butchers.

RESTAURANTS

The best way to step inside Russian-American life is to spend a weekend evening at one of the Russian restaurants along Brighton Beach Avenue, such as **Odessa** (1113 Brighton Beach Ave. [BBA], Tel.: 718/332-3223) or **National** (273 BBA, Tel.: 718/646-1225). The decor runs to garish, with smoky mirrors and gaudy colors dominant. Long linen-decked tables line the rooms. Don't arrive too early: Even at 9 P.M. there likely won't be more than a handful of diners in the National, which holds 200 people. (Odessa gets going a bit earlier than the National.) But come prepared for a long haul. You can order a la carte, although you're better off ordering the prix fixe dinner. (You're certainly encouraged to: One night at the National, the waiter only managed to rustle up one dog-eared menu.) So go with the buffet, which runs between $26 and $35, depending on the restaurant and the musicians. The price includes your music charge, a bottle of vodka for every four people (you're not obligated to drink it all!), and an assortment of two score dishes.

Cold appetizers come first, two trays of them, with waiters piling dish on top of dish to fit them all onto the table. Horse-milk cheese fights for table space with beef tongue, homemade ham, and mushrooms pickled with dill. Salmon roe and smoked

Under the el on Brighton Beach Avenue.

fish (sturgeon, whitefish, and salmon) will probably look familiar. Baked eggplant smeared with a garlic-nut sauce will delight the more adventurous, while some might feel like sticking with the tried-and-true gefilte fish and cold salads like herring, egg, and turkey. "In about one-and-half hour come the hot appetizers," warns the waiter as the diners gape in amazement. There's a gap in the translation: "Appetizer" doesn't mean in English what it means in Russian.

Before you've made much of a dent in the appetizers the band will be playing, and you'll notice that the restaurant is quickly filling up. The musicians are pros—party bands used to playing the circuit of weddings, birthdays, balls, and, perhaps, bar mitzvahs. They play a whole range of American and Russian pop songs (including the Russian original of "Those Were the Days"). They're as infatuated as an American teenager with their synthesizers—although much more competent—and they fondly show off electronic effects like echoes. There's usually a female singer—and sometimes a pair of short-skirted sultry Russians. Or, you might find a Polish singer performing, and tables of Polish revelers scattered throughout the crowd. There are birthday and anniversary parties at the long tables, and perhaps you'll see a crowd celebrating a wedding. This is a big night out, and the Russians are determined to make the most of it. The sequined-gowned ladies swirl around the dance floor with their dark-suited partners as the band plays faster, the house lights dim, and the dancing lights flash. It's tempting to surrender to the

Taking an order.

frenzy of the dance and the flush of the vodka, but remember there are still the hot appetizers and the main course to come.

"Here the hot appetizers," announces the waiter, and the food-laden platters descend: stewed chicken and ribs with potatoes, *pirogen*, popovers . . . and remember, these are allegedly appetizers. Fortunately, the main meat dishes are served in small portions—roast chicken, lamb kebab, and chicken kebab. But they're a rich postscript to the appetizers. After all this, and coffee and dessert, you can go out into the cool ocean air, the quiet street, and stroll along the boardwalk by the beach.

Other, smaller restaurants include **Primorski** (lunch specials start at $3.99) across the street from National at 282 BBA (Tel.: 718/891-3111); **Kavkas** (a.k.a. **Kaukaz**), 405 BBA (Tel.: 718/891-5400; **Café Zodiac**, 309 BBA (Tel.: 718/891-2000); and, for a down-home informal place, **Café Armenia** (daytime only, no entertainment, Tel.: 718/743-2444), on Brighton Fourth St., just off Brighton Beach Avenue. Armenia is a homey place, serving mostly coffees and teas and some stews and soups. Almost everything on the menu is less than $5 and it's a great place to stop if you're at the beach. **Gas-**

tronom Moscow, 31-52 Brighton 6 St. (Tel.: 718/934-8027), is a boardwalk café, serving tea and vodka with a view of the ocean. It's something of a somewhat disheveled, dim place, a bit of the old world on the western edge of the Atlantic. Gastronom is best in the spring and fall, when the beach crowd has retreated.

The Russians dominate Brighton Beach now, but traces of the area's earlier Jewish heritage remain. There are, of course, the dairy restaurants and the kosher butchers left over from the heyday Brighton Beach/Coney Island enjoyed after the extension of the subways to the area in the 1920s, until the decades after World War II, when many families began moving to the suburbs. But, above all, there is **Mrs. Stahl's Knishes** (1001 Brighton Beach Ave., Tel.: 718/648-0210), an eatery that dishes out overstuffed knishes. Packed with fillings like kasha, potato, spinach, cherries, and cheese, these knishes are the kinds that ex–New Yorkers pine for. More than a half-century old, Mrs. Stahl's commands a following that lures travelers and natives alike. "It's an everyday occurrence that people stop in here on the way from the airport," says Les Green, whose family recently took over the store. "The other day a guy came in, I think he said he was a deputy consul general. He'd spent the last three years in Beirut and said he'd been dreaming about our knishes the whole time. This was the first stop he made after the airport." Sip a lime-cherry rickey or chew on a potato-kasha *pletzel*, and you'll know why Mrs. Stahl's remains a New York archetype and why all those people whose parents and grandparents grew up in Brighton Beach keep coming

Deli counter at M&I International Foods.

back from the suburbs—of New York, Miami, or Los Angeles—for another taste of old New York.

MARKETS

M&I International Foods (249 Brighton Beach Ave., Tel.: 718/648-8847), fondly known as the Zabar's of Brighton Beach, features a bounty of foods imported from Eastern Europe and the Soviet Union. Russian women crowd aisles lined with jars of pickled tomatoes, gooseberries, plums, greengages, and currants in syrup; round, Siberia-size loaves of white bread; glistening caviar; fruit nectars from Yugoslavia; and big glass jars of plump apricots and sour cherries. The women—and the few men among the shoppers—cluster around the meat counters where scores of sausages dangle from the ceiling and bagels are strung up as decorative baubles. It's anyone's guess how many kinds of sausages there are. "If you said we had fifty, sixty kinds of sausages, it would be too little," laughs Sophia Vinokurov, who has run the store with her sister and brother for the past decade. "If you said a hundred kinds, it would be also be too little."

Sausages line one wall, fish another. In another case lie salmon roe, imported Russian caviar, smoked sturgeon, salmon, whitefish, herring, sable, eels, and other fish. The fish, which is cold-smoked at a Russian-run smokehouse in Borough Park, is so prominent because many of Brighton Beach's Russians are from Odessa, a city on the Black Sea whose inhabitants eat a lot of seafood.

M&I opened an upstairs annex in 1983 that is devoted to satisfying the legendary Russian sweet tooth. You'll find a staggering assortment of candies from Western and Eastern Europe, the Soviet Union, and the United States. And, of course, there are pastries and cakes made right in Brighton Beach.

When the store opened in 1975, Brighton Beach was a very different neighborhood, remembers Sophia. "Everyone was very old, the neighborhood was very poor." Although Brighton Beach is a long way from affluent, rents are rising and the thriving commercial activity testifies to the area's resurgence. How much longer it will last is anyone's guess, since many younger people are moving out. "The young people, when they finish school they want to go different places, better to make some money," says Jay, a young Russian who works at Feldman & Taub butchers. "The old people, they just speak Russian and stay here." Although the typical immigrant pattern of assimilation and dispersion may be at work, for now Brighton Beach is a thriving Russian neighborhood.

Don't let all the Russians make you forget about the ocean. Brighton Beach was named after the English seaside resort, and it enjoyed a flurry of popularity in the late nineteenth century as a moderately posh bathing area. One block south of Brighton Beach Avenue is the recently renovated boardwalk, which runs along the beach to Coney Island. At the corner of Coney Island Avenue is the Brighton Beach Baths, a sprawling 15-acre recreational complex for area residents. On the other side of Brighton Beach Avenue are cramped blocks of wood-frame houses, many of them quite badly run-down, although rehabilitation efforts are under way.

CONEY ISLAND

To Get There

By subway: Take the B, F, or N train at all times to the end of the line, Coney Island/Stillwell Ave. You can also take the D train (except weekdays, 6:30 A.M., when it terminates at Brighton Beach); the M train (Mon.–Fri., 6 A.M.–9 P.M. only); or the QB train (P.M. rush hours only).

New York Aquarium: Take the F train at all times to W. 8 St. The D, M and QB trains also stop here during the Coney Island service hours (see above).

The amusement arcade area has lost some of the luster it enjoyed during its heyday as the home of the 5-cent frank, but its funky honky-tonk charm lives on. Stroll along the boardwalk and buy a Hygrade frankfurter at **Gregory & Dave's** nosheria. Wonder at the huge red, white, and blue missile that perches on the top of their stand, where they sell everything from frog legs to pizza to beer. If you're up for it, the rickety wood-frame roller coaster is still a thrill—before you eat, please. Or try a tamer ride, like the Wonder Wheel. Ride the rotating glass donut that travels up and down a shaft for a view of the beach. Or simply wander through the New York Aquarium. Neon, pressed stainless steel, and cotton candy—this is a honky-tonk delight.

RESTAURANTS

The queen of Coney Island restaurants is **Gargiulo's** (2911 15th St., between Mermaid and Neptune, Tel.: 718/266-0906). If you insist on defying the spirit of the place by eating a fancy meal while in Coney Island, you'll do fine at Gargiulo's.

More appropriate, however, is **Nathan's**. Nathan's is Coney Island. At the end of the subway line, Nathan's has been selling all-beef franks since 1916. Back then, a subway ride was 5 cents and so was the hot dog. Today the subway fare is $1 and the hot dog costs $1.30. But it's still the real Nathan's, filled with swarms of beachgoers. Hurry out there, since even Nathan's is endangered by food faddism: The venerable establishment recently put out a cookbook with 150 recipes for the common frank, including hot dogs au vin blanc and hot dogs amandine. Is nothing sacred?

Totonno Pizzeria Napolitano (1524 Neptune, Tel.: 718/372-8606; open Friday, Saturday, and Sunday, only from 2 P.M. until the pizza runs out—which can be as early as 7 P.M.) would be worth a trip even if Coney Island weren't there. This is one of the only pizzerias in New York that use a coal-fired oven (it's hotter and the pizzas are crisper), and it may be the only one that uses fresh mozzarella and freshly chopped garlic on its pizzas. Jerry Peno, whose father, Anthony, started the restaurant (and whose nickname provided the pizzeria's name), refuses to put up any kind of sign announcing the restaurant. "If you don't know we're here after 59 years, we don't deserve to be in business." The walls are framed with old newspapers announcing the end of World War II, and the original blue pressed-tin ceiling is still intact. The pizza is simply incredible.

A sausage seller's work is never done.

SHEEPSHEAD BAY

To Get There

By subway: Take the D, M, or QB train to Sheepshead Bay. Walk east on Neptune Ave. for about five minutes and you'll be on the Bay. (Neptune Ave. becomes Emmons Ave.)

Sheepshead Bay eschews the frivolity of its Coney Island and Brighton Beach neighbors. Sheepshead Bay is knots of old people clustered on park benches by the bay; it's the raspy honking of party fishing boats coming in at midafternoon, or hulking three-foot bluefish sold for $5 each by a bearded fisherman out of his cooler. It's a strip of mostly overpriced restaurants interspersed with abandoned houses, clam bars, and a fast-food joint that proclaims, "We put the knish in the pizza."

RESTAURANTS

All those fishermen tramping off the boats would like you to believe they're here to work, but they're really just out for a good time. Sheepshead Bay is best savored with some clams on the half-shell at **Joe's**

Clam Bar & Restaurant (2009 Emmons Ave., Tel.: 718/646-9375). Choose either the clam bar or the restaurant, depending on your price range and how you're dressed, or have a cup of cappuccino at the **Gangplank** (2020 Emmons Ave., Tel.: 718/332-1919) on the water. The city is planning to develop a waterside complex of shops and restaurants during the next several years, perhaps hoping to spruce up Sheepshead's slightly tawdry seaside demeanor.

Jordon's Lobster Docks is located at Knapp Street and the Belt Parkway (Tel.: 718/934-6300). William Jordon now runs a retail operation not far from the wholesale store his family has operated for years. There's a variety of good seafood at reasonable prices. The best value is lobster: Jordon's tanks hold up to 25,000 pounds of lobster at once!

CROWN HEIGHTS: CARIBBEAN CALYPSO

To Get There

By subway: Take the A or C train to Nostrand Ave. (If it's more convenient, take the 3 or 4 train to Nostrand Ave. or the 2 or 5 train to President St. You'll be on Nostrand Ave. farther along the tour.) Walk south, slightly uphill, along Nostrand Ave. You'll know you're going the right way if the next block is busy Atlantic Ave.; the Long Island Railroad runs overhead. (Atlantic Ave. is the dividing line between Bedford-Stuyvesant and Crown Heights.)

By car: Start at Grand Army Plaza in Brooklyn. Take Eastern Parkway to Nostrand Ave. To go to Stuyvesant Heights Historic District continue on Eastern Parkway. Turn left on Troy. Park on Fulton St. on the southern edge of the district. Take Flatbush Ave. from Grand Army Plaza to Church Ave. to explore the Caribbean section of the community.

By bike: See instructions for the "Moveable Feast Tour" on page 244.

Orientation: The Caribbean section of Brooklyn is diffuse. The most prominent commercial areas are centered around Flatbush Ave. and Church Ave., and Nostrand Ave. between Empire Blvd. and Fulton St. The IRT 2, 3, 4, and 5 trains go to various parts of this area.

A word of caution: Although touring Bedford-Stuyvesant and Crown Heights is safer than the popular stereotype allows, you'll probably feel more comfortable if you go with someone else and you don't dress ostentatiously or wear expensive jewelry. A bicycle is the best way to cover the large area, but we've designed these introductory tours for walkers. By the way, most stores and restaurants are closed on Sunday. Saturday is the best time to visit.

Brooklyn has no palm trees, no papayas, no bananas growing among the asphalt. No trade winds wash across the borough. But there's a tropical heat along Nostrand Avenue, a hip-hoppin' beat that rocks the street. Caribbean voices lilt above the traffic, curl around Bed-Stuy's brownstones and Crown Heights' houses. Fruit stands are piled high with cassava, sweet

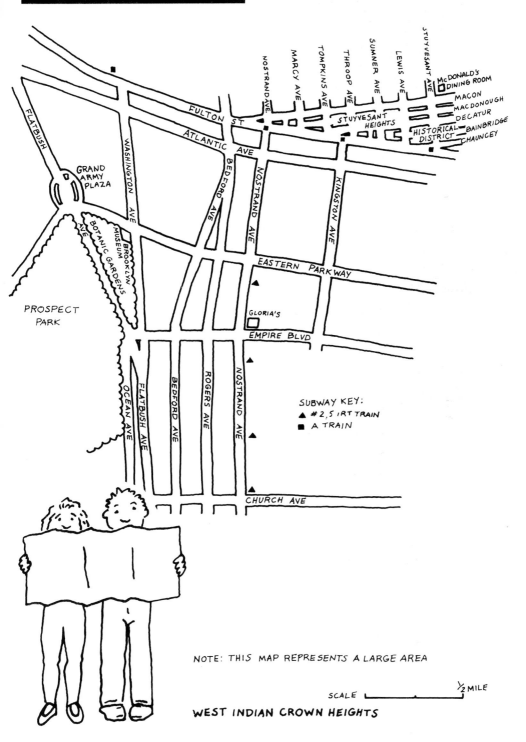

NOSTRAND AVE.

MARCY AVE.

TOMPKINS AVE.

THROOP AVE.

SUMNER AVE.

LEWIS AVE.

STUYVESANT AVE.

McDONALD'S
DINING ROOM

MACON

MACDONOUGH

DECATUR

STUYVESANT
HEIGHTS

BAINBRIDGE

HISTORICAL
DISTRICT

CHAUNCEY

FULTON ST.

ATLANTIC AVE.

FLATBUSH

GRAND
ARMY
PLAZA

WASHINGTON AVE.

BEDFORD AVE.

NOSTRAND AVE.

KINGSTON AVE.

BOTANIC GARDENS

BROOKLYN MUSEUM

PROSPECT
PARK

EASTERN PARKWAY

GLORIA'S

EMPIRE BLVD.

OCEAN AVE.

FLATBUSH AVE.

BEDFORD AVE.

ROGERS AVE.

NOSTRAND AVE.

SUBWAY KEY:

▲ #2,5 IRT TRAIN

■ A TRAIN

CHURCH AVE.

NOTE: THIS MAP REPRESENTS A LARGE AREA

SCALE   ½ MILE

WEST INDIAN CROWN HEIGHTS

pumpkins, mangos, and coconuts. Goat curry, conch, and garbanzo beans are wrapped in a crepelike *roti* at dozens of food stands; every restaurant's cook has his or her own version of the fragrant cook-up rice; and it's all washed down with exotic drinks like peanut punch, mauby, and sorrel.

The New York area is home to about 1 million immigrants from the Caribbean, including a large Haitian community. Brooklyn has the largest number; the borough's West Indian population is concentrated in Bedford-Stuyvesant, Crown Heights, Brownsville, and Flatbush. Scattered along the main commercial streets—Nostrand Avenue, Church Avenue, Fulton Street, and Flatbush Avenue—are dozens of West Indian bakeries, markets, meat stores, roti shops, and restaurants. For the less gastronomically inclined who have a hankering after the Caribbean, there are reggae shops and *botánicas* (metaphysical religious stores). There isn't a lot of money in most of these neighborhoods, so you won't find fancy eateries. What you will find are plenty of lively, friendly people.

Almost every culture has a dish that uses bread to hold some favorite food. In the West Indies—and in Caribbean Brooklyn—that bread is most often roti. Roti is simple enough: a pancakelike bread fried on a griddle and filled with meat, vegetables, or seafood. You'll usually have a choice of fillings like curried chicken, curried goat, conch, shrimp, potato, chickpeas, and vegetables. The roti dough is made with a mixture of white flour and split yellow peas; after a short rising time it is rolled flat and cooked quickly over a griddle. The fillings are folded in as the pancake comes off the stove.

Roti, like much Caribbean cooking, reflects the influence of Indian workers and merchants who settled in the islands, both in terms of the curry spices and, often, the Indian ancestry of the people who run many of the roti shops. You don't even need to taste roti to see its Indian roots. "Hurry, hurry, come for curry" urges a sign outside a roti shop; another restaurateur bills himself as "Singh the Roti."

West Indian drinks are, however, uniquely Caribbean. In most eateries you'll find beverages like sorrel, mauby, sea moss (or Irish moss), and peanut punch on the menu. Here's a brief idea of what to expect from these libations: Sorrel is a carbonated (usually canned) drink made from the sorrel plant; it has a fragrant, fruity taste with an aftertaste the reminds some people of bubble gum. Mauby is altogether different: It is made from the bark of the tree bearing the same name and has a strong medicinal flavor akin to old-fashioned cough syrup. Indeed, its adherents swear by it to cure stomach troubles. (You can find the bark in some markets in the area.) Sea moss is made from a seaweed base and whipped into a frothy, milkshake-style concoction. Peanut punch is similar, except that ordinary store-bought peanut butter is the ingredient used to whip up the shake. Both sea moss and peanut punch are sweet and both generally have what those behind the counter mysteriously term "oils and essences" blended in.

Although there are several commercial hubs in the Flatbush, Crown Heights, Bedford-Stuyvesant, and Brownsville neighborhoods, we've chosen to concentrate on Nostrand Avenue and some of the surrounding blocks to give you an introduction to the area. A tour of the Nostrand

Avenue area offers both a lively commercial strip and, on the side streets, some of New York's most stunning blocks of brownstones. Once you've covered this area, you might also want to explore the blocks around the intersection of Flatbush Avenue and Church Avenue, which is becoming increasingly developed as a commercial center.

RESTAURANTS

Don't miss **Sybil's West Indian American Bakery & Restaurant,** located at 2910 Church Avenue, just east of Flatbush Avenue (Tel.: 718/469-9049). You can take out baked goods like cassava pone, cheesecakes, and pineapple turnovers, or relax with Guyanese or American food.

Molly's West Indian restaurant is on the corner of Nostrand Avenue and Bergen Street. The small shop has a luncheonette-style counter, the better to watch Molly and her energetic crew of women knead and roll the roti dough before they slap it on the griddle. While you're waiting for roti, you might snack on *pulowrie*, a mildly spiced cornmeal dumpling. Other treats at Molly's are pastry and ice cream; try the mango, guava, banana, or coconut ice cream for another taste of the Caribbean. If you'd rather nibble a pastry, Molly's has a good sample of sweet treats—coconut macaroons, coconut sugar cakes, and sweetened chick-peas.

The block between Bergen and Dean Streets has two characteristic storefront eateries. At 664 Nostrand Avenue, **Negril**, a jerk chicken store, recently opened up. Jerk chicken and pork are Jamaican specialties: The meat is slowly barbecued. The flavor of jerk meats is strong and spicy, and the sauce penetrates the meat in a way most barbecues don't. Across the street is the **Port Royal**, at 609 Nostrand Avenue. Port Royal serves Jamaican food, takeout only. Try *bamy* (fish wrapped in a bread turnover), ackee and cod, jerk chicken, cow foot and beans, and oxtail and bean stew.

Next you'll cross Eastern Parkway, a busy thoroughfare that is worth a visit. It is one of the city's grandest boulevards, cutting from Grand Army Plaza almost to the start of the Interboro Parkway at the edge of East New York. Designed in 1868 by Frederick Law Olmsted and Calvert Vaux, who were also responsible for Central Park and Prospect Park, Eastern Parkway and Ocean Parkway were supposed to be the beginning of a network of efficient roadways through the city's residential area. To look at the clusters of people who sit on the benches along the tree-shaded parkway socializing with their neighbors is to realize the city's loss in not building those arteries.

Dewar's is a homey Jamaican restaurant at 807 Nostrand Avenue (one block south of Eastern Parkway, Tel.: 718/773-8403) with a counter and booths, a low-key atmosphere, and dozens of potted plants. Try the traditional "rice 'n' peas," with coconut milk cooked in the dish, to give it a creamier, richer taste. "Peas 'n' rice" has no coconut milk in it. Making it all more confusing, none of the dishes has any peas. The "peas" are garbanzo beans (chick-peas). Verone Dewar-Hollis has been running the restaurant since 1978. "We've got the original spices," she says. "We import them from Jamaica. When we make pudding, we don't use nutmeg from a can. We only use fresh nutmeg." One of the restaurant's specialties

You might plan a visit to Eastern Parkway on Labor Day, when the annual West Indian Carnival takes place. Every year hundreds of thousands of dancers, stilt-walkers, musicians, and animated revelers snake down Eastern Parkway in a carnival frenzy that ranks as one of New York's most dynamic ethnic events. We've never seen anything like these costumes: Most of them are animals, with everything from a queen bee to a dragon (along with lots of devils) represented. The getups are huge, garishly colored (such as orange and green) and amazingly light, allowing their wearers to dance to the music. There's music aplenty: Huge flatbed trucks with entire reggae and steel bands crawl down the parkway. There are people scattered along the route selling food they've made, so this is a good place to try homestyle Caribbean cooking. Want to join the parade? There's little separation between the crowd and the paraders, so you're welcome to wade onto Eastern Parkway and boogie with the marchers.

is homemade fruitcake. Although it's especially popular around Christmas, you can get it all year, although you must order ahead. Dewar's is the best place in the area to get a true Jamaican breakfast: codfish and ackee. Dried codfish is cooked with ackee, the Jamaican national fruit, which is soft and custardy. It's delicious, but watch out: Some people are very allergic to ackee. (The Food and Drug Administration prohibits the introduction of fresh ackee into the United States, because unripe ackee can produce toxic reactions.) If you don't want to try ackee, other breakfasts include liver and banana, codfish and banana, codfish and dumplings, or a vitamin-filled liver breakfast. Dewar's side orders include dumplings and plantains.

Most of the area's eateries are quite simple and superficially rather similar. One of the most popular of the storefront eateries is **Gloria's West Indian Restaurant In & Out** (991 Nostrand Ave. at Empire Blvd, Tel.: 718/778-4852) and, if you're hungry, it's the best place to end a tour of Nostrand Avenue. Like many of the area's other roti stores, Gloria's serves mostly takeout food. Gloria Wilson and her son Larry hail from Trinidad. Cumin is a dominant flavor in the curry used in Trinidadian cooking; most of the curry here is pungent, but not spicy hot. If your tastes run toward hotter food, such as Szechuan cuisine in Chinese cooking, you might ask for "pepper," as in "pepper chicken." For dessert you'll find carrot cakes along with more exotic treats, such as bread pudding Trinidad style and passion fruit.

There is a pair of tables at Gloria's, but most people use them simply to take a break while they wait for their order to get dished up and wrapped in foil. You'll get a good sense of what's happening in the neighborhood by reading the leaflets on Gloria's big front windowsill: Everything from reggae dances to church retreats is advertised. On the wall is the latest copy of the *TnT Mirror*, the Trinidad and Tobago paper, one of the many West Indian papers sold in New York.

Every restaurant's curry is unique; you'll

notice a big difference between the curry at Gloria's and that in Jamaican restaurants. If you like Gloria's curry—and it's hard not to—you can take home some of the madras curry powder sold at the eatery.

Most roti shops are storefront operations, usually geared to a takeout clientele, with no more than a couple of tables at most. One surreal anomaly is an operation called **B's Castle** (718/638-6687), a fast-food roti stand perched incongruously on the rough-and-tumble corner of Bedford Avenue and Fulton Street. Like any other fast-food franchise, this shop is complete with back-lit, full-color photos of roti platters, kingfish, codfish, and the like. Behind gleaming metal counters cashiers punch orders into electronic registers while customers sit around the antiseptic plastic-lined counter. Across the street is an Islamic temple with women in *chadors* milling around outside—a clash of cultures!

If you can't go to the islands, just take the train to Brooklyn.

MARKETS AND BAKERIES

There are perhaps a half-dozen produce stands along the stretch of Nostrand Avenue this tour covers, but they're not to be taken for granted. Korean greengrocers came to Nostrand Avenue in the early 1980s; today they provide perhaps the most familiar sight to many first-time visitors. Typical is **Yong Fruit and Vegetable** (842 Nostrand Ave.) just south of Eastern Parkway, a sizable market run by Koreans, which offers a good selection of West Indian foods. Some of its more unusual offerings include sweet potato relish, candied fruits, sugarcane juice, and coconuts.

Next door to Dewar's is the bright, new **Johnson Central Bakery** (803 Nostrand Ave.). If you're lucky, Trinidadian proprietor Al Johnson may have just pulled some of his fine coconut bread out of the oven. A few blocks further along is **Ronnie's Bakery** (892 Nostrand Ave., Tel.: 718/756-4435), which is run by Veronica Zyns. Like Johnson's, Ronnie's serves typi-

Preparing roti dough.

cal island pastries and breads: rolls filled with fruits and currants, heavy on the molasses; coconut and currant turnovers; beef and vegetable patties; spice buns; cheesecakes; cassava pone; and bread pudding are all worth a taste.

Farther along Nostrand Avenue is a Haitian store, **Au Petit Marché** (Tel.: 718/773-7275), which sells French magazines and a half-dozen kinds of dried fish. Joe Baptiste, who works in the store, shows off the fish arrayed in boxes: Gaspé cod, smoked herring, filets of cod, and conch. One of the store's more unusual items is flat cassava bread. It also sells hot fish-filled turnovers; bags of sea bush, an herb used to make medicinal tea; dried mushrooms; and fresh cotton. Although the store is small, it manages to squeeze in a rack for Haitian records.

Mara's is at 718 Nostrand Avenue. Once the jewel of Nostrand Avenue's markets, Mara's has fallen on hard times. A fire upstairs in the building caused extensive water damage, effectively cutting the store's size in half. But people in the neighborhood say Mara's has also suffered because many Korean merchants have moved onto Nostrand Avenue since the early 1980s, offering some of the same kinds of foods on which Mara's once had something of a monopoly. "Everybody sells the West Indian products now," says Joe Mara, who has run the store since the early 1950s. Mara's is worth a visit, though, because the store still offers the best selection of Caribbean spices in the area. It has four kinds of West Indian dried curry, mauby bark, changy root, and other tropical herbs and spices not easily found anywhere else. You can also find syrups to make sweetened drinks—mauby, apple, and orzapa (cane syrup), for example—along with other tropical sweets like candied fruits, guava jelly, and creamed coconut. Jamaican sodas like ginger beer, coconut, cream, and banana line the shelves.

WALKING TOUR

Bedford-Stuyvesant's reputation notwithstanding, the area has some of the loveliest brownstone neighborhoods in New York. The Stuyvesant Heights Historical District, most notably, has blocks of brownstones that would shame any on Manhattan's Upper West Side. Walking these streets will give you the best sense of the great middle-class neighborhood that still makes up the heart of Bed-Stuy. Dozens of churches and freshly painted townhouses are punctuated by boarded-up buildings and vacant lots. Children in their Sunday best sweep off storefront church steps on a squalid street. It's a neighborhood that takes these contrasts in stride. As one local church sign sums up: "Why Worry When You Can Pray?"

Start the walking tour of Bedford-Stuyvesant at Fulton Street and Nostrand Avenue (A or CC IND subway to Nostrand Ave.). Walk one block north to Macon Street and turn right. Walk along Macon Street; if you'd like to make a short loop, turn left at the second block onto Tompkins Avenue; turn left again onto Hancock Street, the second block north, and left back onto Nostrand. Better yet, continue on Macon Street to Stuyvesant Avenue and turn right. You'll be in the historic district; explore cross streets such as McDonough, Decatur, Bainbridge, and Chauncey for a better sense of the distinguished blocks in this area of Bed-Stuy. There's a subway stop at the corner of Stuyvesant and Fulton (A and CC lines). The shorter loop takes about 15 minutes; the longer one at least a half hour.

One of the only real restaurants in the area of Stuyvesant Heights is **Mc-Donald's Dining Room** (327 Stuyvesant Ave. at Macon St., Tel.: 718/574-3728). The restaurant fortunately bears no resemblance to its better-known namesake. This family-style dining room is a charming oasis. The eatery is now run by Clara Walker, who was one of the original waitresses when it opened in 1948. The restaurant serves typical country-style southern food, from grits to smothered chicken. Don't miss the deep-dish peach cobbler or the sweet potato pie if you have a sweet tooth. There is live jazz sometimes: Call ahead for details.

POLISH GREENPOINT: PIROGEN AND MORE

To Get There

By subway: Take the IND G train to Greenpoint Ave. To reach the G line from Manhattan, take the L train, which runs along 14th St. in Manhattan, to Lorimer St.; or take the E or F train to Queens Plaza.

By car: Exit the Brooklyn-Queens Expressway at McGuinness Blvd. Follow McGuiness Blvd. north for about one mile; turn left on Greenpoint Ave. to Manhattan Ave.

From the Queensborough Bridge, turn right at Jackson Ave. and follow signs for the Pulaski Bridge, which becomes McGuinness Blvd. in Greenpoint. Continue to Greenpoint Ave. and turn right one block to Manhattan Ave.

By bike: See directions for the ''Moveable Feast Tour'' on page 244 (to come from Queens). From Manhattan, take the Williamsburg Bridge. Turn right at Driggs Ave. and take the first right at Broadway and right again on Bedford Ave. (Note the landmark Victorian bank building on the northeast corner of Broadway and Bedford Ave.) Remain on Bedford Ave. until it ends at Manhattan Ave. in Greenpoint, and turn left on Manhattan Ave. Lock the bike near the Greenpoint Ave.–Manhattan Ave. hub.

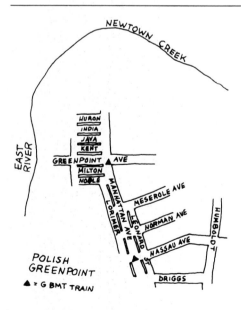

Across the East River from the high-rise and high-tech of midtown Manhattan, the low-rise community of Polish Greenpoint seems much like a bustling Eastern European village in comparison. English is the second language in much of the area, and sausage stores are as abundant here as fast food is on 42nd Street. More than a century ago, when the communities were about the same height, you could reach Greenpoint from Manhattan by a 10-minute boat ride. The journey by subway takes

The service can be fast at Henryk's Delicatessen.

longer today, and though the distance hasn't changed, Greenpoint feels an ocean away.

"Green Point" (as it was first spelled) was once known as the "Garden Spot of the World." In the 1830s, however, the farms and meadows were plowed under, the first streets laid out, and the first homes built. The Polish families who have lived in the community since the 1950s, plus a new wave who've been coming since 1981, have created a new, if more subtle, garden spot. Almost every patch of land along the quiet residential side streets has been planted: Tiny plots of bushes, trees, and flowers abound. Peek into backyards and you'll likely see grapevines, flower gardens, or vegetables growing. The facades of the two-, three-, and four-story homes in Greenpoint appear to have been freshly painted or just restored. On weekends, restoration seems to go on everywhere.

Polish Greenpoint has two hubs. The busier is at the intersection of Manhattan and Greenpoint Avenues, where workers on their days off crowd the markets, the credit union, the *piegarnias* (bakeries), and the restaurants. The other is **St. Stanislaus Kostka Church** at 607 Humboldt Street at Driggs Avenue. Although it is some distance away and the area even a bit sleepy, the church is in many respects the heart of the Polish community. It was to "St. Stan's" that Cardinal Karol Wojtyla of Krakow paid a visit in 1969. Now, at the corner of Broome and Humboldt Streets in front of the church, the intersection has been renamed "Pope John Paul II Square" to honor the community's most famous visitor. (Look beyond the intersection and you'll see the almost ghostly vision of the two World Trade Center towers in the distance.)

The Pope's portrait, by the way, is almost everywhere. In the carpet shop on Nassau Avenue, for instance, a rug remnant with the Pope's face hangs in the window. The Pope's chief competition comes from the Polish workers' hero Lech Walesa, whose round, mustachioed face stares from posters along Manhattan Avenue and in the shops on the side streets. While you hunt for produce at **Manhattan Avenue Fruits and Vegetables** (928 Manhattan Ave.), Walesa will glare down as you handle the tomatoes and cabbages. "Solidarity Needs You," the poster declares: "*Solidarnosc.*"

RESTAURANTS

On a Saturday morning in Polish Greenpoint—the best time to start your tour—you'll want to walk on Greenpoint Avenue, just west of Manhattan Avenue. The **Polish & Slavic Credit Union** (138 Greenpoint Ave.) is packed with fund depositors, and the cramped adjacent dining room, with informal cafeteria service (and almost no English spoken), rewards the thrifty—or just hungry—with full platters of dumplings or beef stew. If you want something a shade fancier, go next door to **Polska Restaurant** (136 Greenpoint Ave., Tel.: 718/389-8368), a popular neighborhood eatery. Here you can negotiate an inexpensive, filling meal with owner Jadwiga Ziemianowicz, a plump woman with blond hair wrapped into a tight bun. She speaks little English, but with finger-pointing and the help of other patrons—the menu is bilingual, even if Jadwiga is not—she will take your order. Unless you eat and drink enough for two, you'll be hard put to spend more than $5 or $6 here—including a bottle of dark Polish beer. You can get platters of *kopytka* (potato dumplings), pirogen (the popular Polish dumpling with potato, cheese, or meat filling), or *placki* (potato pancakes), with a recommended side order of sour cream. You might, however, prefer to start your meal with *zupa* (soup): mushroom-barley or a serving of rich sour soup, with white sausage and potatoes. Polska also serves more substantial meat platters, like beef goulash or beef stroganoff, and its house specialty is European veal shank. You can finish your meal with homemade sugar cake or apple strudel. There are a counter and four booths in the front, where patrons

Stuff yourself with stuffed cabbage.

gather and talk among themselves (this is the kind of place where everyone knows each other), and a large, austere party room in the back. If you want to bring a group, call in advance, but don't expect to get someone who speaks English on the first try; Jadwiga will do her best or grab an English-speaking customer to help out—if she can find one.

You have to move away from the hub to find other good places to eat; Polska is often crowded and service may be slow. So walk back toward Manhattan Avenue and continue one block further to quiet Leonard Street. Turn right and walk three blocks until you reach Norman Avenue. There are two pleasant and inexpensive eateries here. **Henryk's Delicatessen** (105 Norman Ave., Tel.: 718/389-6859) is a family affair: Henryk acts as cashier in front while family members prepare meals in the rear kitchen. The front area is a small market: You can buy mleko (milk), jaja (eggs), and maslo (butter). In the dining room, you can have a meal at one of seven tables. The menu offers three soups to start—schav (sour-grass soup), fruit, and mushroom barley—and pirogen platters and three or four meat dishes. The fruit soup, served summers only, has a cherry base and is flavored with pears, but there are many variations: Fruit soup is simply water boiled and thickened with cornstarch and mixed with fruit juice or syrup; fresh fruit is added later, and the dish is served chilled. Egg noodles make it richer and more filling. A plate of eight pirogen is a good complement. Fillings include cheese, potato, meat, and sauerkraut. (The cheese used in pirogen is a combination of farmer cheese and Lithuanian andrulis, a dry white cheese that helps keep the filling solid in cooking.)

Diagonally across the street, the **Mona Lisa Polish Restaurant** (106 Norman Ave., Tel.: 718/389-4847) has nothing to do with its eponym in the Louvre, but is a quiet, charming neighborhood restaurant, opened in late 1984 by Danuta Kosar, a young woman who arrived with the new wave of Polish immigrants after 1981. The menu has a small but tasty selection of veal, pork, and beef entrées costing no more than $4, and rich, homemade desserts: napoleons, rum cakes, and cheesecakes.

A half-block from St. Stan's is the surprising **Continental Restaurant** (11 Newel St., just north of Driggs Ave., Tel.: 718/383-2768). Opened in 1982, the Continental hides behind a nondescript front door and barred windows, which give the impression that it is closed. Far from it: Enter and you'll discover Greenpoint's jolliest eatery and nightclub. Inside, the front bar and large rear dining room can accommodate one hundred people, beckoning large parties out for a

In Greenpoint, kielbasy is as American as apple pie.

raucous good time. The menu has the largest selection we've seen in the area, with an ample choice of soups, snacks (including a herring dish and caviar with eggs and onions), and main dishes ranging in price from $2.50 to $6, including an appealing platter of apple-stuffed blintzes. A stage in the rear holds the live dance band, which plays Saturday and Sunday nights.

MARKETS AND SHOPS

Greenpoint's food centers are its meat markets, and about a dozen are spread through the area, mainly on Manhattan and Nassau Avenues. They offer not only a huge selection of meats, but also a wide variety of imported Polish foodstuffs, including dried soups, honeys, fruit syrups, chocolate, canned goods (like mushrooms and pickles), and other condiments essential to Polish cuisine, as well as breads and

pastries from local bakeries. Perhaps the best-known bakery—though the hours make a visit difficult unless you live in Greenpoint—is **White Eagle** (600 Humboldt St., Tel.: 718/389-2214), across from St. Stan's. Open Tuesdays through Thursdays from 7 A.M. to 2:30 P.M., it specializes in sweet, crusty *chruscik*, a light deep-fried pastry dusted with confectioner's sugar. Many meat markets also sell fresh and frozen pirogen.

One of the most typical markets is the bustling **R. Nassau Meat Market** (121 Nassau Ave., Tel.: 718/383-3476). Although older clerks speak only Polish, the younger employees are American-born and bilingual. The shop is a sausage museum: Sausages fill the store windows, hang from ropes suspended wall-to-wall, and line the rear wall, too. As in all the Polish meat markets in Greenpoint, all smoking, grinding, and wrapping takes place on the premises. The most popular item is *kielbasy*, a finely ground pork sausage flavored with garlic and other spices. Variations include the narrow, 2-foot-long *kabanosy*, which tastes like a "Slim Jim," and "tastes great with beer," young Richard Karniewicz told us. (Mr. Karniewicz, now in his mid-twenties, is perhaps typical of his generation: He grew up in Greenpoint, works part-time in the neighborhood, and studies law, which he hopes to practice here someday.) Less garlicky than kielbasy, the kabanosy is hung to dry, and reaches optimal flavor in about three days, as the fat drips out and the sausage hardens. *Mysliwska*, or hunter's sausage, resembles a frankfurter and is ideal for barbecuing. The *jalowcowa*, which looks like a salami, is the only sausage without garlic; it is also sold when drier and tangier. Other Polish meat spe-

cialties include *krakowska* (sliced kiel-basy), *kiszka* (a combination of blood, buckwheat, pork skins, fat, and liver), *flaczki* (tripe soup made from the cow's stomach, sold by the container), and smoked and cured raw kielbasy. The store also sells several types of bacon, Polish ham, and veal. The equally busy **W. Nassau Meat Market**—no relation—is at 915 Manhattan Avenue (Tel.: 718/389-6149).

While you're on Nassau Avenue, you might want to explore local shops, for the greatest concentration of Polish-owned stores is here. On the corner of Nassau Avenue and Leonard Street you'll find **Nassau Pharmacy—Murawski Apteka** (566 Leonard St., Tel.: 718/383-0236), an old family establishment that not only caters to the needs of the Polish community but also exports pharmaceuticals to the old country.

WALKING TOUR

Despite its village air and the seeming ordinariness of much of Greenpoint's buildings, the neighborhood boasts some fine nineteenth-century architecture, as well as idiosyncratic treats for those wanderers who relish the eccentricities that make New York's neighborhoods so special. Begin your tour at Manhattan and Greenpoint Avenues. The spire of **St. Anthony—St. Alphonsus Church** (862 Manhattan Ave.) serves not only as the symbolic town center—much the way a church is the centerpiece of a small European village—but points out the finest

Greenpoint's hero—and its best-known visitor.

block in the neighborhood. Milton Street has a must-see row of homes just one block south of Greenpoint Avenue which boasts the area's lushest architecture. In particular, note the houses from 117 to 149 Milton Street, with mansard roofs and spacious front lawns. Turn right on Franklin Street, where the neighborhood reflects Hispanic settlement in Greenpoint (though you'll pass the "Chopin Democratic Club"), and walk two blocks until you reach Kent Street, and turn right again. Not quite as elegant as Milton Street, Kent Street is special because of the graceful brick churches along this Victorian, tree-lined block. Java Street, one block north of Kent Street, is the last of the fine brownstone blocks in Greenpoint. (The streets were laid out to be alphabetical in the original plan, and Greenpoint Avenue was to have been named Lincoln Street.) At Franklin and Java Streets, take a look at **The Astral Apartments**, occupying the full block between Java and India Streets. Built in the mid-1880s, these apartments were an innovation in their time. Intended to provide modern, humane housing for Greenpoint's Irish working class—who supplied labor for the nearby factories producing porcelain, glass, and iron, as well as for oil refineries and printing shops—the building had an airy and light central inner courtyard, a rare alternative to the dark, crowded tenements that housed much of New York's working classes. Unfortunately, the entrances leading to the courtyard are today closed off with metal doors, so you can't see inside.

A bit further north on an otherwise nondescript block, don't miss 109 Huron Street, one of the great oddities and pleasures of the community. With four grand columns, this tiny two-story house, with a postage-stamp-size front lawn, looks like a miniature plantation manor caught by fate in the middle of the city.

The needs of Greenpoint's Polish residents—especially the 50,000 who regenerated the aging, Americanized population after 1981, when the imposition of martial law in Poland prompted many young people to flee—are met through a variety of organizations and resources. **The Polish-National Alliance** at 155 Noble Street (an area, by the way, that contains fine rowhouse architecture) is the community's "glue," providing social services and information for older Polish Americans and younger immigrants.

But most interesting, in our view, is the **Pol-Am Bookstore** (946 Manhattan Ave., Tel.: 718/389-7790) which provides a visitor with a window into the world of the more recent Polish emigré. Darius and Krystyna Kruk opened the store in April 1985 to fill the needs of younger Poles who are new to New York and still have strong ties to their homeland even as they try to become Americanized. Krystyna, an artist in her twenties, is one of them; she arrived after 1981. Darius, now in his thirties, was brought to the United States at age 12 and has ties to both the old and new Polish-American communities. The store sells a wide variety of Polish-language newspapers, magazines, and books, including children's primers; cassette tapes of popular and rock music, Polish folk music, and English lessons to accompany the many English-language books in stock; medals and buttons of Pope John Paul II and Lech Walesa, and decorative Polish folk papercuts. Several magazines, like *Tygodnik Nowojorski* (literally, *New York Weekly*,

Inside the Pol-Am Bookstore.

though the publication is monthly), are written by and for the politically oriented younger generation; even if you can't read Polish, the graphics tell much. In one issue, a blindfold Statue of Liberty and photo essay of New York's homeless provided the graphic emphasis to a feature. English-language columns are in the back of the magazine. English and American literature translated into Polish is also available: Harriet Beecher Stowe's *Chata Wuja Toma* (*Uncle Tom's Cabin*), Nathaniel Hawthorne's *Dom o Siedmiv Szczy* (*The House of the Seven Gables*), and Mark Twain's *Tajemnıczy Przybysz* (*The Mysterious Stranger*). A very thorough *Polish Cookbook* in English, published in Warsaw, is available for about $20. Pol-Am sponsors a Klub Polska, a "cinémathèque" showing Polish movies (with English subtitles) every Friday and Saturday at 8 P.M. in a makeshift auditorium around the corner.

If you're looking for Polish folk gifts (carved boxes, wooden spoons, dolls) or imported candies, you can find them at a spacious gift shop called **Zakopane** (714 Manhattan Ave., Tel.: 718/389-3487), which has been in the neighborhood for 20 years.

ITALIAN BROOKLYN

CARROLL GARDENS

To Get There

 By subway: Take the F or GG train to Carroll St. Walk one block uphill to Court St.

 By car: Take the Battery Tunnel to Brooklyn. Exit immediately after the toll booth onto Hamilton Ave. Go straight; make a left on Smith St. Park on Smith St. anywhere between Fourth Place and Union St. Court St. is one block to the left (west).

 By bike: See the instructions for "Brighton Beach K'nish K'nosh" on page 232.

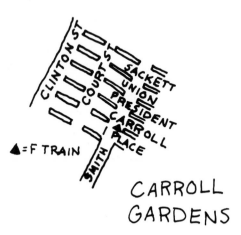

▲ = F TRAIN

CARROLL GARDENS

Carroll Gardens is the center of a tight-knit, thriving Italian community. As you'd expect, the smell of fresh semolina bread wafts out of bakeries; calves' liver and homemade sausages fill the butchers' cases; pasta and pastry stores line the streets. **Vinny's Pizzeria** is on one block and **Sal's Barbershop** on another. This is one of the few quarters where you'll still find Italians, not Koreans, running the fruit and vegetable stands—and don't pick out the fruit yourself, thank you, unless you're a long-time customer.

The neighborhood is more than green-grocers and pasta makers, more than *salumerias* and *latticinis*. Shrines to patron saints dot the neatly kept front yards, where families pass summer afternoons on shaded benches. A pastry shop displays a son's athletic trophies; faces peer from long, narrow brownstone windows.

Carroll Gardens' singularity was formally recognized in 1973, when it was designated a landmark historic district. The neighborhood's treasure is blocks of late-nineteeth-century brownstone row houses, with deep yards, sliced by narrow, tree-lined streets. Land surveyor Richard Butts laid out the area in 1846 so that each block would be wider—and have more room for front and back yards—than elsewhere in the city. Almost all of the blocks between Fourth and President Streets, bounded on the west and east by Henry Street and Hoyt Street, respectively, are worth a stroll. Until recently, Carroll Gardens was considered part of rough-and-tumble Red Hook, and many of the neighborhood's men worked on the docks there. As Red Hook, it was the setting for Arthur Miller's play *A View from the Bridge*. Local property-owners adopted the moniker "Carroll Gardens" in the 1960s as part of their effort to raise real estate values. They succeeded, and urbanites fleeing Manhattan's steep prices have created a property boom here, but the invasion has not yet spoiled the community.

Today, Carroll Gardens is one of the few remaining New York neighborhoods where shopkeepers still willingly extend credit—a little village where residents can call up the local deli to have their shopping done and delivered. If you're short of cash, the fishmonger may tell you to pay tomorrow; shopkeepers greet many of those ambling down the street by name. "It's like a small town," says Sheryl Fragin, who moved to the neighborhood in 1980. "Everyone knows everyone else."

The spine of the neighborhood is Court Street. In the five short blocks between Sackett Street and Second Place, the street is lined with bakeries, pastry and pasta shops, delis, and luncheonettes. Buy some fennel sausage, some fresh mozzarella, and a loaf of Sicilian bread. If the weather is nice, stroll over to Carroll Park (between Union Street and First Place) and watch the old men playing boccie.

RESTAURANTS

Wandering along Court Street you won't go wrong to pop into almost any store that catches your eye. If you want to sit and watch the neighborhood rhythm, the place to start is at **Joe's Luncheonette**, an old-fashioned luncheonette (349 Court St. between Union and President Sts., Tel.: 718/624-9358). Egg creams, Italian dishes like chicken parmigiana and rice balls, along with a full complement of neighborhood regulars are here.

MARKETS AND BAKERIES

"Nobody has better store like mine," boasts Dmitri Medvedev, the Russian owner of **Aiello's** (335 Court St., Tel.: 718/624-1439). Aiello's Italian heritage is apparent in the dozens of kinds of pasta, fresh and smoked mozzarella made in the back, olives, and antipasto which are all jammed into this store. Since taking over the store in 1985, the Medvedev family (Dmitri runs the store with his wife and daughter) have added some Russian dishes, such as *borscht*. Recently added is a restaurant (mostly takeout) next door that specializes in Russian food, an offering he hopes will appeal to the tastes of this increasingly gentrified neighborhood. "More and more they come here, young

American people," says "Dima" in his exuberant English.

"Years ago it was all Italian," remembers John Caputo, the fourth generation of Caputos to bake bread in Carroll Gardens. **Caputo's** (329 Court St., Tel.: 718/875-6871) is best known for its semolina, which is baked in the back along with rye and pumpernickel (for the area's non-Italians), and a dry, dense sourdough Sicilian bread that few other bakeries make. Caputo's makes bread for stores and restaurants all over Brooklyn, as well as for the family's shop. Although the Caputo family hails from Palermo, Carroll Gardens draws its residents from all over Italy. In recent years, many new residents have come from Bari, in southern Italy, spurring the bakery to begin baking *caralla*, a hard fennel-seed biscuit that's a Bari staple. The bakery sells a wide variety of other biscuits and Italian pastries; try the giant cheese horns, filled with ricotta.

G. Esposito Jersey Pork Store (357 Court St., Tel.: 718/875-6863). The Espositos have been turning out handmade sausages since 1922. John and George, grandsons of the founder, are running the business now, while their father, Frank, handles accounting. Come in the summer and try the sausage made with basil, tomatoes, and mozzarella; you can sample provolone with parsley or fennel, and four other kinds of fresh pork sausage, as well as a variety of dried sausage, year-round.

There are also a few stores on Smith Street one block east of Court Street. Don't miss the other **Joe's** at the corner of President Street; this deli has a good selection of cheeses and antipasto, and specializes in small, deep-fried rice balls and prosciutto balls that the regulars toss back as if they were tumblers of whiskey.

A DETOUR TO BENSONHURST

To Get There

By subway: Take the N train to 18th Ave., and you'll exit by 65th St., in the thick of the action. (Exit from the front of the train if you're coming from Manhattan.)

By car: Take the Belt Parkway to Bay Parkway. Take Bay Parkway to 86th St. You can park anywhere here; 18th Ave. is four blocks to the left.

By bike: Follow directions for "Brighton Beach K'nish K'nosh" on page 232. Turn right off Ocean Parkway onto Ave. P. Bear right onto 77th St., when Ave. P ends at Bay Parkway. 18th Ave. is four blocks ahead.

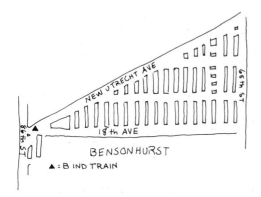

BENSONHURST

▲ = B IND TRAIN

Bensonhurst is a sprawling neighborhood filled with well-kept single family and row houses, each with its own tiny front lawn. Only 50 years ago, there were truck farms in Bensonhurst. Later, "The Honeymooners" was set here. Today, Bensonhurst is *Saturday Night Fever* land: The movie was shot in **Lenny's Pizza** parlor on 86th Street. But the Sicilian roots of most of Bensonhurst's Italians and Italian Americans are evident, especially in the late-summer Feast of Santa Rosalia, when the neighborhood honors the Sicilian saint. Stroll the commercial strip, 18th Avenue between 64th and 75th Streets, to see how the old country and the new world mix. Young girls strut in tight jeans while their grandparents amble along the crowded street dressed in black.

Eighteenth Avenue has food shops, of course. It's also lined with bridal shops, video and record shops, hairdressers, florists, the Brooklyn Italians Soccer League ("1979 U.S. Challenge Cup Champions," boasts the sign), social clubs, catering halls, and photo galleries whose windows are filled with photos of wide-eyed brides.

The liveliest street in Bensonhurst is 86th Street, but we've found 18th Avenue to be more fun for a visitor. You may also want to explore little enclaves like Avenue U, just east of McDonald Avenue, where there is a nice concentration of Italian food shops. (If you go there, don't miss the unassuming Sicilian restaurant **Joe's of Avenue U,** 287 Ave. U, Tel.: 718/449-9285.)

"Do you have a problem with sizes?" asks a hand-lettered sign at Castle Clothes. "Most men who have picked up some weight in the gut do." Walk along 18th Avenue and you'll know why that sign is there: latticinis, salumerias, pork stores, cafés, pastry stores, bakeries, pizza shops. "*Qui si fa da mangiare*—We serve food," says the neon at **Tony's**, on 70th Street.

CAFÉS

If you only go to one café, try the **Gran Caffè Italia** (6921 18th Ave., Tel.: 718/232-9759, which has a large selection of imported Italian pastries and *spumoni* as well as coffee and a warm, homey atmosphere. **Alba Pasticceria** (at the corner of 70th St., Tel.: 718/232-2122) is showy, big and glittery, with a wide selection of pastries. **Caffè Mille Lucci** (corner of 72nd St., Tel.: 718/232-9159), is a fancier restaurant/café. **Da Gino's** (7118 18th Ave., Tel.: 718/232-9073) is a focac-

ceria (informal little restaurant serving primarily pasta dishes).

MARKETS AND BAKERIES

There are a dozen or so good Italian food markets on this stretch: pork stores with sausages dangling to the counter and windows filled with orange, green, and red pork cartoon cutouts advertising the week's specials; latticini, with deli counters filled with cheeses and antipasto; pasta stores stuffed with dozens of flat, round, and corkscrew-shaped pastas. **Queen Ann Ravioli & Macaroni** (7205 18th Ave., Tel.: 718/256-1061) has the best selection of pasta. **La Bella Sicilia** (6110 18th Ave., Tel: 718/837-9070) is a well-stocked latticini/salumeria that serves a special hot ricotta hero sandwich on Sundays only.

As you walk down 18th Avenue past 64th Street, Italian Bensonhurst merges with Jewish Borough Park. The **International Bakery & Bagel** (6104 18th Ave., Tel.: 718/837-6431) boasts both hot bagels and Italian pastries. **Achim Foods** (5906 18th Ave., Tel.: 718/232-8954) is a strictly kosher bakery. Although some shops on Sicilian 18th Avenue are open on Sundays, Saturday is the day to go to see the neighborhood in full swing.

KOSHER BROOKLYN

New York City's Jewish history is almost as old as New Amsterdam itself; the first 23 Jews arrived on New York's shores in 1654, and formed the foundation for a community that would grow, prosper, and eventually settle throughout the United States.

Brooklyn's Jewish history is almost as old. Around the 1660s, city records noted that a man named Asser Levy owned property in what was then "Breuklen." But permanent settlers didn't cross the East River until about 1834, when German-Jewish communities sprouted in Williamsburg and near the present Borough Hall. In 1865, Abraham Abraham and Joseph Wechsler founded what is now Abraham & Straus, although the Straus name didn't appear until 1893, when Isidore and Nathan Straus, Macy's founders, became partners. The first Jewish cemetery in Brooklyn, Union Fields near Cypress Hills, opened in 1848. You can see a monument to Jewish Civil War veterans there, as well as the graves of U.S. Supreme Court Justice Benjamin Cardozo and poet Emma Lazarus, whose sonnet, "The New Colossus," is engraved on the Statue of Liberty. The opening words, "Give me your tired, your poor," greeted millions of weary newcomers as they came to the "Golden Land" in hope of a new life.

The heart of early Brooklyn Jewry was Brownsville, a farm village that attracted

Watching the camera.

Jewish workers when Jacob Cohen, who had bought a house in the area in 1885, became the first of many manufacturers to move his factory there as well. By 1917 Brownsville was home to 115,000 Jews, and within 30 years the number peaked at 400,000. The neighborhood once even had its own Yiddish theater—now a Baptist church—and from Brownsville emerged such luminaries as scholar Louis Finkelstein, comedian Danny Kaye (né David Kaminsky), composer Aaron Copland, and critic Alfred Kazin, as well as the not-so-luminous crime ring Murder, Inc. You can read Kazin's memoir *A Walker in the City* to get a vivid picture of a Jewish Brownsville that is no longer. Once home to more than 200 synagogues, today it has none. And its Jewish population has shrunk to a bare handful of elderly hangers-on.

Brooklyn was the birthplace, too, of many Jews who made their mark far beyond the reaches of Brownsville, Canarsie, Crown Heights, or Williamsburg. Native son Allen Konigsberg's self-deprecating Brooklyn humor catapulted him to fame as writer and filmmaker Woody Allen. The late impresario Sol Hurok, opera star and company manager Beverly Sills, and singer Barbra Streisand are also products of Jewish Brooklyn.

Jewish Brownsville may be gone, but other Jewish neighborhoods have sprouted, many made up of the tens of thousands of refugees who fled Nazi persecution during the 1930s and 1940s. Among these are Polish and Hungarian Hassidim who built up communities where they could carry on their highly ritualized religious observances. Since the 1940s, Brooklyn has also been home to about 25,000 Jews of Syrian descent, who have retained many of the native traditions they brought with them from Damascus and Aleppo—often by way of Alexandria, Cairo, or Beirut. Although in their dress and mannerisms they appear much more assimilated into American culture than the Hassidim, many of their customs are strange to Jews of Eastern European (Ashkenazic) backgrounds.

An estimated 500,000 Jews live in Brooklyn, linked by a common heritage and, in the 1980s, an apparent renaissance of Jewish consciousness and culture. Yet they celebrate their heritage in diverse ways. Our introduction to kosher Brooklyn focuses on four of the most distinctive neighborhoods, the ones we think offer the greatest variety of Jewish expression and the widest choice of food and sights.

Note: Remember that if you take your tour on a weekend, you must go on Sunday. From sundown on Friday until sunset on Saturday—*Shabbat*—these neighborhoods close up, except for the synagogues. In midsummer, you'll find that even on Sundays the neighborhoods are very quiet, as families escape en masse to summer colonies. You can visit all four neighborhoods in a day if you go by bike, as The Hungry Pedalers tours do, or by car. But we recommend that you do one or two at a time, and allow yourself leisure for the random discovery of shops and buildings that we haven't listed, as well as to explore those we have.

WILLIAMSBURG

To Get There

By subway: Take the J or M train to Marcy Ave. (first stop in Brooklyn). Transfer free to the B24 shuttle bus, or walk south to Division Ave. and turn right (west) to Lee Ave.

By car: Exit the Williamsburg Bridge at Division Ave.; drive west (right) to Lee Ave.

By bike: See the instructions for "Kosher Special," tour on page 238.

By foot: You can walk over the Williamsburg Bridge from Manhattan's Lower East Side, following the same route many of the early Jewish residents of Williamsburg took. Walk up the stairs in the center of Delancey St. to the pedestrian promenade. At the exit, turn right on Driggs Ave., and continue for four blocks to Division Ave. Walk left to the intersection with Lee Ave. and bear right. (One of the first sights that tells you you've arrived is a clinic with signs in Yiddish, Spanish, and English. You'll know you're on Lee Ave. when you see the yellow school buses with Yiddish lettering—some used to carry students to yeshivas, others to ferry workers to Manhattan's diamond district.)

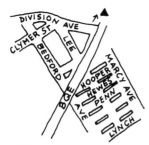

KOSHER
WILLIAMSBURG

▲ = J BMT TRAIN
(BROADWAY +MARCY)

Little boys with *yarmulkes* (skullcaps) and *payoth* (earlocks) ring a schoolbell to beckon their classmates from the playground back into the boys-only *cheder* (day school). Pairs of little girls walk hand-in-hand in long, high-necked dresses along Lee Avenue on the way to the girls' school. Men in clusters of two, three, a half-dozen sport broad fur hats or black top hats, ankle-length overcoats, black trousers, black shoes, and perhaps a ceremonial black and white *tallith* (prayer shawl)—even in summer. Women, heads covered by wigs or wrapped in tight kerchiefs, wheel baby carriages, a gaggle of children at their side. The language? Yiddish.

How did Williamsburg become a Hassidic haven? That history began only in the 1940s, but Jews started moving here not long after 1903, when the Williamsburg Bridge was completed and offered a way out of the crowded Lower East Side for those who could afford it. Even earlier, the area had been a fashionable gaming and resort area, and some of the mansions on Bedford Avenue, one block west of Lee Avenue, were once private clubs. By World War I, the area was largely populated by German Jews, and after the war by poorer Eastern European Jews. The area suffered a decline during the Depression years of the early 1930s, but was revived by the influx of Satmar Hassidim in the early 1940s. Perhaps the most insular of Hassidic groups, the estimated 45,000 Satmar are staunchly anti-Israel and do not proselytize. They also tend to resent other Hassidim. In the early 1980s, a feud erupted between the Satmar and the Lubavitchers of Crown Heights, whom the Satmar accused of trying to lure away some young men. A Satmar rabbi asserted, "We resent the missionary activities of the Lubavitch as much as we would resent the Hari Krishna and Reverend Moon." Kidnappings, including beard-cuttings, made these Hassidic groups *New York Post* material for a while, but in general, the Satmar shun the media and only hesitatingly open up to strangers.

When you visit Hassidic Williamsburg, it is easy to forget that there is a large Hispanic neighborhood there, too, and a smaller, older Italian one to the north. Once you cross Division Avenue from the north, or Lynch Street from the south, you will be immersed in an ancient culture: Stepping into Hassidic Williamsburg is, perhaps, a step back in time.

RESTAURANTS

At the northern border of Williamsburg at Division Avenue, you'll know you've arrived in the Hassidic area when you see the first Hebrew signs or Yiddish names: Yankel's Shoe Store, Mazel (Hebrew for "luck") Variety Store. You also won't be far from one of the better eateries in the area, **Weiss Restaurant Caterers** (187 Clymer St., Tel.: 718/384-8126). A large, modern dairy/vegetarian eatery, it has about ten Formica tables and aisles wide enough for the neighborhood's ever-present baby strollers. Photos of Hassidic rebbes stare down at eaters, who savor Eastern European potato or sweetened noodle pudding (*kugel*), blintzes, Israeli salads (tomatoes, cucumbers, green peppers), and kosher pizzas and danish. Weiss's serves many flavors of the kosher soft drink "Mayim Chaim," Hebrew for "water of life."

Return to Lee Avenue and head south, and you'll soon hit **Itzu's** (45 Lee Ave., Tel.: 718/384-8631), the Hassidic equivalent of a greasy spoon. It's fun for the atmosphere: the crowded tables filled mostly with black-garbed neighborhood men crouched over Yiddish newspapers. But the food selection is good, too. Walk toward the rear, where you can see the selection of vegetarian casseroles, blintzes, and salads, but if you're so inclined, you can get scrambled eggs and "a cup coffee," too. Service is friendly, and there always seem to be a few non-

Hassidic regulars in for an early breakfast. Around the corner is **Williamsburg Kosher Dairy Restaurant** (216 Ross St., Tel.: 718/ 384-2540), a converted pizza parlor (the old decor is little changed) that is now a large, animated, family-oriented eatery. You can get a filling fish entrée (gefilte, flounder, carp, or whitefish), stuffed peppers, blintzes, thick soup (mushroombarley, pea, or diet vegetable), and cheesecakes and coffee cakes. A sink near the door serves the ultrareligious Hassidim, who are required to wash their hands and pray before they eat. If you crave Jewish delicatessen, head toward **Landau's Glatt Kosher Deli** (65 Lee Ave., Tel.: 718/782-3700), where you can sit with a thick sandwich of your favorite cold cuts or platters of meat loaf or pot roast, or buy food to take out.

Families crowd a Williamsburg restaurant.

BAKERIES AND SHOPS

Williamsburg is not so much a place for eating out as for buying Eastern European specialties to take home: Whitefish, stuffed cabbage, fruit soups, rich mocha cakes, and other fattening delights line the shelves of the area's delis, groceries, bakeries, and candy shops. **Flaum Appetizers** (40 Lee Ave., Tel.: 718/387-7934) is a throwback to another era. But its smells and wares are very much of the present. As you enter, you'll relish the aromas of pickles, sable, smoked whitefish, and Nova Scotia salmon on the right-hand side; on your left, you'll no doubt *kvell* (burst with delight) over the selection of loose chocolates, kosher candies from Israel, and old-fashioned sweets reminiscent of childhoods long past: shoelace licorice, bubble gum cigars, chocolate-flavored coffee beans, and mint lentilles (nonalcoholic liqueur-flavored candies). Get a pound of *mitzvah* (good luck) disks, sweet pastel-colored candies with Hebrew words marked on them.

For baked goods, you have a selection of about six fine bakeries, all on Lee Ave-

nue, but the most alluring for us was **Sander's Kosher Bakery Shop** (159 Lee Ave., Tel.: 718/387-7411), whose service is friendly and selection of coffee cakes, cookies, pastries, and iced cakes is excellent.

At **Moskowitz Candy Land** (165 Lee Ave., Tel.: 718/387-7195), we reveled in five flavors of chunk chocolate: sweet, bittersweet, white, lemon, and peanut butter. The last two kinds are used generally for baking, but you can, of course, eat them plain: The flavors are subtle, not too sweet, and (chocoholics beware!) potentially addictive. Of course, you'll find lots more here than just chunk chocolate. **Shufra Candy Co.** (866 Lorimer St., Tel.: 718/383-5760) is a major supplier of rich, European-style loose chocolates and other candies to New York's kosher neighborhoods, and you'll have a mouth-watering choice of goodies to buy there.

You can't eat books, but you can take them home, and a visit to **Beis Hasefer** (House of the Book) at 75 Lee Avenue will be rewarding. This store has a large selection of Hebrew and Yiddish books, but also has educational materials for children, including coloring books concerned with biblical subjects (in Yiddish) and baby bracelets with names like Faigy, Goldie, Pessie, and Malky. For kosher people on diets, the store carries *Kosher Calories*, a book that lists the caloric content of more than 10,000 brand-name kosher foods. At **Religious Books and Articles** (163 Lee Ave., Tel.: 718/388-5574), a similar store a few blocks down, you can find various religious toys. Just before the holiday of Purim, for example, there are Queen Esther puppets and *graggers* (noisemakers) for sale.

WALKING TOUR

Food, of course, is not all there is to Williamsburg, so stroll along Lee Avenue to get a better feel for the area. There are several wig stores and hat shops, like **Feltly Chassidic Hats** at 185 Hewes Street (at Lee Avenue), but the wigs and hats serve the particular needs of ultra-religious men and women in the area. Take a stroll along Bedford Avenue. You'll see outstanding examples of turn-of-the-century mansions that once housed wealthy Brooklynites and later became resorts. Today, those that are serviceable function as synagogues or Jewish day schools, while others are being restored. Many side streets between Bedford and Lee Avenues (among the most attractive are Penn, Heyward, and Hooper Streets south of the Brooklyn-Queens Expressway overpass) are lined with immaculately kept row houses with stoops and small apartment buildings. *Shteblach*—small congregations—dot the streets; they are usually entered through basement doors. Don't be surprised, as you wander around, to discover dozens of children staring at you from apartment windows or front porches.

Come to Williamsburg in autumn, during the harvest holiday Sukkoth, and you'll see roofs, porches, and fire escapes enclosed by small huts made of pine branches and wooden planks, and in some cases decorated with fruits and vegetables to celebrate the harvest. You'll find larger huts on the sidewalk, outside restaurants, which patrons use as a modified alfresco area for prayer and dining. For families unable to build their own sukkah, there's the **Deluxe Awning** shop at 33 Lee Avenue, which specializes in sukkah awnings.

CROWN HEIGHTS

To Get There

By subway: Take the IRT 3 or 4 to Kingston Ave.

By car: Take Eastern Pkwy. from its beginning at Grand Army Plaza and drive about a mile and a half to Kingston Ave.

By bike: See "Kosher Special" tour directions on page 238. From the Brooklyn Bridge, follow the "Brighton Beach K'nish K'nosh" directions (page 232) to Grand Army Plaza, then cycle to Eastern Pkwy., which begins in front of the Brooklyn Public Library at the Plaza, and head toward Kingston Ave.

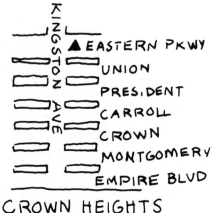

CROWN HEIGHTS

▲ = 3,4 IRT TRAIN

Crown Heights is the hub of New York's population of about 15,000 Lubavitchers. Unlike the Satmar Hassidim, the Lubavitchers have not staked out an exclusive territory; West Indian and American-born blacks live side by side with them, although their worlds and lives barely intersect.

"Are you Jewish?" Many New Yorkers have been asked this question by young, earnest-faced Lubavitcher men stationed at one of the "mitzvah (good deed) mobiles" in Manhattan's business districts, and it is a question you might be asked in Crown Heights too. For most people, it's the only contact they've had with the Lubavitchers, who use special vans to carry on their proselytizing. Unlike Williamsburg's insular Satmars, these Hassidim are anxious to invite other Jews to join them in prayer and observance. Preadolescent and teenage boys are the Lubavitcher soldiers: If they think you might be Jewish, they'll try to draft you with literature and perhaps recruit you inside the van to say a prayer. If you're a woman, they'll give you a pair of Sabbath candles.

The Lubavitchers trace their roots to the eighteenth-century revivalist movement of Rabbi Ba'al Shem Tov in Poland. Also known as Chabad (a Hebrew acronym for "wisdom, understanding, and knowledge"), the Lubavitchers came to Brooklyn in 1941, following the route of their rebbe, Menachem Mendel Schneerson, who established a world headquarters at 770 Eastern Parkway on the corner of Kingston Avenue. It seems always to teem with activity and even houses a radio station and videotape facilities.

RESTAURANTS, BAKERIES, AND SHOPS

The five-block stretch of Kingston Avenue is the commercial spine of Crown Heights. Start at **Lubavitcher World Headquarters** at the corner of Kingston Avenue and Eastern Parkway, and you'll likely see many Lubavitcher men standing in front of the building davening, bowing up and down rapidly, as they pray. Then walk south (uphill for two blocks, then downhill). Up the block is **Ess & Bentch** (Eat and Pray) **Luncheonette** (299 Kingston Ave., Tel.: 718/771-9323), a three-table, mostly takeout eatery. Should you eat in, notice the red, eight-sided "Stop—Don't Forget a Brocha Achrona" signs imploring you to remember your grace after your meal. (Copies of the grace—in Hebrew— are on each table.) For more substantial eat-in meals, try **Mermelstein's** (351 Kingston Ave., Tel.: 718/778-3100) or **La Gvina Pizzeria** (379 Kingston Ave., Tel.: 718/788-9500). At Mermelstein's, also the local caterer, you can satisfy a craving for traditional Jewish deli: stuffed roast beef

sandwiches, stuffed peppers, boiled chicken, pot roast. La Gvina is an Israeli-run modern-style pizzeria where you can also feast on dairy dishes, as well as glatt kosher knishes, calzone, and felafel. The **Shabbos Fish Market** (417 Kingston Ave., Tel.: 718/774-1659) advertises "Life Fish," and **Oneg Bakery** (425 Kingston Ave., Tel.: 718/493-2627) is the best place for traditional Eastern European–Jewish pastries, breads, and cakes: the not-too-sweet crumbly rugelach (small, dry, honey-splotched pastries), poppy-seed pastries, apple strudel, challah, and chocolate cakes.

The attraction of Crown Heights, however, lies not so much in the food—you'll find many more eating places in Orthodox Borough Park—but in the nonedibles you'll discover there. The Lubavitchers have long campaigned to preserve Jewish learning and customs, but with a creative and sometimes whimsical approach that often integrates modern styles. You can get a sense of how this is done at **Crown Heights Judaica** (327 Kingston Ave., Tel.: 718/604-1020), where you'll find stuffed Torahs and giant mezuzahs for children; schoolbags with tzedakah (charity) pockets; Jewish board games like "Kosherland" (for children aged 6 to 120, the box says); "Mendy and the Golem" comic books; and musical cassettes featuring the Miami Boys' Choir, Country Yossi and the Shtebel Hoppers, and A Wedding in Jerusalem. Bookshelves are packed with Orthodox and Hassidic philosophy and instruction, in English and Hebrew.

Across the street is **Machne Israel** (332 Kingston Ave., Tel.: 718/493-9250), headquarters for Tsivos Hashem, or Army of God, the Lubavitcher equivalent of boy and girl scouts for children under 13. Its ground-floor annex teems with children's Judaica, from bibs and *mitzvah* straws to Hebrew Sesame Street stickers and educational materials. A local craftswoman who carves miniatures frequently has her extraordinary handiwork on display there. On one visit, we saw a three-story dollhouse, complete with tiny mezuzahs. On the second floor, the father read Talmud (elaborate interpretation of Jewish law); on the first floor, the mother blessed the Friday-night candles at a dining-room table set for a big dinner. The bathroom had a clawfoot tub, and the toilet had a pull-chain. Nearby was a one-story miniature synagogue chapel. Unfortunately, the house was not for sale. Also visit the **Chassidic Art Institute** (375 Kingston Ave., Tel.: 718/774-9149), which features many painted portraits of the rebbe and religious motifs. **The Kochleffel** (369 Kingston Ave., Tel.: 718/493-3960) is a modern housewares stores specializing in kosher kitchen needs. (*Kochleffel* means mixing spoon.)

WALKING TOUR
Don't leave Crown Heights without strolling along the two blocks of President Street between Kingston and New York Avenues. President Street is at the crest of Crown Heights, and sports the area's most gracious homes. The street itself is also wider than the parallel streets. The astonishing brick mansions with expansive front lawns date from before World War I, when this area was a genteel, well-to-do "doctors' row." Professionals still live here, but so do large Hassidic families, and at least one mansion is now a dormitory for a local Hassidic girls' school.

KINGS HIGHWAY: SEPHARDIC BROOKLYN

To Get There

By subway: Take the F train to McDonald Ave. and Kings Highway. Walk west.

By car: Follow Ocean Pkwy. to Kings Highway (just after Ave. P); turn right and continue two blocks to E. 5th St.

By bike: See instructions for the "Kosher Special," on page 238 or follow "Brighton Beach K'nish K'nosh" on page 232 to Ocean Pkwy., and turn right onto Kings Highway, after Ave. P.

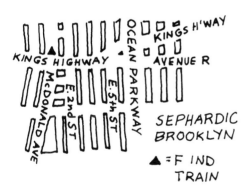

Arabic and French in a Jewish neighborhood? Yes, in this close-knit community of 25,000 Jews whose roots are in Damascus and Aleppo, Syria. The first of this group came to New York after the turn of the century, when the yoke of the Ottoman Empire tightened for religious minorities. (Christian Arabs suffered the same fate, and some of their descendants are storekeepers on Atlantic Ave.; see page 7.) Others came later, after living in Iraq, Egypt, Lebanon, or wherever they could find refuge when Muslim rulers made life difficult for the minority Jews. The earliest settlers came to New York when the Eastern European Jews did—at the turn of the century—and also settled on the Lower East Side. They've been in Flatbush since the 1940s. In their homelands, the Sephardic Jews grew up surrounded by dominant cultures whose languages and traditions they adopted. So don't be surprised to hear Arabic and French here as well as Hebrew—but no Yiddish.

RESTAURANTS

Stop here for lunch, where you can choose from about a half-dozen informal restaurants. The fanciest area eatery is **Lee Levach** (487 Kings Highway, Tel.: 718/336-6658), a Syrian-Israeli establishment that opened in August 1984. Its tablecloth-and-chandelier setting belie the informality of the place; Israelis rarely dress up, so you won't be out of place if it's a hot day and you're in shorts and a T-shirt. A glatt kosher restaurant, Lee Levach has a generous selection of meat entrées, but you can also indulge the Israeli passion for salads and vegetables: The menu lists 12 different salads, including hummus (mashed chick-peas) and babaganouj (mashed eggplant) dips, as well as avocado, Greek, Turkish, Moroccan, red cabbage, eggplant in sauce, and other selections, and eight varieties of stuffed vegetables. A small combination salad has samples of eight salads and is recommended for one person; the large salad, with even more samples, is recommended for two.

At **Shalom Israeli Oriental Foods** (542 Kings Highway, Tel.: 718/339-8085) and **David Restaurant** (547 Kings Highway, Tel.: 718/998-8600) nearby, you'll find many of the same salad and meat

Kings Highway noshery.

dishes for slightly lower prices and in an even more informal setting. Shalom, owned by an Egyptian, specializes in *mouloukhia*, a thick, vegetable-based meat soup. At David, a cup of Turkish coffee, sweet, strong, and flavored with cardamom pods, will round off a felafel platter, or a plate of stewed okra, or you can have any of the popular Israeli dips or several soups.

MARKETS

Several markets on Kings Highway cater to the Sephardic palate, and import specialties from Israel and elsewhere in the Mediterranean. You'll see the same selections of olives, nuts, spices, tahini, dried fruits, chick-pea flour, and other cooking ingredients that abound on Atlantic Avenue. Items of particular interest are imported Israeli soups, including an instant Hebrew "alef-bet" (alphabet) soup; *salep*, a sweet pudding flavored with orchid bulb (a "digestif," one merchant told us); packages of dried eggplant skins from Syria, ready to be boiled and stuffed; *doa*, a brown, crumbly bread spread, which is a mixture of sesame seed, crushed walnuts, cumin, and a touch of salt and coriander that are machine-ground and

Glatt kosher self-service.

Shalom Israeli Oriental Foods.

refrigerated. We found homemade doa at **Phoenicia Middle East Foods** (551 Kings Highway, Tel.: 718/645-2466). Food shops include **Bat Yam Middle Eastern Groceries** (525 Kings Highway, Tel.: 718/998-8200) and, next door, **Holon Middle Eastern Groceries** (527 Kings Highway, Tel.: 718/336-7758).

How can two almost identical stores exist side by side—and two or three other Sephardic groceries with many of the same products survive within three blocks of each other? We asked Camille, a proprietor of Phoenicia. "No problem," she replied. This is the only neighborhood that caters to the culinary desires of Syrian Jews, or the many Israelis in the metropolitan area who are kosher and have a passion for Mediterranean cuisine. "They come from all over," she said.

While in the area, you may wish to visit the modern Sephardic Center at Ocean Parkway and Avenue S on the other side of Ocean Parkway. If you're even more ambitious, continue on Kings Highway east of Ocean Parkway to an Orthodox Ashkenazic area, and note the contrasts to the Sephardic section. Eateries include **Moishe's Glatt Delight Fast Food** (627 Kings Highway), **Reich's Dairy Restaurant** (702 Kings Highway), and **Feigenblum's Bake Shop** (712 Kings Highway).

BOROUGH PARK

To Get There

By subway: Take the B train to the 50th or 55th St. stop at New Utrecht Ave.

By car: Follow the Brooklyn-Queens Expressway to Prospect Expressway, and continue to Church Ave., which, turning right, becomes 14th Ave. Park when you reach the forties or fifties, and walk one block to 13th Ave.

By bike: Follow "Kosher Special" (page 238) or "Brighton Beach K'nish K'nosh" (page 232) map to Ocean Pkwy. Turn right at Church Ave. and continue as it becomes 14th Ave., until you reach 49th St. Turn right onto 13th Ave.

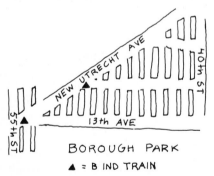

BOROUGH PARK

▲ = B IND TRAIN

Borough Park is the late-twentieth-century, urban version of the Eastern European *shtetl*, the self-contained village where Jews lived—often by fiat—for centuries. In Borough Park, however, the *shtetl* has grown by an act of will. Although 13th Avenue is the main (and thriving) commercial strip, the neighborhood stretches as far east as Fort Hamilton Parkway, as far west as 18th Avenue, as far north as 36th Street, as far south as 55th Street—and it's dribbling over these borders. The streets are often jammed with shopping carts, baby carriages, hurried (and harried) shoppers, and worshippers. Borough Park is the city's most populous Jewish neighborhood—and the most crowded. In the early 1980s, according to one estimate, about 100,000 people lived in Borough Park, a majority of them Jewish, 60 percent of them Orthodox. Since then, the number of Orthodox has probably increased: We've seen the construction of new synagogues, schools, and stores built by the Orthodox community in recent years.

Borough Park has long been a place for

Shopping on 13th Avenue (Borough Park).

Out for a stroll (Borough Park).

people seeking to prove their upward mobility; when built up in the 1920s and 1930s, its first residents were secular Jews moving from the Lower East Side or from elsewhere in Brooklyn. It also was, and remains to a lesser degree, home to middle-class Italians, some Irish, and a sprinkling of Hispanics and Chinese. Its transformation into an Orthodox neighborhood has been gradual, but accelerated when Hassidim and other observant Jews seeking refuge from the Holocaust came to the area in the 1940s. Some Williamsburg Hassidim fled to Borough Park in later decades, when they felt their own neighborhood had become too crime-plagued. New York today has about ten Hassidic sects, and about eight are represented in Borough Park.

RESTAURANTS

"Do I like Borough Park? It's just like Israel," said Tel Aviv–born Rachel Schlyfer, whose family, including two daughters, has transplanted itself to Brooklyn. "You can leave children in their strollers outside on the sidewalk when you go shopping—it's so safe. Where else in New York can you do that?" And there are children galore here. When we spoke with Rachel, she was seven months pregnant with her third child.

And that's perhaps key to your visit: Borough Park is a family place for "modern" Orthodox Jews, and the many restaurants tend to be simple and family-oriented. You can satisfy all your eating and shopping needs on 13th Avenue between 39th and 55th Streets, although if you visit on a Sunday, you'll have to compete with crowds of families—and strollers (the four-wheel kind).

The area's dozens of food emporia offer a diverse choice of cuisines—all, of course, glatt kosher. The typical menu features Middle Eastern dishes like felafel, hummus, and eggplant salad as well as kosher pizza, knishes, and calzone. Eateries of this sort are on almost every block.

The "in" place in Borough Park these days appears to be **Kosher Castle** (5006 13th Ave., Tel.: 718/871-2100). Borough Park's McDonald's, it is a sparkling new, mobbed, fast-food eatery with a very substantial menu of soups, salads, and entrées, and family-size seating arrangements. It's noisy and packed. Don't expect a restful lunch here.

If your palate tends to the exotic, you might try **Nosheria Glatt Kosher Chinese Restaurant** (4813 13th Ave., Tel.: 718/436-0400), where the menu features sweet-and-sour bass, wonton soup, Man-

darin or Cantonese duck, egg rolls, and other Chinese goodies. There's also a delicatessen selection for more provincial tastes. For so-called "American" cuisine, though, try the slightly more upscale **Adelman Original Delicatessen and Restaurant** (4514 13th Ave., Tel.: 718/853-5680), which serves the standard kosher meat platters—and southern fried chicken with french fries.

MARKETS, BAKERIES, AND SHOPS

If you want ice cream, you can get it at **Fine-Ess Quality Ice Cream** (4906 13th Ave., Tel.: 718/436-1909). In case you're wondering whether Jewish dietary laws forbid meat eaters from consuming a dairy product so soon after a meat meal, don't worry: Fine-Ess has not only 20 dairy ice cream flavors, but 20 pareve—nondairy—flavors, too. This "ice cream" is soybean based, like the popular Tofutti. And, by the way, Tofutti was developed by an entrepreneur seeking to accommodate kosher diets. Fine-Ess also has sherbet and frozen yogurt.

For sweets and takeout specialties, one of the best places is **Weber's Appe-tizers** (5502 13th Ave., Tel.: 718/435-2490), which is just across from the subway exit. One of the featured selections is a pizza knish, a tomato knish covered with cheese. The pizza knish originated at **Mom's Kosher Knishes** (4410 16th Ave., Tel.: 718/853-7178), on another commercial strip in Borough Park, which is less busy and less appealing. Weber's offers superb chocolates by the jarful; old-fashioned penny candies; a novelty, "Doggie-Man Bubble Gum"—gum shaped like a hot dog with a squiggle of candy mustard, if you can believe it; and more substantial edibles, including lox, sable, herring, pickles, and salads-to-go.

Closer to the center of Borough Park is **Candy Man** (4802 13th Ave., Tel.: 718/438-5419). As you trip over crowds of children reaching into cubbies of candies, you'll find an enormous selection of domestic and imported kosher chocolates (many from Israel) and other sweets. Specialties include chocolate-dipped glazed fruit, including kiwi and pineapple, and a marzipan *challah*: a sweet almond paste confection molded in the design of the traditional braided bread of Eastern European Jews.

The **Shmura Matzoh Bakery** (1285 36th St., Tel.: 718/438-2006), which

Making deliveries in the neighborhood.

opens only to make Passover matzoh, is located at the fringe of Borough Park. Most of the year, it looks like an abandoned store—but wait until the holiday.

For all your kosher needs, you can shop at the **Super K Market,** a gigantic supermarket (formerly known as **Kosher Revolution**) on 13th Avenue between 39th and 40th Streets (Tel.: 718/853-0337). Here you'll find a huge selection of frozen blintzes, fish, noodle pudding, potato pancakes—everything you need that you don't want to cook—plus a large selection of Israeli imports. But you won't find the atmosphere as chatty as in the smaller markets nearby. This area of Borough Park also has a few eateries catering to Sephardic Jews.

Borough Park is a politically active community: You can't miss signs and posters plastering the neighborhood exhorting residents to this rally or that protest, or the huge signs indicating the offices of local representatives. Borough Park may be a *shtetl,* but it's an all-American one. On the Fourth of July, you can still buy poppy-seed or walnut strudel or diet rugelach at **Franczoz Kosher Bakery** (4623 13th Ave., Tel.: 718/438-8978), but if you're feeling proud and patriotic, you can also buy a sweet layer cake decorated with an American flag.

Why is glatt kosher meat different from all other kosher meat? In the ultra-Orthodox neighborhoods of New York, you'll see signs indicating that a delicatessen or butcher sells glatt kosher meat only. Because it's glatt kosher, however, doesn't mean that it's any "more" kosher than kosher meat not marked glatt. *Glatt* is the Yiddish word for "smooth," and describes the smoothness of an animal's lungs during the slaughtering. In order to qualify for glatt stamping, the lungs must have no cysts or scabs. The tradition of eating glatt kosher is based on ancient biblical law; however, as *The Third Jewish Catalog* points out, major scholars all the way back to Maimonides have rejected the need to follow the glatt kosher standard. Probably the chief difference between meat that's kosher and meat that's glatt kosher is price.

AN ANOMALY GROWS IN BROOKLYN

South of the majestic Grand Army Plaza, on the other side of Prospect Park, and sometimes described as the "flip side" of the elegant Park Slope area, is that urban phenomenon known as the "changing neighborhood." Once a bedraggled collection of not-too-well-maintained brownstones and unkempt apartment buildings on the fringe of Bedford-Stuyvesant and Crown Heights, the area now has a fancy name—Prospect Heights—and a surging real estate market: The brownstones are being resold and renovated, the apartment buildings converted into market-rate co-ops, and genteel cafés and boutiques are moving onto nearby Flatbush Avenue and other streets. In the midst of this change is **Restaurant Cuscatlán** (626 Vanderbilt Ave., Tel.: 718/789-9306), just two blocks from Prospect Park. Carmen Rivas, who migrated to the United States from El Salvador, opened Cuscatlán in 1982, before the gentrification began. It is the largest of the handful of Salvadoran restaurants in New York, says Carmen's son Tony, Cuscatlán's manager. Many Salvadoran families come to the restaurant not only to savor such specialties as *pupusas* (cornmeal patties with meat or cheese stuffings, topped with peppery shredded cabbage), sweet plantains with *frijoles* (beans) and sour cream, *tamales,* and *orchata* (an icy almond-flavored drink), but to buy souvenir gifts imported from El Salvador and to dance and party to live Salvadoran music—until recently. With the change of the neighborhood has come pressure to gentrify its ambience, too, and Cuscatlán was threatened with being closed if the "noise" from the weekend dancing continued. Cuscatlán's jukebox still bounces with Salvadoran rhythms, but the dancing has stopped. Tony Rivas shrugs his shoulders when he talks about it. "We make a living here," he says, "but . . ."

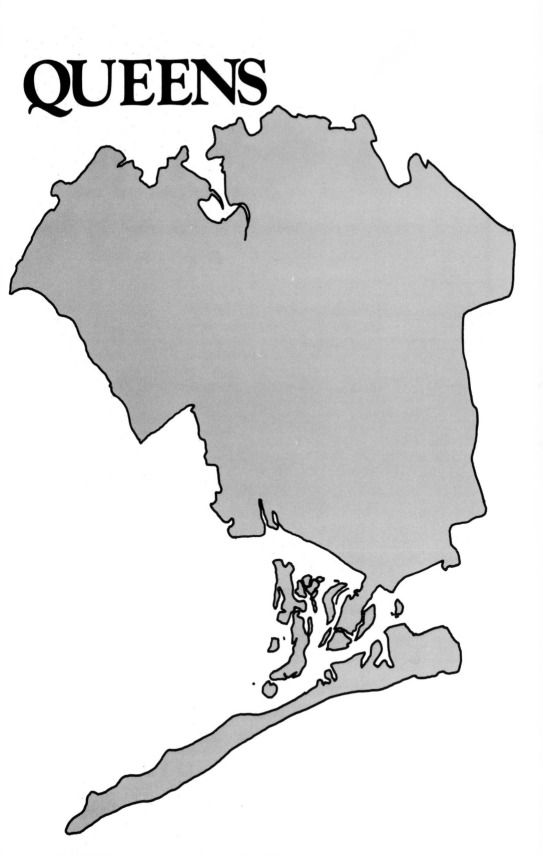

QUEENS

Queens has none of Fifth Avenue's classical glamor, none of Brooklyn's glorious blocks of Victorian brownstones, no Parisian-style boulevard like the Grand Concourse in the Bronx, lined with landmark Art Deco apartment houses. Unlike Staten Island, Queens can't even complain of being New York's neglected stepchild.

And it's not the land of Archie Bunker, either. While its homey ordinariness may be one of Queen's greatest strengths, the borough has many personalities. For decades, its quiet middle-class neighborhoods have been magnets for hardworking immigrants seeking a better life as well as for city folks seeking a more suburban ambience but not quite ready to abandon New York City altogether.

Today Queens consists of neighborhoods like Elmhurst, where Southeast Asian faces and dialects mingle with those from the Indian subcontinent, Iran, Afghanistan, and all over Latin America; Malba, a wealthy, semiprivate beachfront community; and Astoria, a Greek neighborhood, where Mediterranean folkways still have their place amidst the urban hustle. During the 1986 World Cup soccer games, you need not have gone farther than Jackson Heights to cheer the brilliant victory of the Argentinian team along with thousands of Argentinian-Americans who call Queens their home. What Manhattan's tenement-thick Lower East Side once represented to the fresh-out-of-steerage "greenhorns" a century ago, the quieter streets of Queens now offer to people who have made their way to New York from all different areas and by many means of transport.

The borough of Queens was named after Catherine of Braganza, wife of Charles II, when the British drove out the Dutch in 1683. It was one of ten counties that formed New York State, and its original borders included portions of what is now Nassau County. Although Queens was incorporated into New York City in 1898, its older families for quite some time considered themselves residents of the much more chic Long Island; when Malba, just west of the Whitestone Bridge, was being developed in 1907, it was advertised as being on "Long Island's North Shore."

The borough remained quite rural through the early 1900s even though factories had begun sprouting in western Queens in the 1840s. But after the completion of the Queensborough Bridge in 1909 and an underground tunnel for the Long Island Railroad the following year, people began migrating to Queens in droves. That movement accelerated when the subway system reached Flushing in 1929, and, once again, in 1939, when LaGuardia Airport, built to accommodate visitors to the 1939 World's Fair in nearby Flushing Meadow, opened for service. The postwar baby boom was a boon to Queens, and garden apartment communities and high-rise apartment clusters rose around the borough.

With 1.8 million people, Queens has the second-largest population of New York's five boroughs and is geographically the largest. With more than one-third of New York City's land, it has some of the city's loveliest parks.

It may seem difficult at first to get a handle on Queens because of its many faces. Try to describe the United Nations, with all its conflicts and diversity and its goal of

The latest news . . . from Greece.

trying to make the world a better place, and in a sense you've got Queens. But instead of ambassadors, politicians, and diplomats, you've got, for the most part, fairly ordinary, idealistic, and ambitious people trying to preserve what matters most to them from their home cultures and yet at the same time trying to become American.

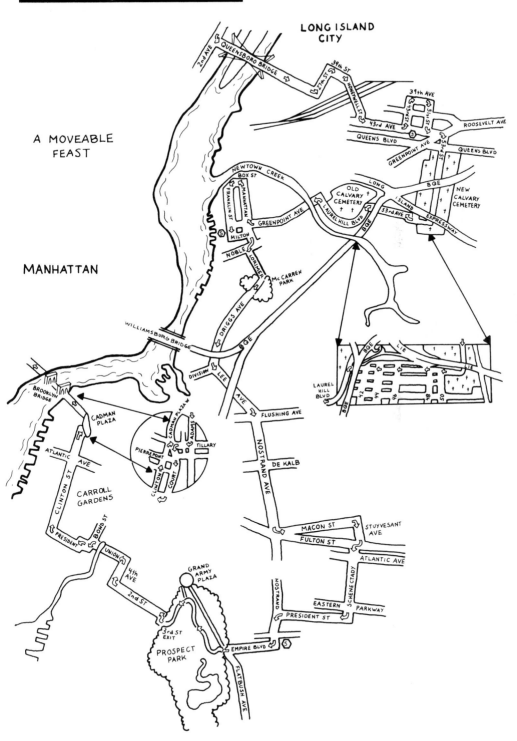

A MOVEABLE
FEAST

MANHATTAN

ASTORIA: BOUZOUKIS & BAKLAVA

To Get There

By subway: Take the N train toward Ditmars Blvd. Get off at any of the following three stops: Ditmars Blvd., 30th Ave., or Broadway.

By car: Exit the Triborough Bridge at Hoyt Ave. South; turn left on 31st St. to get to Ditmars Blvd., or turn right on 31st St. for 30th Ave. or Broadway. (You can park anywhere in the area; everything is within walking distance.)

If you take the Queensborough Bridge, exit at Queens Plaza and turn left on 31st St.

By bike: From the Triborough Bridge, follow the bike path and exit down the stairs at Hoyt Ave. South; continue east on Hoyt Ave. toward 31st St. and turn right or left depending on destination.

From the 59th St. Bridge, exit from the bike lane on the south side; turn left on 27th St. to Broadway; turn right to 31st St.

If you take the Roosevelt Island tram, follow the Island road to the 36th Ave. Bridge; turn left on Vernon Blvd. to Broadway; turn right to 31st St.

Also see tour directions for "Queens Cornucopia" on page 250.

GREEK ASTORIA

▲ = R BMT TRAIN

"Astoria is Greektown, USA," declares Christine Sariyannis, owner of the Kentrikon Center gift shop, and no sooner do you turn a corner here than signs appear to bear out her claim: Venus Fashion Imports, Athenian Dry Cleaners, Odyssey Optical—even Mt. Olympus Bagels. But facades tell only half the story: Come here on Greek Orthodox Good Friday during the traditional outdoor funeral processions when thousands of Astoria's Greeks stream from the dozen or so churches in the area. Bands play a *kaden*, a slow funeral march, fragrant incense fills the air, and priests flank a casket bearing a symbolic Christ while thousands of parishioners follow, holding lighted candles. This is the evening, says Christine, when you realize at last how large the Greek population is in Astoria. The estimates range from 60,000 to 200,000, but ask a shopkeeper like Konstantinos Tsirbas, who owns the Café Hilton, and you'll soon hear that Astoria is the third-largest Greek city after Athens and Salonika. During summer evenings, when the weather most closely resembles its Mediterranean counterpart, the streets and parks are packed with Greeks young and old. Bouzouki music from the restaurants is piped outdoors; Greek Astoria takes on a festive air. And all year round, the *kaffenions*—coffeehouses—scattered around the area are packed with young Greeks—mainly men—who passionately discuss politics and soccer amidst the intertwining aromas of Greek coffee and tobacco. They keep up with the goings-on back home by reading the dozen or so newspapers flown in daily, plus another dozen or so magazines available all over the neighborhood.

A stroll along Astoria's side streets shows how village traditions have been transported across an ocean: You'll see grapevines on trellises, vegetable gardens, even orange and fig trees—and flowers everywhere. The sense of family in Astoria overlaps into the way restaurants are set up: People tend to go out in large groups, and you should, too. There's a wide variety of flavors in Greek food, and to get the best out of your meal in Astoria, go with several people.

Freshness is the essence of the food, whether in homegrown herbs (dill, rosemary, sage, and oregano are among the most common), or just-ripe produce, or

All in the family.

newly caught fish—some flown in from Greece—or just-slaughtered meat or poultry. Dips and cold appetizers are popular preludes to a large meal; a platter of assorted appetizers is a good beginning. This usually consists of up to four dips—*taramasalata* (caviar spread), *tzatziki* (cucumber and yogurt flavored with garlic, mint, and dill), *skordalia* (potato and garlic), and *melizanosalata* (eggplant and mashed chick-peas)—and *dolmades* (stuffed grape leaves), cubes of feta cheese, and tomatoes and olives. Spinach and cheese pie appetizers, *spanatirokopita*, baked in *fillo* dough are also popular, and you might prepare yourself for an entrée with popular *avgolemono* soup, a chicken broth flavored with lemon. Greek salads with anchovies, tomato, feta

Business partners.

cheese, onion, cucumber, and greens, with a light oregano-flavored dressing, are ample in Astoria: A "small" one easily feeds two people. You'll find meat or fish entrées fairly simple: Lamb, the Greek staple, is often spit-roasted and served with braised vegetables, including artichokes, asparagus, string beans, lima beans, okra, or spinach, as well as rice or orzo, a popular Greek pasta. Beef is often served ground with vegetables, or in loaves, as in *moussaka*—a layered "pie" with eggplant, cheese, and eggs—or as the stuffing for eggplant, peppers, and other vegetables. Fish entrées are often broiled with olive oil and lemon, braised in tomato sauce, fried—sometimes with skordalia—or baked. If you're still hungry, typical Greek desserts include baklava (nut-filled pastries wrapped in honey-soaked fillo), rice pudding, or halvah.

You can put the finishing touch on your meal by lingering over a tiny cup of Greek espresso that has been boiled in a *briki*, an enamel or metal urn. There isn't much per cup, but you won't need or want much; Greek coffee is *very* strong. Greeks also drink herbal infusions called *tisanes* to aid digestion or relieve headaches or

Basting the beef.

other ailments. Among the more common teas are chamomile, geranium, rosemary, parsley, dandelion, thyme, and the Mediterranean standby, mint. And don't forget your Greek wines and liqueurs: *Retsina* is a resin-flavored white wine, often bitter to the tongue, but nice chilled, and *rodytis* is a refreshing rosé. *Ouzo*, an anise-flavored aperitif, is well named, for it oozes down your esophagus and gives you a little spin before your meal.

RESTAURANTS AND CAFÉS

Note: The N train, which takes 20 minutes to get to Ditmars Boulevard from Times Square, runs along 31st Street, the "spine" of Astoria. Major commercial avenues off the spine include Ditmars Boulevard, 30th Avenue, and Broadway. The eateries and shops described in this section are in each of these areas.

You'll quickly feel at home in **George's Hasapotaverna** (28-13 23rd Ave., Tel.: 718/728-9056), simple, wood-paneled restaurant with folk decor. Sitting on a quiet side street near Ditmars Boulevard, George's serves a capacious Greek salad, the best spinach pies we've had, lightly spiced meatball appetizers, and finely cooked entrées. Service is relaxed and friendly, and, perhaps because we were non-Greek visitors, we were treated on several occasions to desserts on the house: once, a dish of halvah sprinkled with cinnamon and lemon juice; another time, yogurt with honey and nuts.

Taygetos (30-11 30th Ave., Tel.: 718/726-5195) has an ample selection of vegetable dishes offered as main courses as well as on the side, and on request they once prepared a special platter of spinach, lima beans in tomato sauce, and green beans, plus a side order of orzo. Their tzatziki (spicy cucumber dip) and skordalia were superb eaten as dips or with fresh-baked Greek bread or pita bread.

Roumeli Taverna (33-14 Broadway, Tel.: 718/278-7533), an Astoria institution by now, takes its name from a famous mountain range in Greece. Rather fancier and priced slightly higher than George's and Taygetos, it attracts perceptibly more non-Greeks, perhaps because of its location in a more commercial area of Astoria (and not far from the Museum of the Moving Image, formerly Paramount Studios; see box on page 83). The menu selection covers Greek standards, with an extra touch of lemony garlic sauce on the vegetables. The artichokes were a rich and perfect accompaniment for baked lamb.

In case you prefer to snack in Astoria, the area is dotted with wonderful cafés where you can get a cup of cappuccino and pastry and forget about watching the clock. The glitziest is the two-story **Café Hilton** (22-06 31st St., Tel.: 718/274-6399) near Ditmars Boulevard, which Mr. Tsirbas opened in 1980. "I liked the name Hilton from the hotel," confessed this native of Athens. The ground floor is the retail selling area, and here you can purchase such specialties as baklava; *kantaifi,* honey pastries cooked in butter and covered with shredded dough; *touloubaki,* small ovalshaped fried semolina cakes dipped in honey syrup; *melomakarouna,* orangefilled pastries covered with walnuts; and different kinds of almond cookies, like *kourabiedes,* with whole almonds and covered with confectioner's sugar, and chewy *amigdalota,* which we particularly liked because they're not as rich as the other cookies, and are wonderful for dunking in coffee. Mr. Tsirbas also sells a sweet holiday bread called *tsoureki,* which during Easter is sold braided with colored hardboiled Easter eggs on top.

You can also find many rich, calorie-laden chocolate-covered, cream-filled, layered pastries at Hilton and in bakeries all over Astoria. At Hilton, you can order desserts to take home, or eat upstairs in a crowded café that has a large picture window overlooking the busy intersection outside. Among the better bakeries is **Schoenberg's Bakery** (33-18 Broadway, Tel.: 718/728-6892) technically in Long Island City but spiritually in Astoria. Owned by George Bitsanis, it has luscious fruit-piled tarts and pies and specializes in rich wedding and birthday cakes and coffee cakes.

On 30th Avenue, we rather like **HBH European Café** (29-28 30th Ave., Tel.: 718/274-1609), across the street from Taygetos and located in a quiet residential part of Astoria. One of the "most Greek" of the area's cafés—we came in once

when a young Greek filmmaker was using the rear of the café to shoot a scene—it has a fountain and dark wooden tables, and a lush selection of baklava and chocolate cakes. Across the street is a playground that the Greek-American Homeowners Association has been trying for years to renovate into a park called Athens Square—if it can raise $1 million. Further east on 30th Avenue, try **Galaxy Greek Pastry** (37-11 30th Ave., Tel.: 718/545-3181), a quiet, homey coffeehouse with chocolate specialties. **Omonia Café** (32-20 Broadway, Tel.: 718/274-6650 or 718/728-9024) combines a contemporary look with traditional Greek cookery. After substantial renovations, it reopened in mid-1985 with an enclosed plant-filled sidewalk café and classy beige interior decor. The pastry offerings include so-called "light" pastries (custard and nut) and rich, creamy cheesecakes and tortes. Wine and liqueur-flavored coffees are served along with American and Greek coffees, and at night—7 P.M. to 4 A.M.—

We *like* our work!

Omonia also serves salads, pizzas, and spinach pies.

Tropicana Café & Patisserie (31-14 Broadway, Tel.: 718/728-4170) is the unlikely name of one of Astoria's newest and perhaps trendiest late-night hangouts. Rock music and video images replace the bouzouki-filled ambience of the area's other cafés, but the selection of pastries, cordials, and coffees is similar—and there's also an ample selection of Greek appetizers and salads for a light dinner out. This is where young Greeks and Greek Americans can go for a night out—and not worry about seeing their parents or grandparents in the same place.

Astoria has several nightclubs that keep the neighborhood dancing long after much of Queens has gone to bed. **Taverna Vraka** (23-15 31st St., Tel.: 718/721-3007) is a Cypriot nightclub where one can eat or just drink, and perhaps happen in on a family celebration. You might find a christening party going on, as we once did. Family members formed a long line and danced around the tables to the music of a live bouzouki band; dollars were thrown in appreciation to various soloists. On other nights, you might hear an entertainer from the homeland or a local Greek or Cypriot group. **Café Acroama** (29-35 Newtown Ave. at 30th St., Tel.: 718/204-1727), which opened in early 1984, is run by two young Greek Americans, Julie Ziavras and Evangelos (Evan) Fampas, who sing and perform there, too. But they're also trying to make it a more international club; Monday is jazz night, and other evenings the program is apt to include Latin American music or offerings from other countries, as well as Julie singing Greek folk tunes to Evan's accompaniment. **Bohemian Hall** (29-19 24th Ave., Tel.: 718/728-9327) is a small Eastern European bar with an enclosed beer garden—possibly unique in New York—that doubles during the spring and summer as the site for bazaars and folk festivals, often Greek or Cypriot. Local church groups use the garden for special saints'-day celebrations. Every year in early September, the Manhattan-based Ethnic Arts Center sponsors an international folk festival. Folk musicians, mainly of Balkan origin, though Eastern European *klezmorim* (Jewish wedding musicians) have played, too, perform live music for the hundreds of folk dancers who participate. Many of the older performers are laborers who have preserved their music as a serious sideline, while some of the younger ones are making a living from their music. Watch as grateful dancers—often compatriots from the "other side"—place dollar bills, moistened with a lick of the tongue, on the instrumentalist's forehead. Folk clothing and gifts, as well as Greek food, are often for sale during this festival.

MARKETS AND SHOPS

Astoria has dozens of markets offering good selections of feta and *haloumi* cheeses, olive oil, herbs and spices, beans, pastas, and imported canned and bottled goods from Greece and elsewhere in the Mediterranean. There are also many fine produce markets run by Greeks, and the prices are generally lower than in much of the borough, while the quality is high. The greatest concentration of markets is on 30th Avenue between 32nd and 36th Streets. **Mediterranean Foods** (33-20 30th Ave., Tel.: 718/728-6166) is a large, comprehensive store. Specialties include Greek pastas, fresh

Fresh from the oven.

herbs, and pastries (including the recommended tahini bread, a flat, circular sweet bread), Greek and Italian ground coffees, and a good selection of brikis. In the dairy bin are fresh cheeses, including Greek yogurt—homemade for the store. Be prepared for the thick, bitter taste; it's often used in making sauces.

The king of Greek food markets in Astoria is **Titan Foods** (25-30 31st St., Tel.: 718/626-7771), which Kostas Blafas opened in March 1985. Titan has been importing and distributing Greek food products for years, and its supermarket is the largest retail outlet of its kind in America, according to Mr. Blafas. As in a typical American supermarket, the shopper takes a shopping cart down numbered aisles. But at Titan, product names are listed in Greek, and here one can stock up with large quantities of all the makings of Greek cuisine. There's a cheese, fish, and meat counter in the rear—there are six different fetas, from dry, bitter Bulgarian to blander Greek-style fetas—and a good choice of frozen foods, including spanakopita (spinach pies ready to bake) or frozen fillo dough for the more ambitious cook. Titan also sells hard-to-find herbs and spices, about two dozen brands of olive oil, and, among the coffees, a Greek

decaffeinated brand called *Venezios.*

Certain kinds of fish favored in Greek cooking, including *barbuna, maridas,* and *langostinos,* are flown in daily to **Ocean #11 Fish Market,** also known as **Poseidon Fishery** (35-08 30th Ave., Tel.: 718/721-2391). The area's largest, busiest, and most comprehensive fish market, it supplies local restaurants as well as individual shoppers, so the selection is wide.

Jolson's Liquors (22-10 31st St., Tel.: 718/728-2020) sells Greek wines and aperitifs, including several novelties. A red *bouzouki* dessert wine is sold in a bouzouki-shaped bottle. You can buy Aphrodite white wine or Othello red wine from Cyprus, and some of the ouzos and retsinas are sold in bottles encased in plastic *amphorae* (Grecian urns) or miniature Greek temples.

Greek pottery, folk clothing, and jewelry, and various wedding and religious gifts, as well as Greek videocassettes, audiotapes, books, and magazines, are, not surprisingly, widely available in Astoria. Mrs. Sariyiannis's **Kentrikon Center** (31-12 23rd Ave., Tel.: 718/721-9190) has a broad and tasteful selection of gifts, especially traditional folk clothing, including costumes for Greek Independence Day in May, and religious accessories, such as *lambades* (baptismal candles) and the wedding crowns worn by bride and groom, which someday will be buried with them. Also available are many children's books, including *Classics Illustrated* comics—in Greek, of course. **Corfou Center** (22-13 31st St., Tel.: 718/728-7213) houses the Hellas Video Club and sells lovely ceramics, as well as books, key chains, decals, greeting cards, and religious icons, plus a very large selection of Greek newspapers and magazines.

THE "OTHER" ASTORIA

It is easy to overlook the fact that Astoria is not exclusively Greek. Italians have long made Astoria their home, and smaller Czech and Ukrainian communities also lay claim to the area. Be sure to visit the shops and restaurants in the "other" Astoria.

MARKETS AND BAKERIES

La Guli pastry shop (29-15 Ditmars Blvd., Tel.: 718/728-5612) is a superb Italian bakery with miniatures; you take a tray and put together your own assortment. There's also a fine stand-up espresso and cappuccino bar: a nice break during a neighborhood walk. At **Liguria Italian Delicatessen** (35-13 Ditmars Blvd., Tel.: 718/728-5311), you'll find such Italian specialties as sun-dried tomatoes, plain or in olive oil, and homemade mozzarella and ricotta cheeses. At **Cassinelli Food Products, Inc.** (31-11 23rd Ave., Tel.: 718/274-4881), you can buy fresh pasta every

day, including capelletti with meat or cheese; *cavatelli* with cheese; *gnocchi* and *cappelloni*; fresh spinach, meat, or cheese *ravioli*; and *manicotti*. Also available at Cassinelli's are Italian fruit syrups (*granata, tamarindo, orzata,* and *menta*), basil sauces, and other Italian imports. **Mario Tenaglia Latticini and Fresh Sausage** (22-75 31st St., Tel.: 718/728-2920), a 35-year-old Astoria institution, is one of the rare delicatessens that don't compromise: Only Italian food is sold here—except Coca-Cola—and a wide selection, too. At **John & Angelo** (29-03 Broadway, Tel.: 718/728-4210), there's a superb selection of prepared pasta and vegetable dishes and salads, many cheeses, and cooking accessories: pasta makers and cutters, meat and cheese graters, and espresso makers.

René Seiler Meat and Poultry Market (29-11 Broadway, Tel.: 718/278-8189) is a Swiss-owned, old-fashioned meat and

Three of the guys at the S&M Pork Store.

cheese shop: Take a look at the ancient cash register and telephone in the little booth near the rear of the store. You can buy very high-quality poultry and sausage, but you may not know Monsieur Seiler has it unless you ask: The store seems rather spare, at first glance, but the inventory is there. Monsieur Seiler also sells imported French *chevre* and *brie* cheeses, and an eclectic selection of vinegars, mustards, syrups, and preserves. **Astoria Meat Products, Inc.** (35-09 Broadway, Tel.: 718/726-5663) is a Ukrainian-owned shop that specializes in kielbasy (sausage), but also sells a large selection of Eastern European groceries. We especially like **S&M Pork Store** (35-10 Ditmars Blvd., Tel.: 718/278-8468), a busy Czech market that doubles as a meeting place for the small Czech community in Queens. Shelves are lined with canned and bottled imports from Hungary, Rumania, Czechoslovakia, and

Yugoslavia. Meat specialties include *jaternice,* a pork sausage stuffed with rice, bread, or blood; gypsy meat or bacon, dark smoked spiced steak and bacon; and *debrecina,* pork-and-beef frankfurters spiced with garlic. There's also a large selection of hams, salamis, bolognas, headcheese, liverwurst, and homemade meat loaf. The market had been operating under another name in Astoria for 33 years and had become a bit sleepy, until early 1984, when two young men, Josef Skrkon—a new immigrant from Czechoslovakia—and his partner, Henry Michtalik, took it over. Now it's a lively place once again, says Rudy Gregorovic, a police detective who, in his spare time, dons an apron and helps out. Why the new interest? It's because Josef brings a friendly, old-fashioned European style to the place, says Rudy, and Josef is proud of his success. "So far I'm well and I'm happy, thank God," he smiles.

Long before many people knew the difference between dolmades and debrecina, celebrities like Rudolph Valentino, Gloria Swanson, W. C. Fields, and the Marx Brothers were making the trip out—or, probably, being chauffeured—to Astoria, where Famous Players–Lasky Corporation, later to become Paramount Pictures, had opened studios in 1919. The U.S. Army took over the studios in 1942 to make propaganda films (Paramount had already relocated to Hollywood), but in 1971 the property was abandoned.

The good news is that restoration of the renamed Kaufman-Astoria Studios began in 1976. Its sound stages have since been used for films like *Hair, The World According to Garp, All That Jazz,* and *Kramer vs. Kramer.* A new **Museum of the Moving Image** offers exhibitions of movie memorabilia, film series, and occasional film courses, too. The entire complex, including federally landmarked buildings, is known as the **Astoria Motion Picture and Television Foundation** (34-31 35th St., Tel.: 718/784-4520), and is within easy walking distance of Astoria's restaurants, markets, and cafés.

FLUSHING: LITTLE ASIA IN QUEENS

To Get There

By subway: Take the IRT 7 line to the last stop, Main St.

By car: Take the Queensborough Bridge and follow signs to Northern Blvd., which will take you directly to Flushing. Park near Main, Union, or Bowne Sts.

By bike: For the most direct (and least picturesque) route from Manhattan, begin by crossing the Queensborough Bridge and follow Northern Blvd. directly to Flushing. A more pleasant alternative is to follow Northern Blvd. to 76th St., turn right onto 34th Ave. and continue to 114th St., then turn right for three long blocks to Roosevelt Ave. (under the el), which you should follow east until you reach Main St. The "Queens Cornucopia" bike tour (see page 250) weaves around quiet residential areas and leads into Flushing via Flushing Meadow Park and the Botanical Gardens (potential picnic sites).

ORIENTAL FLUSHING

▲ = #7 IRT TRAIN (LAST STOP)

The Orient Express leads to Flushing, and if you have any doubt about that, take the IRT 7 train to Main Street, and watch (and listen) as you get closer and closer to the last stop. The faces—and conversations—will remind you more of the Far East and India. As you climb the exit stairs, you will see that the advertising posters in the station are in Chinese.

If, however, you come by bike or car, and then walk along Main Street or Roosevelt Avenue, you'll find yourself in New York's second Chinatown. Walk a few blocks to the north to Union Street, and you'll come upon a flourishing Korean and Japanese mini-mall. Head east on Main Street, over a slight rise past the Flushing post office, and you'll hit some of the most comprehensive Oriental food and house-wares stores around. But keep going: As the road starts to dip you'll find yourself in Flushing's Indian bazaar. Clustered within one block are a dozen stores selling all kinds of Indian groceries, appliances, and saris.

Long-time Flushing residents like to brag about their town's role in early American history, and they're right to do so: **The Bowne House**, built in 1661 as a sanctuary for fellow Quakers by John Bowne, and the Friends' Meeting House, built in 1694, recall Flushing's beginning as a haven for seekers of religious freedom. The huge weeping beech tree near Parsons Boulevard and 37th Avenue was planted in the late 1840s, and Flushing's landmark Town Hall building, an example of early Romanesque revival, was erected in 1862.

But the real revolution in Flushing began in the mid-1960s, when the easing of immigration laws led to streams of Chinese, mainly from Taiwan and Hong Kong, Koreans, and, to a lesser extent, Indians and Japanese, who settled in this appealing community, which offers fine transportation and schools, good housing, and nearby parks.

These new arrivals now make up nearly half of Flushing's population of 200,000: According to the 1980 census, there were 40,000 Chinese, about 40,000 Koreans, and around 8,000 Indians and 7,000 Japanese. The numbers have surely grown since then; you'll likely see newly opened shops catering to this thriving community: Mikado Realty, State Bank of India, Koreana Boutique.

In many of the shops, you'll feel like a foreigner, lacking in language, unfamiliar with the food. But Flushing's new citizens

Vegetable shopping in Flushing.

seem anxious to become Americanized, even if they continue to cook their traditional cuisine: Visit the Flushing Branch Main Library at Main Street and Kissena Boulevard, and head down one flight to the New Americans Program. Here, a thriving—and oversubscribed—program helps with English lessons, citizenship training, and coping in New York. And take a peek into the children's library right beside the entrance. Although the parents may stumble over their English, the children—the huge majority Oriental and Indian—revel in their own native English.

The Asian markets and restaurants are all within walking distance of Flushing's hub at Main Street and Roosevelt Avenue, but don't expect to cover everything in a day. You might want to split your visit into two, or even three, parts, as we have outlined.

CHINESE FLUSHING

MARKETS, BAKERIES, AND SHOPS

Flushing's Chinatown is packed into one block of Roosevelt Avenue between Main Street and Prince Street, one block west of the Main Street subway stop. (There's a growing overflow onto parallel side streets.) You'll see markets, bakeries, a few restaurants, the Chinese-owned **TLC**

Fresh fish!

Pharmacy, a music store specializing in Chinese audiocassettes and records, and other businesses. Worth a visit is **Yi Mei Fung Bakery Co.** (135-38 Roosevelt Ave., Tel.: 718/886-6820), which has a Manhattan Chinatown branch; it sells a good selection of traditional Chinese mooncakes, lotus-bean cakes, pineapple and coconut cakes, and vegetable *dim sum* buns. **Maria's Bakery** (135-50 Roosevelt Ave., Tel.: 718/539-3111), part of a popular chain with branches in Hong Kong, Taiwan, Manhattan, and Los Angeles, is a combination sit-down/takeout coffee shop where you can buy vegetable, meat, and sweet Chinese pastries; its popularity is signaled by the double-parked cars outside and the lines of people buying boxes of pastries to go. **Flushing Seafood** (135-17 Roosevelt Ave., Tel.: 718/353-8585) is the major Oriental seafood market in the area, with a full aquarium in front and a selection of fresh fish and frozen goods from Ecuador, Panama, and Canada. **Flushing Food** (135-18 Roosevelt Ave., Tel.: 718/445-0444) is a clogged grocery stocked half with Chinese, half with Thai foods.

Return to Main Street and turn left (west) for several long blocks toward busy Northern Boulevard, where Main Street ends. (Take note of the monumental RKO Keith's cinema at the intersection.) If you turn left you can quickly visit the large **Wah Keong Book Co.** (135-18 Northern Blvd., Tel.: 718/762-8889); it will be of little use if you don't speak Chinese, but re-

Yes, this is what you think it is.

flects the flavor of the neighborhood. Note the shelves of airmail stationery for writing to the folks back home.

You'll find many multipurpose Chinese markets in Flushing, but you can satisfy all your food and many household needs at the modern, busy **Kam Sen** (41-79 Main St., Tel.: 718/939-2560). In the store's right-hand section as you enter are shelves of dishware and cookware: teapots and tea sets, thermoses, ceramic ware, woks, spoons, etc. There are also tables and chairs. In the right rear is a stationery section and miniapothecary, with jars of dried medicinal and cooking herbs. Tapes and magazines (including "girlie" publications) from Hong Kong and Taiwan line the rear shelves. In the food section—about 75 percent of the store—you may be overwhelmed by the breadth of the display: *tofu*, sauces, frozen dim sum buns, a fresh fish counter, Chinese vegetables (water chestnuts, broccoli, squash, and many roots), a meat counter, and then shelves of noodles, oils, dried spices, crackers, and on and on. You'll find a small selection of food from the Philippines, Thailand, Vietnam, Japan—and even the United States: Spam is a best seller here, apparently. Along the left wall are canned and boxed Chinese fruit juices, including *haw*, blackcurrant, and sugarcane juice, and bottles of soy milk. Among the novelties you'll find here are ginseng toothpaste from China and Chinese vegetable seeds from California (Chinese leek, long radish, amaranth, bitter gourd, Chinese mustard, asparagus bean, and pickling cucumber).

For a picnic, you can buy containers of ready-to-eat (and delicious) smoked duck, as well as fish and rice cakes, pickled vegetables, sprouts, and even *sushi*. In the warm weather, you can buy Taiwanese ices: Served in heaping giant-size cups like the Latin American snow cones, they consist of syrups poured onto shaved ice, but with different kinds of flavors, including peanut, fruit preserves, tamarind, and red bean. The ices are often flavored with sweet evaporated milk and banana flavorings.

Before you leave Kam Sen's, take a look at the window display; the electric rice cookers, pots, and tea baskets (containing thermal teapots and tumblers) are not displayed inside the store but are some of the loveliest products Kam Sen has to sell.

RESTAURANTS

When **Stony Wok** (137-40 Northern Blvd., Tel.: 718/445-8535) opened in 1984, it was the first restaurant in the New York area to offer "hot wok" dishes, cooked at the table on built-in gas burners. The concept is that you create your own casserole: Order four or five different dishes, and mix them together on the spot. The menu is unusual: soups like ginger-flavored clam, ginseng-flavored venison, duck with Chinese herb in casserole; appetizers, including winter bamboo in lemon sour cream, a traditional sauce of Taiwan, or squid roll with ginger sauce; a seafood selection, including eel, sautéed snails, cuttlefish and lily flower with sea cucumber; and raw a la carte dishes for at-table wok cookery, including mutton, venison, oysters, quail eggs, *tong ho* (garland chrysanthemum leaves and stalks, a seasonal offering), ox stomach, bean thread, *taro* root, and dried lily flower. (Each of the Stony Wok dishes costs less than $5, some as little as $1; you normally order at least three to make your casserole.) Larry Cheng, the restaurant's young manager, moved to Flushing from Los Angeles in 1984; he notes that in less than two years, the Taiwanese community has boomed; real estate values have skyrocketed—next door, a building was being renovated as the Taiwanese fraternal association.

Further north is **Mei Wei Shiang,** also known as **House of Hand-Made Noodle Co.** (138-12 Northern Blvd., Tel.: 718/961-9811). "Noodles are like pizza in Korea!" explained its Korean-born owner, James Liu, who opened the restaurant a few years ago. The whole wheat noodles are made in the restaurant's kitchen in the rear, and you can select Peking-style dishes, such as noodles in bean sauce with seafood in garlic sauce, and so on. All come with side dishes of pickled vegetables. There are more standard seafood and beef or poultry entrées, too. The servings are very ample; we couldn't finish ours, and James gave us sticks of chewing gum when we finished!

KOREAN AND JAPANESE FLUSHING

The Korean Produce Association is based in Flushing, and even the most casual visitor can't help but be struck by the Korean presence. The Koreans have become affluent here, and run almost every kind of business, from nail salons (over which Koreans have a monopoly) and driving schools to dentists' offices and stationery stores. There are four Korean-language newspapers published in New York alone. And you'll see about a half-dozen 24-hour Japanese-Korean restaurants with sushi bars, and several fine Korean crafts stores.

MARKETS AND SHOPS

Head north on Roosevelt Avenue from Main Street and turn left (west) on Union Street. Between 37th Avenue and Northern Boulevard is a compact, three-story shopping complex of several dozen Korean and Japanese stores. Its anchor is **Daido-Main Street Foods** (137-80 Northern Blvd., Tel.: 718/961-1550), which is both a social center and food emporium: Note the bulletin board advertis-

In Flushing, English is a second language.

Hosing down the produce.

ing real estate, English lessons, and music instruction. Japanese magazines, comics, pharmaceuticals, and videotapes are for sale (the last, for rent) here, as well as all the makings for sushi—fresh and frozen fish, huge packages of dried seaweed for wrapping, and pickled vegetables—and a $99 sushi maker. There are dozens of varieties of noodles, including Japanese carrot and spinach noodles, freezers full of spring rolls, fish cakes, or frozen *gyoza* (dumplings)—or the makings to prepare your own—boxes and cans of green tea, plenty of instant foods (plastic containers of different flavors of *ramen* soup noodles and boxes of curries), and a wide selection of soup stocks, sauces, and other condiments. In the front of the store are the fresh meat and fish counters.

Aliya Mart, Inc. (41-75 Bowne St., Tel.: 718/939-0666), **Kuhwa Oriental**

Food (142-10 41st Ave., Tel.: 718/961-0996), and **Sam Bok** (42-21 Main St., Tel.: 718/359-7345) are mainly Korean groceries, with ample Japanese offerings, located about 10 minutes from Daido. At Aliya, the huge selection of foods, cooking and eating utensils, and children's toys is complemented by a welcome sight for the foreign visitor: Japanese cookbooks in English. Kuhwa, on the corner of Union Street, has a huge selection of fresh fish, and prepares frozen and ready-to-eat Korean seafood specialties and fresh salads. Sam Bok sells produce as well as Korean food, and has a separate seafood store next door, where you can sit at a counter and get fried or sautéed dishes, or purchase fresh fish. All three stores also have bins of Korean seafood and pickled salads and spicy fish dishes; you can fill up containers to go. Be careful; if you haven't acquired a taste for these, you may find them extremely salty or spicy, especially pickled cucumber, squid in pepper sauce, tiny shrimp salads, hot *kimchee* (spicy cabbage), and other combinations.

Korean handicrafts are available at **Rose Handicraft** (422-22 Main St., Tel.: 718/359-0430) and **G. Youn Co.** (36-14 Union St., Tel.: 718/359-1187—near Daido Foods). Both sell lovely lacquered wood furniture and jewelry boxes with inlaid mother-of-pearl, ornate curtain decorations, embroidered silk house slippers, and ceramics. At Rose, you can also select from decorative, colorful silk Korean quilts, blankets, and pillow covers. For about $175, each store has an ornate lacquered push-button telephone, with mother-of-pearl inlays of birds and floral designs.

What did you say you want?

RESTAURANTS

Flushing has about six 24-hour Korean restaurants, with sushi bars in front and tables with built-in burners to prepare Korean barbecue: beef, seafood, and chicken dishes marinated in special sauces and cooked at the table. ("Why 24 hours?" we asked. Many Korean and Japanese businessmen put in long hours, we were told, and there's nowhere else to eat.) Typical of these is **Seven Seas** (42-05 Main St., Tel.: 718/762-7214), a spacious restaurant with airy, modern decor and an artificial rock garden. The menu offers a huge selection of sushi, *teriyaki*, and Japanese entrées, as well as Korean appetizers and specialties. Among the Korean barbecue dishes are steak, pork ribs, kingfish, herring, and eel. A large selection of noodle platters or broths include shrimp, beef, or vegetable bases. The more unusual seafood dishes include Korean sea leaves, abalone and rice, spiced crab, and Korean caviar.

Open 24 hours.

INDIAN FLUSHING

MARKETS

You'll find six almost identical Indian markets packed into the area of Main Street between Franklin and Holly Streets: **Ganesh Groceries** (42-75 Main St., Tel.: 718/961-9311); **House of Spices** (42-92 Main St., Tel.: 718/539-2214); **Bharat Bazar** (42-71 Main St., Tel.: 718/445-4231); **Dana Bazar** (42-69 Main St., Tel.: 718/353-2818); **India Bazar** (42-67 Main St., Tel.: 718/358-5252); and **India Health Food** (42-45 Main St.). We found Ganesh to be the most comprehensive. In the freezer in the front, you can buy frozen appetizers and entrées (curries, *pullaos*, and *samosas*—tiny savory pies), as well as Indian ice cream in flavors like fig, rose, and mango. In the rear are fresh fruits and vegetables: chilies, *karela* (bitter melon), *tindora* (cucumber-like vegetables), long beans, coriander, and jackfruit, as well as ginger root, and *arvi*, a smaller but more pungent gingerlike root. The shelves are stocked with canned vegetables, ginger paste, chutneys (coriander, mint, and coconut relish), and huge, clear plastic bags full of nuts; seeds (dill, poppy, sesame, and cumin); dried mint, curry, and bay leaves; different kinds of *dal* (sauces made from lentils or other legumes), flours, and powders. Tiny bottles of essence of rose, vanilla, mixed fruit, or raspberry flavor the legendary Indian sweets, which you can select, by the pound, from display shelves by the cashier in front. Be forewarned: What looks like a small, modest sweet is deceptively rich and filling—one piece at a time should be enough. We're partial to *kheer mohan*, a rich, honey-soaked, milky cake covered with thick cream; *pista burfi*, a pistachio nut fudge; and *cham cham*, an oozy honey cake.

For your medicine cabinet.

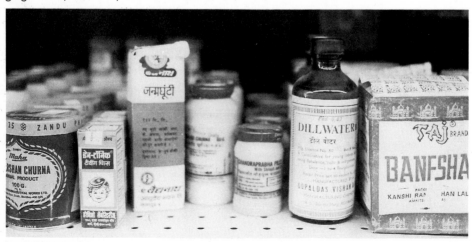

You can get it wholesale.

Although Flushing's Indian community is much smaller than the one in Jackson Heights (see page 109), it boasts something Jackson Heights doesn't have: **The Hindu Temple of New York** (45-57 Bowne St., Tel.: 718/961-1199), which is the only classical Hindu temple in North America. You can reach it by walking north on Franklin Avenue from Main Street for one block to Bowne Street; then turn right (east) for four-and-a-half blocks to Hawthorne Avenue, where you'll find the temple among a cluster of old, small one-family homes that have seen better times. Even the temple, which was built for $900,000 in 1978, already seems a bit worn: Its exterior gray paint is peeling; inside, ceiling tiles are missing, and parts of the temple are illuminated with bare bulbs. Never mind: Walk in, leave your shoes on a shelf downstairs, and wander through the incense-drenched main sanctuary, where strains of Indian music provide a mystical backdrop for the abundant sculptures of Indian gods. The bas-relief murals along the walls were carved by temple *shilpis*—sculptors from India who specialize in religious themes and whose trade is passed from one generation to the next. A *sthapathi*—an artist-designer—sketched out the murals, which depict Hindu legends and scenes of daily life, on which the shilpis based wire forms that they covered with stucco and then carved. Outside, the temple is covered with more ornate designs, including that of the elephant god Ganesha, to whom the temple is dedicated. Visit the downstairs auditorium and gift shop; if you come on a Saturday, you may see Hindu dance classes in progress. This isn't the only Hindu temple in Flushing; another is up the street, at 43-38 Bowne Street. The Sikhs also have a sanctuary nearby; they pray at a *gurudwala* at Parsons Boulevard and Roosevelt Avenue.

JACKSON HEIGHTS: THE OTHER AMERICA

To Get There

By subway: The best bet is to take the IRT 7 along Roosevelt Ave. Get off at 69th St./Fisk for the Filipino area; get off at any of the next four stops (74th St., 82nd St., 90th St., or Junction Blvd.) for the Latin American section. You can also take the E, F, GG, or R train to 74th St./Broadway. Exit there or, if you're going further into Queens, transfer to the IRT 7. All of the places we mention are within about a 15-minute walk of the stop.

By car: Take the Brooklyn-Queens Expressway to exit 37, which is Roosevelt Ave., if you're coming from Brooklyn or middle/lower Manhattan. If you're coming from the Triborough or Bronx-Whitestone Bridges, get off at Broadway. Turn right onto Roosevelt Ave., if you're coming from Brooklyn or lower Manhattan. From the Triborough Bridge, turn left onto Broadway and, a few blocks later, left onto Roosevelt Ave.

By bike: The quickest route is to take the Queensborough Bridge to Northern Blvd. Cut over any cross street between 75th St. and Junction Blvd. to get to 37th and Roosevelt Aves. (For a more leisurely ride, see our "Salsa & Spanakopita" tour on page 253.)

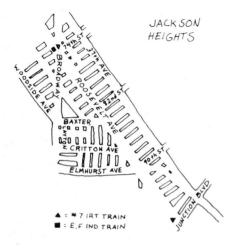

JACKSON HEIGHTS

▲ = # 7 IRT TRAIN
■ = E,F IND TRAIN

Dígame!" "Tell me what you'd like!" The next time someone tells you New York isn't really America, point him or her toward Jackson Heights: This is the real America, an American stew simmered in Spanish and Indian blood. This is an America of blue corn flour, of quail eggs, and of kidneys sizzling on a grill—an America of steaming tamales, of huge loaves of Uruguayan bread and bowls of peppery Peruvian seafood soup. It's a neighborhood where the newsstands may sell more copies of *El Diario*

Shelly's.

than they do of the *New York Times* or the *Daily News*, where you can buy *La Nación*, *La Prensa*, *El País*, and dozens of other Spanish-language newspapers and magazines, rent a videocassette in Spanish, or watch a Spanish-subtitled American movie at the local theater. Even the drought emergency signs a few years back were in Spanish.

You don't have to be a demographer to know that New York's Latin American population is growing. On the subway or in the street, you've heard the staccato rhythms of Spanish with a dozen different accents, accents as different as the countries that these immigrants come from. Our section on Spanish Harlem (page 142) is an introduction to Puerto Rican New York. This section concentrates on South Americans, especially Colombians, although we've included some of the Asian, Indian, Irish,

and West Indian influences in Jackson Heights. We focus on Jackson Heights and its two main thoroughfares, Roosevelt and 37th Avenues, because it's both a pleasant neighborhood and also a bustling, dynamic commercial area. This is a sprawling area; if you want to explore further, Northern Boulevard and Corona Avenue are also major commercial streets.

The street system here is simple: avenues (Roosevelt and 37th) run east-west and streets run north-south, exactly the opposite of Manhattan. Like Manhattan, however, most businesses are on the avenues. Street numbers get higher as you travel farther from Manhattan. Most of the area we discuss falls between 74th Street and Junction Boulevard (just past 95th Street). Addresses are a snap: The first part tells you the block. For example, 86-14 is between 86th and 87th Streets.

Jackson Heights' immigrants are layered on top of an older Irish and Italian neighborhood. Larded among places like **El Triunfo Argentinian Bakery**, and **El Templo de la Salsa** record shop (*los últimos hits del momento*) are holdovers like **Budd's Bar**, **Continental Restaurant**, and **Rendez-vous Cocktail Lounge**. Keep your eyes peeled, and you'll find some bizarre hybrids of the sort that New York's shifting populations seem to produce in such abundance, like a *croissant de queso crema* (cream cheese croissant) at **Shelly's Bakery**. Around the corner at **Tom's Pizzeria** the sign says *Tenemos Empanadas* (we have empanadas) while the signboard on an Indian restaurant advertises both a juicy burger and a vegetarian special (complete with samosa, *poori*, and the like). No surprise that one of the self-described "narrowbacks" (native New Yorkers) at Liffey's Pub grouses, "We're the ones that have to carry passports these days."

If you've read about drug arrests in Jackson Heights, you'll be surprised at this largely middle-class neighborhood. This is an area of solid six-story apartment buildings—the first co-ops in New York were built in Jackson Heights during the 1920s—and small detached homes, of quiet side streets cut through by busy avenues. Almost every block has a travel agency with brightly colored signs advertising bargain fares to Bogotá, Cali, Lima, and Santo Domingo. This is also a neighborhood in a state of unending flux. Immigrants who established themselves often use Jackson Heights as a springboard to the suburbs.

The Cubans and Argentinians, who led the tide of Spanish-speaking immigrants here in the 1960s, have mostly moved on. Although their restaurants and markets are still in Jackson Heights many have settled in Long Island or New Jersey. Today, Colombians, Peruvians, Salvadorans, and other Latin Americans stream in to Jackson Heights and the surrounding neighborhoods. Because these cultures—and their cuisines—are so varied, we've split this chapter up into sections on Argentinian, Colombian, Peruvian, and Salvadoran food. We've also included information on Asian, Indian, Filipino, West Indian, and other establishments.

ARGENTINIAN JACKSON HEIGHTS

Argentinian food? "It's 95 percent Italian," boasts Marcelo Amormino, whose family runs the **Argentina Delicatessen** (95-27 Roosevelt Ave., Tel.: 718/672-3556) and lives above the shop. That's an exaggeration, but not too much of one, as a glance around the store shows. There's fresh pasta of all sorts—gnocchi, fettucine, spaghetti, and cannelloni—made by Marcelo's mother, Rita. There are olives and antipasto, along with imported Italian cheeses and fruitcakes.

Argentina's cuisine developed quite separately from that of most of the rest of South America. Although there are Spanish influences, the huge numbers of Italians who began emigrating to Argentina beginning in the mid-nineteenth century exercised a strong influence. The result is mouth-watering national cuisine based on pasta and steak. In fact, Argentinians consume more pasta per person than any other country in the world—except Italy.

Ten or fifteen years ago there were many more Argentinians living in Jackson Heights, according to Marcelo. Most have moved to Forest Hills, Kew Gardens, or farther away, although they still come to the area to shop, and on weekends the store is jammed.

If you want to try only one delicacy here, make it *matambre*. This Argentinian cold cut is made of a filet of boiled flank meat, with eggs, parsley, spinach, carrots, and grated cheese wrapped into a roll and cut crosswise, with the hardboiled egg in the center. Other specialties include tongue and eggplant (both in oil), vinegared pigs' knuckles, and fresh mozzarella. The store also carries more typically Latin American items, including *mate* tea, *paella* mix, and *masa harina* (the fine corn flour used in Latin cooking). There are also tins of the typical Argentinian *dulce* (sweet), a custardlike dessert made of sweet potato, guava, quince, or simply flavored with vanilla or chocolate. It's generally eaten with cheese. The store also sells an intriguing sparkling wine (like champagne) made from pineapple.

RESTAURANTS

Walk by on the street and you'll see the white-suited grill chef on public display at **La Cabaña Argentina** (95-51 Roosevelt Ave., Tel.: 718/429-4388). A large plate glass window shows him at work, cooking up endless portions of beef for the patrons of this justifiably popular restaurant. This is one of those places that manage to hang wine bottles in netted ropes on the ceiling and cover the walls with hand-lettered poetry without having it look like kitsch. Maybe that's because it's a friendly, down-home place with big portions of good food and no pretense. A big favorite among the Argentinians is the huge mixed-grill platter (*parrillada*). If you're with a group and you want to sample the full range of Argentinian meats (including innards), that's the platter to get; otherwise, you're best off sticking with the

Peppers and cucumbers at Top Tomato.

steak. Argentinians eschew hot sauce in favor of a garlic, basil, and oil combination that's lathered on meats. If you don't want beef, get the fine crepelike cannelloni filled with spinach and ground chicken. Best for dessert are the flaming fruit-filled crepes.

Che! Bandoneon (40-20 Junction Blvd., Tel.: 718/429-8435) has similar food and a tango show nightly. It's a good idea to call ahead as hours are irregular.

La Fusta (80-32 Baxter Ave. across from Elmhurst Hospital, Tel.: 718/429-8222) is a favorite among many people in the area for good reason. It's a cozy little Argentinian restaurant that serves a finely cooked assortment of grilled meats and pasta.

You can get a quick, simple meal of grilled meat at one of the Argentinian *car-nicerías* that are clustered on 37th Avenue. These are butcher shops—for the most part, simple, plastic-walled, fluorescent-lit stores—that serve grilled meat sandwiches and platters. Prices reflect the lack of pretense. Sandwiches are generally under $2, and a platter of meat is usually under $4 (except the parrillada, a heaping mixed-grill platter). Try **La Portena** (37th Ave. near 75th St., Tel.: 718/335-0909) or **Carnicería "Mi Tio"** (75-20 37th Ave., Tel.: 718/446-3345), which has an eye-catching window display: Various grilled meat cuts circle on a lazy Susan. **18 de Julio** (77-05 37th Ave., Tel.: 718/429-5495) is a bit less austere, more of a restaurant than an extended butcher shop, although prices are very reasonable.

MARKETS AND BAKERIES

Daniel Adur has been working in bakeries for 55 of his 66 years, and his pride in **Confitería El Triunfo** (84-10 37th Ave., Tel.: 718/457-1632) triumphs over his limited English. There is a good selection of Argentinian pastries at the shop. You'll also see an American flag and an Argentinian flag, both on flagpoles and carefully wrapped in plastic dust jackets, brought out only on special occasions. Look more closely and you'll see photos of Señor Adur at the Lions Club (he heads a local Spanish-language chapter in Sunnyside), and a testimonial to his success in protesting electricity hikes in Argentina.

La Uruguaya (77-07 37th Ave., Tel.: 718/424-5339) has both Uruguayan and Argentinian breads, pastries, and newspapers. Don't miss the massive loaves of Uruguayan bread.

The best single store in Jackson Heights for Latin food products is **La Constancia** (95-05 Roosevelt Ave., Tel.: 718/476-1876). A sister store is located at 410 46 Street near 4th Avenue in Brooklyn (Tel.: 718/439-5500). (**Casa Moneo** in Manhattan still wins hands down over this store; see "Little Spain" on page 187.) Behind the cash register is a pastiche of Chilean, Ecuadorian, Peruvian, Colombian, and U.S. bills, a fitting twist on the habit of sticking the first customer's payment on the wall. Here you'll find unusual foods from all over the Americas: everything from Ecuadorian newspapers and records to quail eggs and cakes of brown sugar wrapped in plantain leaves. The selections from Colombia and Peru are best, and on the weekends there's fresh ceviche.

The largest selection of produce is at **Top Tomato**, a large 24-hour produce store (94th St. and Roosevelt Ave., Tel.: 718/457-4004). It has a good selection of fruits and vegetables.

Geier's Meat Market (82-13 Roosevelt Ave., Tel.: 718/639-8410) has one of the best selections of meat. "If it's part of the animal, we sell it," says Joe Zaccheo, the manager of this crowded meat market, which once sold to the Irish and now sells to Latin Americans. He's not kidding: You'll find kidney, tripe, intestines, beef and calf hearts, lambs' heads, beef eyes and beef ears, as well as some even more exotic body parts.

COLOMBIAN JACKSON HEIGHTS

The largest Latin presence in Jackson Heights is Colombian. Colombians started moving to the area in the 1960s, and their numbers swelled during the 1970s. Many of those who came to New York were from the middle and lower-middle classes; they looked north for an escape from their native country's strict class divisions. A growing number set up their own businesses, and they now make up a potent force along Roosevelt and 37th Avenues.

Dozens of Colombian restaurants have opened since the early 1980s, ranging from unassuming cafeteria-style luncheonettes to posh places with linen tablecloths. Many restaurants have oversize windows, lots of blond wood, and tiles. Service tends to be quick. These restaurants can be crowded, especially on a weekend evening, but otherwise it's possible to linger indefinitely over a soup or a *batido* (a milkshake, typically made with tropical fruits), a cup of inky coffee, or a heaping platter of food.

The cuisine of Colombia is quite varied, a reflection of the differences between the high central mountains in the country's interior and its Atlantic and Pacific coastal areas, as well as the mingling of Indian and Spanish influences during the three centuries the Spanish conquistadores made Bogotá their Latin American capital. "The food in Bogotá tends to be more sophisticated," says a friend who hails from the capital. "The way they cook in Bogotá? I wouldn't eat that food," sniffs a teenager who works in his parents' Cali-

style restaurant. To an outsider, the differences are less pronounced: We'll give you the basics of Colombian cooking, and you can figure out the subtleties as you eat your way through the neighborhood. Probably the best thing to say is that we've eaten at many of the restaurants along Roosevelt Avenue and have never had a bad meal.

Most people are familiar with empanadas, a mixture of ground beef, vegetables, and spices folded into a corn-flour dough envelope and deep-fried. It's hard to generalize about empanadas: Not only every region but every family seems to make them differently. They typically have onions, cumin, and other spices: If you want to add some spice to them (or any other Colombian dish), reach for the hot sauce that's on every table.

Tamales are another staple: No two are alike (and none bear any resemblance to the crusty Mexican version). But the basics are a filling of cornmeal, mixed with meat (beef, pork, and sometimes chicken). The variations are endless: Many cooks add chick-peas, while those from coastal areas often sweeten their tamales with raisins. No matter what's inside, tamales are wrapped in a leaf (usually plantain) and steamed. In New York, the leaf is mainly for show: The real wrapping is aluminum foil.

Soups are a mainstay. The classic is *sancocho*, a thick soup with beef, vegetables (usually yucca and plantain—a banana-like vegetable often used in Latin cooking), and, sometimes, chicken and potatoes. Other typical soups are *mondongo* (tripe) and *ajiaco* (chicken and potato, with coriander), along with a variety of fish soups.

Main dishes are typically beef or pork. *Sobrebarriga* is a favorite dish: It is a nice piece of flank steak marinated in spices and then grilled. A typical meal is the *plato montañero*, a huge platter heaped with ground beef, fried egg, fried pork, Colombian bread, and avocado. *Bistec a caballo* is another popular dish: steak with rice, salad, and fried eggs.

Desserts tend to be very sweet. You're probably familiar with *flan* (custard). Figs or guava, usually served with a mild white cheese, are also favorites. Both figs and guava are often cooked with condensed milk and caramelized into a very sweet paste. To most *norteamericanos* it will be too sweet.

RESTAURANTS

Roosevelt Avenue between 74th Street and Junction Boulevard has nearly a dozen good Colombian restaurants. For the most part, we've listed our favorite restaurants geographically, as if you got off at the 74th Street subway stop and were strolling along Roosevelt Avenue. There are differences, but they're as much in style as in quality. Find a place you like the looks of and you won't go wrong. Although English is a second language at best, most restaurants have English menus; you'll likely find a friendly patron who will help you out. People are very friendly and flattered that you're interested enough in their food and culture to come to the area.

Chibcha Restaurant (79-05 Roosevelt Ave., Tel.: 718/429-9033) is a swank Colombian restaurant and nightclub. It features entrées in the double-digit price

range, along with singers and bands from the old country.

Los Arrieros (76-02 Roosevelt Ave., Tel.: 718/898-3359) A cozy, comfortable place decorated with plenty of wood and tiles, offers quick, friendly service, along with a wonderful, spicy flan. This is a comfortable, intimate place to have coffee and dessert, although the entrées are also quite good.

At **Tierras Colombianas** (82-18 Roosevelt Ave., Tel.: 718/426-8812) waitresses in white blouses and blue skirts trimmed with the Colombian national colors (yellow, red, and black) bustle about. On Friday, Saturday, and Sunday there's guitar music. This is a nice place, but it's not one to linger at: There are almost always people waiting to be seated.

La Pequeña Colombia (83-27 Roosevelt Ave., Tel.: 718/478-6528) specializes in food from the Cali and Medellín areas of Colombia. It's more relaxed than Tierras Colombianas, although it, too, has live music on the weekends. As at many restaurants in the area, there's a different soup offered every day.

El Rancho de Jonas (85-08 Roosevelt Ave., Tel.: 718/639-2577) is a small, pleasant, family-run restaurant that features Cali-style cooking: The specialties are *bistec criollo* (beefsteak in a creole sauce) and *cazuela de mariscos* (seafood casserole).

Cali Viejo (84-24 Roosevelt Ave., Tel.: 718/898-9812) is one of two restaurants run by José Bartidas and his wife. (**Cali Viejo II** is located at 73-10 Roosevelt Ave., Tel.: 718/424-2755.) It offers a good assortment of nicely flavored Colombian dishes. The empanadas are some of the best we've tasted, and the combination dinners provide a good introduction to

Cali-style cuisine. Cali Viejo is one of the few restaurants that also serve Colombian breakfasts. The morning choices range from a grilled tortilla with cheese to scrambled eggs with tomatoes and scallions, and are served with *arepas* (thick, corn tortillas used in much the same way as Americans use bread, to eat with food) and rice. You should also try Cali Viejo's rich Colombian-style hot chocolate.

BAKERIES

Neighborhood regulars crowd into **Las Américas Bakery** (93-09 37th Ave., Tel.: 718/458-1638) to get pastries and coffee or perhaps a guava paste and cheese-stuffed plantain with a roll. Francisco Martinez, a baker for 35 of his 46 years, has been running a thriving business at the store since 1971. "We were the first Colombian bakery in New York," he says. Las Americas also does a thriving mail-order business, selling instant packages of some of the more popular Colombian breads, particularly to the thousands of farm workers scattered across the Midwest. "Many Colombians come to this country without papers so they go to work on farms where it's harder to find them. But they like to have some food from the old country."

There are a dozen kinds of bread in this bustling bakery, from the springy *pan de yucca* to the *pan de queso*. Amid all the other treats, don't pass up a slice of the dark fruitcake sold at the counter. There is also some hot food sold at the bakery.

The bread line.

CUBAN JACKSON HEIGHTS

Most Cubans have moved up and out—to other parts of Queens, Nassau County, and New Jersey—but there are still some Cuban restaurants left in Jackson Heights. And there are a number of shops bearing witness to the Cuban presence in the neighborhood. Stroll around and you may see "Los Cubanitos" bodega, "Los Cubanitos" barbershop, and "Los Cubanitos" bakery, although they may no longer be run by Cubans.

RESTAURANTS

Rincón Criollo (40-09 Junction Blvd., Tel.: 718/639-8158) is a little corner of pre-Castro Cuba thriving in Queens. The wall is festooned with a larger-than-life portrait of the nineteenth-century Cuban patriot José Martí and photos of the party times in the Batista days. The Acosta family, who runs the restaurant, had another Rincón Criollo in Havana. It was expropriated when Castro came to power, and the Cuban government now runs it for tourists. A picture of the straw-thatched cocktail patio from the old days adorns the restaurant's business card in case there's any doubt as to where the family's heart lies. Don't miss the place mats: They look like they were printed in the 1950s and smuggled out.

Pork—roasted, fried, or stuffed inside a crusty tamal—is a Cuban specialty. Also good is the *bistec Rincón Criollo*—chopped meat (*picadillo*) sautéed with onions, garlic, and peppers. Cuban cooking, unlike South American cuisine, uses generous amounts of green peppers, reflecting its Spanish heritage. Another trace of Spanish influence is in the *tortillas*, which are omelets, not the corn or flour tortillas most Americans are familiar with.

Cuban frijoles (beans) are different from those of other Latin countries: They're black beans (not kidney or pinto), and they're liberally spiced with vinegar. If you like them, try the black bean soup, served with avocado. This friendly, sedate restaurant might be a good place to bring someone who's wary of eating in some of the more informal Cuban restaurants. Not only is the ambience more toned down than most, but there are familiar stand-bys like filet mignon for the less adventurous. Desserts include both papaya and shredded coconut served with a mild white cheese similar to cream cheese.

El Bohio (85-16 Roosevelt Ave., Tel.: 718/899-7365) is more informal than Rincón Criollo; most of the action takes place at a counter in the front, although there is a separate dining area. Cuban meat sandwiches, such as *medianoche*, are the specialties.

El Sitio (68-28 Roosevelt Ave., Tel.: 718/424-2369 or 429-9474) is less formal still. This is classic Cuban-American lunch-counter dining, and it can't be beat.

BAKERIES

El Yumuri (40-07 Junction Blvd., Tel.: 718/476-8413) is a nice Cuban bakery with a counter where you can tank up on strong coffee or stuff yourself with a Cuban sandwich. In the window are elaborate cakes decorated with trappings such as a baseball field (complete with players), a ship, and dancers. Predominant colors are day-glo green and orange.

PERUVIAN JACKSON HEIGHTS

If your picture of Peru doesn't go much beyond the Incas' mountain cities, it's time to visit Jackson Heights and catch up on the past 450 years. Yes, you'll still find traces of the Incas' remarkable legacy of domesticating plants and cultivating them on their steeply terraced mountains. But what's most characteristic of this cooking culture is spice: Peppers—black, red, and golden—and coriander (*cilantro*) are in almost everything. Although some dishes may look similar, the cuisine is altogether different than that of Peru's northern neighbor, Colombia. Seafood dishes—*escabeche* (fish sautéed in an oil and vinegar sauce and served cold) and ceviche—are most likely to interest *norteamericanos*. Try some of the soups and the potato dishes. (Potatoes in cheese sauce or shrimp sauce are characteristic.) Beef dishes include a

At the griddle.

ubiquitous *lomo saltado especial*, a beef tenderloin fried with onions and tomatoes served with rice and a fried egg, as well as many beef and lamb stews, spiced with cilantro. You may want to sample one or more of the numerous spaghetti dishes found in most Peruvian restaurants, but you'll find them more of a curiosity than a gastronomic treat. If your tastes run to the adventurous, Peruvian food also has several dishes with tripe (*cau cau*) and calves' hearts (usually skewered and grilled).

RESTAURANTS

There are three Peruvian restaurants in Jackson Heights, all within a few blocks of each other. **Pepe's Seafood Restaurant** (95-28 Roosevelt Ave., Tel.: 718/429-8184) is a very informal place where it sometimes seems that they wait until the order comes in before they buy the ingredients. No matter: The *asopao de mariscos*, a rich seafood bouillabaisse, heavy on coriander and garlic, makes it worth the wait. Ceviche and octopus salad are also quite good.

La Ñusta (90-01 37th Ave., Tel.: 718/429-8401) is our favorite, partly due to the homey feeling of the restaurant—although the charm of the proprietor's family watching television on a slow night won't be for everyone—and the rich fabrics hung around the comfortable wooden booths. Service is quick and friendly. And the food is, on the whole, best at La Ñusta. The escabeche is excellent, as is a creamy shrimp soup with huge Peruvian shrimp. A green minestrone, loaded with basil, is blander but worth a try. La Ñusta features traditional Peruvian desserts, notably *arroz zambito* (a very sweet rice dish, made with caramelized sugar, cloves, and coconut) and *mazamorra morada*, a fruit compote made with purple corn.

Inti Raymi (86-14 37th Ave., Tel.: 718/424-1938) is the fanciest (and busiest) of the three restaurants. You'll do best if you come here for the ambience and relative poshness, because the food is no better than at Inti's Peruvian competitors.

FILIPINO JACKSON HEIGHTS

There's not a large Filipino community in Jackson Heights, but on Roosevelt Avenue between 69th and 70th Streets there are two Filipino restaurants and two food stores specializing in Filipino products. Filipino food is heavily influenced by Spanish cooking, although Chinese (noodles and egg rolls) and Malaysian (peanut butter sauce and coconut milk) traces are apparent. It would be hyperbole to claim that the cuisine of the Philippines is as complex or varied as any of those that it draws on, but at its best it can be quite tasty.

Staples of the diet are rice and fish; the national dish is *adobo*, a peppery stew traditionally made with chicken or pork (although more unusual ingredients include anything from squid to okra) cooked with garlic, soy sauce, and vinegar, usually after being marinated. Soups are plentiful enough to make a small meal. One of the best is *tinola*, a chicken soup cooked with plenty of ginger, garlic, onion, and (sometimes) papaya. Don't leave without trying a *pancit* (noodle dish) specialty like *pancit malabon*, which is similar to a Spanish paella, but with noodles as well as rice.

Desserts are typically very sweet and syrupy. If you try only one, make it *halo-halo*, a baroque version of the shaved-ice drinks popular in hot climates the world over. Served in a tall glass, it's a brightly colored (usually red) mixture of candied, canned, and fresh fruits and sweetened kidney or mung beans mixed with a bit of milk. Other typical desserts include *san rival* (a layered napoleon cake) and *brazo de mercedes* (a creamy log roll), as well as *legeplan* (coconut custard).

RESTAURANTS

If you stay too long at **La Cocina Filipina Restaurant** (69-10 Roosevelt Ave., Tel.: 718/651-0594), the electronic organist will begin repeating his limited repertoire. But the food is good, the service quick and friendly, and the atmosphere delightful: Filipino parents sucking on bright red halo-halo drinks while their young children play.

Maharlika (69-13 Roosevelt Ave., Tel.: 718/429-4265) is a very informal and inexpensive restaurant, better suited to a quick bite than a full meal.

The decor and the menu at **Barrio Fiesta** (65-14 Roosevelt Ave., Tel.: 718/429-4878) are similar to those at La Cocina Filipina, but there's disco dancing here instead of just an organist.

SALVADORAN JACKSON HEIGHTS

Salvadoran cuisine is similar to some other Central and South American cuisines: It has plenty of plantains, and it seems almost every dish is served with rice and beans. One dish we haven't found anywhere else is *tamal de elote*. This is a tamal made with young, white corn, and cooked with milk and sugar, so it has a fresh, sweet taste. (In some parts of El Salvador it's sweetened further with raisins.) *Pasteles de carne* look like empanadas, although they're made with corn flour: They're stuffed with ground beef and served with spicy pickled cabbage on the side. *Enchiladas* are unlike what you're used to in Mexican restaurants: They're served on a small, flat tortilla, heaped with ground beef, and topped with a radish and a crumbling of white cheese. *Tacos* are quite good: They're hard, small tortillas, stuffed with chicken, rolled up, and covered with a sauce that includes cilantro. Pupusas, similar to small empanadas, are served with pickled cabbage on the side.

Empanada de leche is a dessert: It's filled with ripe plantains, which have been cooked with milk, cinnamon, and raisins. Salvadoran *refrescas* (cold drinks) are special: *Orchata* is a tan beverage with a medicinal taste. *Cebado* is bright pink, vaguely reminiscent of bubble gum.

RESTAURANTS

Although the Salvadoran population in New York is sizable, there are only a few Salvadoran restaurants. (One, Restaurant Cuscatlán, is in Brooklyn at 626 Vanderbilt Ave. near Grand Army Plaza, at least two others are in Jamaica, and one Salvadoran *pupusería* is on upper Broadway in the heart of Dominican Washington Heights.) José and Rosamelia Tejada, who are from the capital, San Salvador, run **Izalco en New York** (94-16 37th Ave., Tel.: 718/ 672-0853), helped by Rosamelia's mother, Elba Tobar, and the Tejadas' daughter. Izalco is named after an active volcano in El Salvador. (The business card features a volcanic eruption in front of the New York skyline.)

THAI JACKSON HEIGHTS

For your Thai shopping needs, try **Thai Grocery** (37-60 90th St., Tel.: 718/672-2183). This wonderful store is crammed with everything a Thai cook could want—spices, pastries, canned goods, and instant foods. Even the notices and advertisements are written in Thai. **Duang Thai-Oriental Groceries** (77-02 Roosevelt Ave., Tel.: 718/424-0243) has a similar selection, but without the character of Thai Grocery.

INDIAN JACKSON HEIGHTS

"Okra! Fifty cents a pound! Today only!" shouts a brown-skinned vendor on the sidewalk in front of a market on 74th Street between Roosevelt Avenue and 37th Avenue one Saturday afternoon. Women in saris, their arms already loaded with plastic bags full of groceries, hurriedly pick through outdoor bins stocked with eggplant, ginger, long beans, tindora, and okra. Inside, they choose from 5-pound bags of dal (yellow lentils), dried peas, several different kinds of flour, ghee (cooking lard), laxmi, and rice—from 25-pound bags of long-grain to more costly 10-pound bags of basmati.

Service with a smile.

RESTAURANTS, MARKETS, AND SHOPS

All over the neighborhood, Indians, Pakistanis, and other transplanted New Yorkers rush to do their grocery shopping. There are plenty of stores to choose from. A starter might be **Patel Bros.** (37-54 74th St., Tel.: 718/898-3445), which brags about being the largest Indo-Pakistani grocery store chain in the United States. The Patels, who also have stores in Chicago,

Texas, California, and Georgia, have opened a larger one at 71-10 37th Avenue, three blocks away, which, as well as groceries, has stacks of cookware. And nearby there's **Dana Bazar** (73-12A 37th Ave., Tel.: 718/424-1039) and **Ganesh Groceries** (72-26 37th Ave., Tel.: 718/ 458-7100)—companion stores to counterparts of the same name in Flushing.

Jackson Heights has New York City's largest Indo-Pakistani community, and the best time to see it is during the weekend when 74th Street, between Roosevelt and 37th Avenues, and 37th Avenue itself, from about 71st to 76th Streets, are crammed with shoppers crowding into sari palaces and discount luggage stores, appliance outlets, and video shops.

You can meet all your food shopping needs in the area (see also "Indian Flushing," page 92), but if you want a sit-down meal or snack, try any of the restaurants listed below.

Shaheen Restaurant and Sweets (72-09 Broadway, two blocks from the 74th St. IRT or BMT stop, Tel.: 718/639-4791) is a large fast-food-style restaurant,

Sweets galore at Shaheen.

Lovers of Indian food can find anything they want in Jackson Heights.

which also has a huge bakery that supplies many Indo-Pakistani restaurants and grocery stores in the metropolitan area. You can buy Indian pastries and coffee or tea to stay, or boxes of pastries by the pound. There's also an excellent selection of main courses, including chicken, lamb, and vegetable curries; *biryani* (rice stews); and *tandoori* or *kaharee* chicken (the latter cooked in ginger and tomato).

The fancy **Delhi Palace** (37-33 74th St., Tel.: 718/507-0666) has an extensive selection of northern and southern Indian cuisine, with a moderately priced lunch menu and bargain-priced weekday and weekend luncheon specials. Featured are tandoori dishes (cooked in a clay oven over charcoal) of chicken or shrimp; you can also select *ghosh ka pakwhan* (spicy beef and lamb dishes), vegetarian entrées (lentil-based vegetable balls, mixed vegetable dishes, or *paneer*—a solid Indian cheese something like a cross between cottage and ricotta), and Indian soups, including *mulligatawny* (spiced vegetable broth) and coconut. Southern Indian specialties include *uthappam* ("pancakes" with a range of vegetable and spice flavorings), *dosai* ("crepes" with lentil or vegetarian fillings), samosas, and roti (a kind of Indian bread).

Lower key and lower priced is the

surprising **Jackson Diner** (37-03 74th St., Tel.: 718/672-1232). Mahendra Chikara—nicknamed Bob—bought the diner in 1983 and now offers both a traditional selection of American diner food and a wide Indian menu, with curry dishes, spicy chicken specialties from Peshawar, and a good list of paneer and vegetarian dishes, as well as chicken, shrimp, and lamb tandoori specials. Servings are ample, and the food is excellent. The interior was renovated in mid-1986 and offers a less dinerlike ambience than what Bob started with.

Udupi is the name of a religious town in southern India renowned for its vegetarian cookery. It's also the name of a popular modest-priced vegetarian restaurant at 35-66 73rd Street (Tel.: 718/478-8822). Varieties of lentil and potato appetizers start your meal; dosai are among the popular entrées. Uthappam come with tomato

and pea combinations, onion fillings accented with hot chili, and mixed vegetarian combinations. You'll also find a good selection of rice dishes and cauliflower, chick-pea, and vegetarian curries. Indian breads include *poori*—light whole wheat puffed breads—and *batura*, large puffed breads.

Shamiana Sweet Center (72-27 37th Ave., Tel.: 718/458-8512) has an extensive assortment of takeout savories, prepared dishes, and sweets, and also has informal seating in the rear of the store. You can try *patra*, a spicy dish made of long patra leaves, green chilies, and mustard seed; *dali-wada*, fried lentil balls in yogurt, similar to Middle Eastern felafel; *khanavi*, a concoction of gram (chick-pea) flour and pepper; or *dokhla*, spicy cakes made of chick-pea flour. Shamiana's mouth-watering sweets include the ubiquitous *gulabjamum*—rosewater-flavored honey balls—and other popular milky, honey-soaked desserts.

Shamiana serves heavenly sweets.

IRISH JACKSON HEIGHTS

Visitors to the area who think it's mainly an Indian, Latin American, and, increasingly, Chinese and Korean neighborhood should realize that Jackson Heights had long been home to Irish Americans, although the community is no longer so dominant. Still, you can taste a bit of the Irish in Queens with a visit to **Liffey's Pub** (75-15 Broadway, just off Roosevelt Ave., Tel.: 718/429-8005), which claims to serve the best Guinness in the States—and there's no reason to doubt it. Unlike the few surviving old-time Manhattan bars like McSorley's, Liffey has not been afflicted with a cult following, so you can sip your brew in peace here. Even more hometown, perhaps, is **Gibbons' Potchenstill Irish Pub** (72-08 Broadway, Tel.: 718/429-8979), where a good shepherd's pie is one of the Irish specialties served. There's entertainment on Saturday and Monday nights. Just next door is **Gibbons' Queens Irish Import Store** (Tel.: 718/476-0633), which has a rich selection of fisherman knit sweaters; key chains (especially if your last name is Burke, Flynn, Kennedy, or the like); magazines; newspapers; records and videocassettes; religious plaques; and imported foodstuffs, teapots, ceramic gifts, and Cadbury's chocolate.

SUNNYSIDE: AN URBAN JEWEL

To Get There

By subway: Take the IRT 7 to 40th St. or 46th St.

By car: Exit the Queensborough Bridge at Queens Blvd. Turn left on 43rd St. and continue one block to 43rd Ave.

By bike: See the directions for the "Moveable Feast Tour" on page 244.

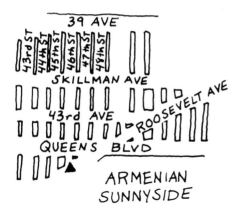

ARMENIAN SUNNYSIDE

▲ = #7 IRT TRAIN

Sunnyside is an urban jewel, highlighted by the oasis of low buildings, tree-lined streets, and common yards of Sunnyside Gardens. There's nothing fancy about Sunnyside. The neighborhood's charm—and the reason Sunnyside Gardens is a landmark historic district—lies in the foresight with which it was developed in the 1920s. Sunnyside was the site of some of the first co-ops in the United States and, during the Depression, of pitched battles between the law and residents who couldn't afford their mortgages. Urban historian and critic Lewis Mumford lived here for some years and held the neighborhood up as a model of sensible city planning.

Sunnyside today is a polyglot neighborhood, filled with working-class Irish, Eastern Europeans, Hispanics, Asians, and Armenians. Rents are rapidly increasing as more professionals discover the area as an alternative to Manhattan, whose skyline shimmers in the distance. Unique to the neighborhood is the large number of Armenians. Most of the more than 50,000 Armenians living in the New York area are scattered, but Sunnyside and nearby Woodside boast the largest concentration.

RESTAURANTS, BAKERIES, AND SHOPS

There are several food stores catering to Armenians and other people from the Middle East. The best is **Pyramid**

Bakery (43-02 43rd St., corner of 43rd Ave., Tel.: 718/392-2702). The selection of Middle Eastern pastries, fresh pita bread, yogurt, olives, feta cheese, halvah, nuts, fresh dates, grape leaves, and other specialty treats puts this store among the top rank of Middle Eastern food stores in the city. Try the *lahmajun*, something like a Middle Eastern pizza. (It's pita bread with spicy ground beef, thyme, and coriander.) Another specialty is *basterma*, a cured meat typically served with cheese and some of the strong *rakia* that Armenians drink. There is a stunning selection of imported and fresh sweets: Pistachio-filled halvah is superb, but don't miss the sweet tahini bread.

Pyramid also features a good variety of feta-type cheeses from the Balkans and the Middle East, including Israel. *Labneh*, a Lebanese spread made of fresh yogurt, is sold at the store. There are the normal gourmet fixings like sun-dried tomatoes from Italy, but Pyramid also has more unusual delicacies like sun-dried sour cherries and walnuts in syrup. The store is run by the Kassabian family, Armenians who lived in Egypt for several generations before coming to the United States. Peek into the back and you'll see them making pita and other bread products, such as the paper-thin *lavash*.

There are several more modest stores selling Armenian and Middle Eastern food products. One, a block away, is **Armen Foods** (42-20 43rd Ave., Tel.: 718/729-3749). Run by a Rumanian-Armenian couple, the store also has some Eastern European foods, such as sausages, in addition to a good selection of grains, spices, and other Armenian and Middle Eastern foods.

If you like strong Latin coffee, **La Flor de Cuba** (49-02 43rd Ave., Tel.: 718/651-6802), just over the Woodside border, six blocks from Armen Foods, serves some of the tastiest cappuccino and espresso in the city. Quirino and Nancy DelGobbo, a husband-wife team from Argentina and Cuba, respectively, brew the coffee at their modest bodega. They also make Cuban sandwiches, tamales, and other snacks.

WALKING TOUR

The heart of Sunnyside Gardens is between Skillman (one block west of 43rd Avenue) and 39th Avenues and between 45th and 50th Streets. (Many of these streets have floral names in addition to their numerical ones—a nice touch in a verdant neighborhood.) All of these blocks are nice: you can also walk into the gardens in the center of the blocks—don't be put off by the discreet entrances that look as if they lead only to private yards. Although some of the gardens were broken up in the past decade—a 50-year clause decreeing they remain common ground expired in the mid-1970s—many of them are still quite open and are now protected as landmarks. (Two good gardens are on the blocks between 45th and 47th Streets, between Skillman and 43rd Avenues.)

RIDGEWOOD ROUNDABOUT

To Get There:

By subway: Take the M train (from lower Manhattan) to Seneca Ave. or Forest Ave. It's about a 10-to-15-minute walk to Myrtle Ave., the main commercial thoroughfare, from the station. The L train, which runs along 14th St. in Manhattan, stops at Myrtle Ave., three blocks west of Seneca Ave.

By car: Follow the bicycle directions below if you take the Williamsburg Bridge. From upper or mid-Manhattan, take the Queensborough Bridge to Queens Blvd. Turn right on 69th St. and right on Grand Ave. Turn left on Fresh Pond Rd. and left on Myrtle Ave.

By bike: The most direct route from Manhattan is via the Williamsburg Bridge to Broadway. Turn left on Myrtle Ave. to Ridgewood, just over the Queens border. It's also possible to take the Queensborough Bridge to Queens Blvd.; turn right to go through the New Calvary Cemetery and continue south through Maspeth to Forest Ave. (Consult a map for details, or follow the simpler—but somewhat longer and more heavily traveled—car directions.)

Orientation: Myrtle Ave. is the main commercial street, but most of the historic district and the best shops are found on the blocks immediately north of Myrtle Ave.

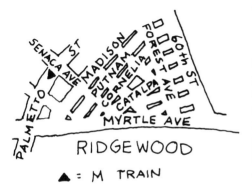

RIDGEWOOD

▲ = M TRAIN

When we moved here 50 years ago, all the Germans looked down on us as dirty Irish," remembers an old woman sitting on her porch. "It wasn't until we scrubbed our stoop every day for years, just like they did, that they warmed up to us." The 50,000 people who live in Ridgewood, a potpourri of Germans, Irish, Yugoslavs, Rumanians, Italians, Hispanics, and Asians, don't scrub their steps or sidewalks much anymore, but the legacy of the tidy, thrifty German ways—dating to the 1850s—still lives in this neighborhood.

Ridgewood's creamy yellow and orange brick row houses make it stand out from the surrounding neighborhoods. Its older German residents still buy flaky *strudels* and spicy *wursts*, and they still have a *Fasching* (Carnival) ball before Lent, but the neighborhood is increasingly inhabited by Eastern Europeans, especially along Seneca Avenue. Now you can buy huge toque-shaped Yugoslav bread at a sleepy bakery or pick up cassettes of Rumanian pop music at corner grocery stores. "The capital of Rumania is somewhere on Seneca Avenue," quips one of the neighborhood's old-timers.

Ridgewood residents worked tirelessly over the past decade to upgrade the neighborhood. They've received landmark status for the old row houses, planted trees, renovated Myrtle Avenue, the busy main strip, and twisted arms to carve out another zip code (so their insurance rates wouldn't reflect the troubles in neighboring Bushwick, just over the Brooklyn line). That Ridgewood thrives in the midst of some rather dreary neighborhoods is testimony to the community's doggedness. Realtors have promoted it as a place where quiche and strudel—young professionals and older ethnics—can coexist. There's not much evidence of the quiche crowd, yet, and if you look carefully enough you might see some of the small knitting mills that have long provided jobs for the neighborhood's newcomers—whether German, Irish, or, today, Yugoslav or Rumanian.

There's no use pretending Ridgewood is a gastronomic mecca. But its restored row houses and the lingering neighborhood feeling of old New York give it charm

so authentic that parts of the movie *Brighton Beach Memoirs* were filmed here. In 1983, almost 3,000 buildings in the area, most of which are built in Romanesque and Renaissance Revival styles, were placed on the National Register of Historic Places, making this area one of the largest Federal Historic Districts in the United States.

What kind of neighborhood is Ridgewood? The kind of place that inspired Fathy Salem, owner of Pyramid Vacuum, to take out an advertisement in the local paper to announce an open house at his vacuum cleaner store to celebrate his American citizenship. This is a neighborhood that still has a place for **Murken's Confectionery** (59-05 Myrtle Ave., Tel: 718/821-9482), a Naugahyde-boothed establishment where the waitresses still dress in crisp white uniforms and white shoes and the countermen greet their customers by name—a place where they still make ice cream on the premises. The walls are mottled gold-and-green plastic and the plants are plastic; there is a candy concession—the kind that sells massive red foil–wrapped chocolate hearts on Valentine's Day—along one wall.

The Germans who began settling in Ridgewood around 1880 were Gottscheers, a group of fourteenth-century religious heretics who bounced around the Austro-Hungarian empire for five centuries before ending up in Queens. Now, Ridgewood and neighboring Glendale brag about being the largest Gottscheer "towns" in the world, according to Joannenne Coppinger, district manager of the local community board. Every three years the community hosts a huge reunion with Gottscheers from Kitchener, Ontario, and Cleveland.

BAKERIES AND SHOPS

Rudy's Pastry Shop (905 Seneca Ave., Tel.: 718/821-5890) has been baking strudel since 1934. Cheese, apple, or cherry—it's all wonderful at this popular bakery off the corner of Myrtle Avenue.

The neighborhood boasts two Yugoslav bakeries that cater to the neighborhood's Eastern Europeans. **International Bake Shop** (719 Seneca Ave.,at the corner of Woodbine St., Tel.: 718/386-9550) is the better of the two. Proprietor Kornel Ardeljan, who started the store in the mid-1970s, bakes a variety of country-style Yugoslav breads as well as *burec*, a pastry filled with apple, cheese, or spicy ground beef and onions.

Forest Home Made Bakery (6864 Forest Ave.) is similar, although it doesn't have the seating for you to sit down and enjoy coffee and a pastry, as the International does. Don't miss the huge toque-shaped bread loaves.

Jobst & Ebbinghaus (676 Seneca Ave., at the corner of Gates Ave., Tel.: 718/821-5747) has few peers: Homemade meat loaf warm from the oven—if you're lucky—is only one of the specialties. "We make everything on the premises, even the babies," says Hans Weindler, the owner, whose sons (a fireman and an attorney) still help out on Saturdays. Other delicacies include stuffed breast of veal, baby Virginia hams with a honey-glaze sauce, headcheese, and other smoked German meats, along with the normal assortment of cold cuts and sausages. **Morscher's Pork Store** (58-44 Catalpa Ave., Tel.: 718/821-1040) also has mouth-watering meat loaf, sausages, smoked meats, and more! It's also located on one of Ridgewood's most charming side streets.

HILLSIDE AVENUE: A NEW MELTING POT

To Get There

By subway: Take the E or F train to Sutphin Blvd. or Parsons Blvd. and walk on Hillside Ave.

By car or bike: From Manhattan; take the 59th St. Bridge and follow Queens Blvd. for about 2 miles until it merges with Hillside Ave. (Cyclists might do better to take a longer, less bumpy ride along Northern Blvd. to Kissena Blvd., and turn right (south). Kissena Blvd. eventually merges with Parsons Blvd.

Hillside Avenue in Jamaica, Queens, from about Sutphin Boulevard to Parsons Boulevard, is a mishmash of real estate offices, car dealerships, restaurants, and markets. But it's also where a number of new immigrant groups to the area have set up an interesting array of shops.

RESTAURANTS, MARKETS, AND SHOPS

At **Sybil's of Guyana West Indian Bakery and Restaurant** (159-24 Hillside Ave., Tel.: 718/297-2359), for example, there's a fascinating assortment of West Indian and Indian selections, including curries, roti, pooris, Guyanese and Jamaican patties, bread puddings, *salaras* (coconut cakes) and fruit rolls, and specialty beverages including sorrel, mauby, and the wonderful peanut punch (made by blending peanut butter, milk, sugar, vanilla, and nutmeg). (Sybil's has another even larger shop on 2210 Church Avenue between Bedford and Flatbush Avenues in Brooklyn, Tel.: 718/469-9049). Head north up Parsons Boulevard (up is literal; it becomes quite a steep hill), and you'll find about a half-dozen Indo-Pakistani shops, a collection of stores run by the followers of the guru Sri Chinmoy, and **Kabul Market** (87-22 Parsons Blvd., Tel.: 718/291-0948), operated by Nor Yakub, an Afghan who came to the United States after the Soviet invasion of his country. About 400 Afghans live in Jamaica, according to Mr. Yakub, and in his shop they can get such specialties as a long, flat Afghan bread; *malahi*, a milky, sweet dessert; and the spicy peppers and roots also found in Indo-Pakistani cuisine.

Returning to Hillside Avenue, you can fulfill all your cricket needs—as well as a craving for West Indian food—at **Soogrim Sports/ West Indian & American Grocery** (164-07 Hillside Ave., Tel.: 718/426-7787). Cricket aficionados can get bats, balls, stumps, pads, trophies, helmets, etc., there, as well as *hawan samagi*, *masala*, and other assorted items and foodstuffs. (Soogrim has another outlet at 35-64 94th Street in Jackson Heights.) Finally, this part of Jamaica has a sizable Central American population, mainly Salvadorans and some Guatemalans, and there's also a substantial Chinese settlement. So if you feel the urge for something just a bit different, explore Jamaica. The languages and foods available within this area make it one of New York City's truest (and possibly its fastest-growing) melting pots.

MANHATTAN

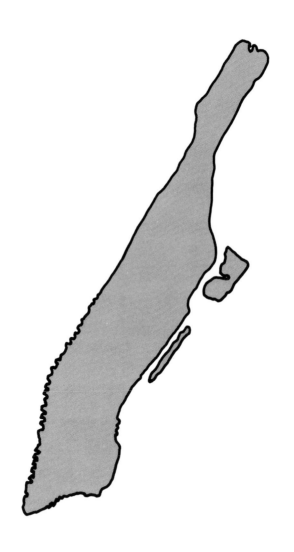

anhattan's crowded, pulsing streets, its pinched buildings, and its rich soup of cultures defy easy description. Chauvinists claim that crowded onto this sliver of land is the sum of human experience. Need we add that it's a food lover's delight?

Everyone has his or her own sensory impressions of Manhattan's gastronomy, from the smell of roasted chestnuts on a crystalline fall day on Fifth Avenue to the cool swallow of Italian ices on a sticky summer evening in Greenwich Village. There are the smoky aromas of Chinatown's tea shops and the plump, hanging mozzarella a few blocks away in Little Italy's cheese stores; on 6th Street Indian waiters scurry from cramped kitchens to backyard eating gardens, while on nearby Essex Street the ritual preparation of kosher dairy products and meats goes on as it has, in other places, for millenniums.

Uptown, nearly a million people jam onto Ninth Avenue in May for a culinary adventure that lets them sample the foods of the world in 20 short blocks. And every day in the grand cafés, oysters arrive from France, salmon from Alaska, and truffles from Italy, while investment bankers and French merchants toast good times and better business. As the gorged and the hungry alike sleep in Manhattan's penthouses and tenements, freezer trucks pull through the tunnels that connect New York to the continent and wend their way to the 14th Street meat market, the last stop on their trip from the cattle plains of Kansas and Nebraska. As the sun rises, rubber-booted fishmongers on Fulton Street are approaching their lunch hour, while the bridges and tunnels and train stations be-gin disgorging tens of thousands of commuters who head for Greek coffee shops, Korean greengrocers, and Indian newsstands. And so it goes, through the lunches and brunches and afternoon teas, through the dinners and after-dinner drinks and the bleary pub crawls, until the meat trucks pull through the tunnel once again, and the city begins waking up, scratching its stomach and yawning, ready to fill its voracious belly once again.

Manhattan has become the world's culinary as well as financial capital, since haute cuisine follows high finance. Escalating rents have forced restaurants to raise prices—and squeezed those that couldn't out of business. A "moderate" meal can run $100 for a couple, and it's easy to drop $50 for a mediocre dinner. Much of the interesting ethnic cooking that was once found in Manhattan is now in the outer boroughs, but there are still tight-knit neighborhoods and inexpensive ethnic eateries that survive. Since there has been so much written about Manhattan's ethnic eateries, we're going to give short shrift to the best-known ones, Chinatown and Little Italy, on the assumption that if you're interested in this book you'll be at least passingly familiar with those areas.

What we will give you is a peek into some of Manhattan's lesser-known corners. From places like Wilson's in Harlem, where waiters wearing black bow ties hurry around a bustling restaurant, to an underground kosher wine cellar that covers the better part of a city block in lower Manhattan, from one of the Lower East Side's last, great dairy restaurants to a bustling Brazilian restaurant in midtown, we want to show even the best-traveled New Yorkers that Manhattan always holds new surprises.

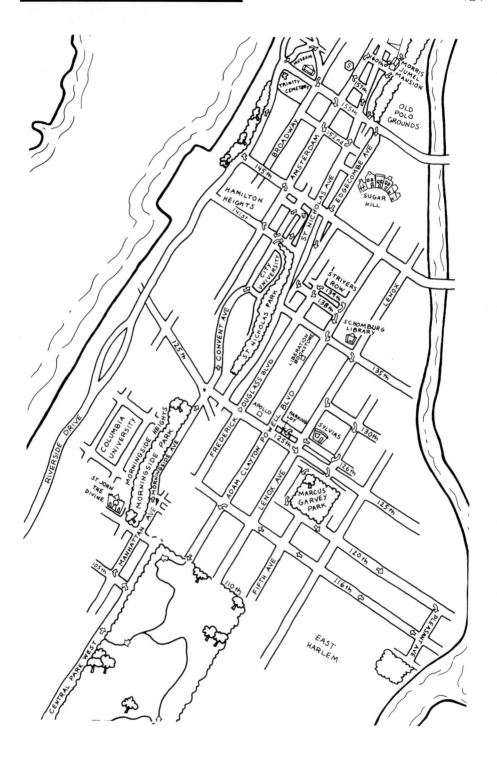

THE HARLEMS: SIGHTS & SOUL

Harlem "is the cosmopolis of colored culture, of gaiety, of art, and the capital of Negro cookery. Harlem's visitors come from the Southern United States, the West Indies, from South America and even from Africa. In what it eats, Harlem shows itself less a locality than an international rallying point. [It] is a haven where food has an odd psychology, where viands solace the mind as well as feed the body. . . .

"The New Yorker does not appreciate the infinite variety of yam and its congeners until he has made the rounds of the Harlem markets. There are red and yellow yams brought from the Southern states for the benefit of those who long for the food of the old plantation. Huge yams from the West Indies, as big as a man's head, are imported especially for Harlem. In some months, they are sold for . . . more than the price of the choicest cuts of meats, because they are eaten as cures for homesickness. . . .

"If jazz is to promote the love of Afro-American fare, then to collards we shall shortly go. . . . Along the line of Lenox Avenue are seen delectable collards foliaged as are cauliflowers, with just a tinge of light purple or lavender. . . . What broccoli is to Park Avenue, the select collards are to the colony of upper Manhattan. . . .

"On Saturday afternoons and nights, the broad sidewalks of Lenox Avenue become groves and gardens and broad fields [with] sugar cane . . . plantains . . . collards . . . and yam. . . . One would go far before finding anything more colorful and picturesque than this weekly food exposition which Harlem stages. . . ."

—from "What Tempts Harlem's Palate?"
New York Times, July 15, 1928

CENTRAL HARLEM

To Get There

By subway or bus: Take the A train, to stops along Frederick Douglass Blvd. (Eighth Ave.), or the IRT 2 or 3, which stop along Lenox Ave. Harlem also has an excellent surface transportation network, and, depending on where you want to go, you can find buses as well as subways traveling on the major avenues. Buses are recommended because you can also see much of Harlem's rich architecture en route to your destination. And they're more fun.

By car: The Harlem River Dr., Major Deegan Expressway, and Henry Hudson Pkwy. all flow into Harlem. A 24-hour municipal parking lot just east of the Harlem State Office Building at 163 W. 125th St. is convenient to public transportation and within walking distance of major sights. Enter on 126th St.

By bike: See the instructions for the "Harlem Sights & Soul" tour on page 247.

Orientation: Black Harlem is spread over an area approximately spanning the Hudson River and Madison Avenue, north of 110th Street from Madison to Manhattan Avenues and north of 125th Street from Convent Avenue to the Hudson River. (Morningside Heights, separated from lower West Harlem by Morningside Park, is an overwhelmingly white area dominated by Columbia University and is not included in this section.) The northern border is roughly at 155th Street.

Nearly 60 years after the *New York Times* caught the essence of Harlem through its food, Harlem remains the capital of Black America. It's perhaps not as exotic today as it seemed in the 1920s, when Harlem was at an artistic, intellectual, and political peak known as the Harlem Renaissance.

Still, it is an area rich in history and continues to be an American cultural center. Harlem produced authors James Baldwin, Claude Brown, and Piri Thomas; it was a hotbed for the Black Nationalist movements of Malcolm X, H. Rap Brown, and Stokely Carmichael in the 1960s; and it's now home to a different kind of black nationalism—the brilliantly successful Dance Theater of Harlem, a ballet company and school with an international reputation, as well as the Black National Theater. Harlem also claims the Schomburg Center for Research in Black Culture, probably the most comprehensive collection of books, periodicals, manuscripts, and artwork of its kind.

Called *Nieuw Haarlem* by Dutch farmers who incorporated their settlement in 1658, Harlem was originally an Indian village on the banks of the Harlem River between what are now 110th and 125th Streets. Slaves held by the Dutch West India Company built a connecting road to New Amsterdam, 20 miles to the south at the southern tip of Manhattan, in 1678. The area's lush soil attracted not only farmers but wealthy merchants, too; the Morris-Jumel Mansion at Harlem's border with Washington Heights is the only relic of the once numerous estates that dotted Manhattan in the eighteenth and nineteenth centuries. Harlem developed a suburban character after the opening of a rail line in 1837, which ran from City Hall uptown along Park Avenue; many of the brick and brownstone row houses built in its aftermath still stand. Although the rail line opened up Harlem for residential development, it also divided the area and created a bleak strip of factories and tenements along the tracks. East Harlem became firmly established as a working-class neighborhood after the completion of the Third Avenue and Second Avenue elevated lines in 1879–80. Russian,

German, Italian, Irish, Hungarian, and Scandinavian immigrants filled the area's tenements and shacks.

To the west, quality residential construction continued. Noteworthy is Hamilton Heights (Convent Avenue between 141st and 145th Streets, just north of City College), with its posh row houses built between 1886 and 1906. So-called "Strivers Row," which got its name in 1919 from the ambitious black American artists and professionals who settled there, is the best other surviving example of the era. Located on 138th and 139th Streets between Adam Clayton Powell and Frederick Douglass Boulevards (Seventh and Eighth Avenues), these lush homes were completed in 1891 and include one block—the northern section of 139th Street—designed by the great firm of McKim, Mead & White.

What is known as "Black Harlem" had its genesis around 1904, about the time the subway finally came uptown. Black real estate entrepreneur Philip A. Payton, Jr., began buying and managing white-owned apartment buildings and renting them—often at inflated prices—to blacks. With the concurrent demolition of black neighborhoods in what was called San Juan Hill (the location of today's Lincoln Center) and the Tenderloin District (today's Herald Square and Penn Station neighborhoods), Harlem became a magnet for blacks; by 1914, Harlem's black population had swelled to 50,000. (Only four years earlier, all of Manhattan had about 60,000 blacks.) Some whites tried fighting the black influx by forming the Harlem Property Owners' Improvement Corporation. But their efforts failed, and little by little they moved out. The formerly white landmark Hurtig and Seaman Theater at 253 West 125th Street became the Apollo Theater; many Harlem churches are former synagogues.

The now-legendary "Harlem Renaissance" flowered just after World War I. There was a black literary intelligentsia, whose core included James Weldon Johnson, W. E. B. Du Bois, Langston Hughes, Zora Neale Hurston, Countee Cullen, and artist Aaron Douglas. Jazz clubs sprouted all over: The names Cotton Club, Savoy, and Smalls's Paradise are synonymous with these magic years, although, paradoxically, some excluded black patrons while welcoming black performers like Duke Ellington and Cab Calloway. The Harlem Renaissance coincided with Marcus Garvey's Black Nationalist "Back to Africa" movement. Although Garvey's movement collapsed, and he was disgraced (and jailed for fraud), the West Indian's efforts have remained a lasting symbol of black pride. In 1973, Mount Morris Park at Fifth Avenue between 120th and 124th Streets was renamed Marcus Garvey Memorial Park.

Further uptown in Harlem, and up a hill on Edgecombe Avenue north of 145th Street, spacious apartments and townhouses were built that attracted more well-to-do blacks. Nicknamed "Sugar Hill" because its residents could afford to live the "sweet life," the neighborhood at different times was home to Cab Calloway, Duke Ellington, Paul Robeson, and Supreme Court Justice Thurgood Marshall. High-rise luxury apartments at 409 and 555 Edgecome Avenue—still towering presences with spectacular views of the Harlem Valley and the Bronx—were then, and remain, two of the area's most prestigious addresses.

For most Harlemites, life has always been more difficult than for the majority of other New Yorkers. When the Depression hit New York, it devastated much of Harlem, and it brought the Harlem Renaissance to an end. As Langston Hughes wrote in his autobiography *The Big Sea,* "The Depression brought everybody down a peg or two," but "the Negroes had but few pegs to fall." (A number of books about the Harlem Renaissance came out in the 1980s, including Jervis Anderson's *This Was Harlem* and David Levering Lewis's *When Harlem Was in Vogue.* Roi Ottley's *New World A-Coming,* published in 1943, has a particularly evocative rendering of Harlem and the black American experience.)

To outsiders, today's Harlem is a patchwork of myths and reality. Although parts of Harlem contain some of New York City's most devastated blocks, others have some of the city's finest turn-of-the-century architecture. In the 1980s, Harlem entered what some have dubbed its second renaissance. New investment has spurred much renovation. Along 135th Street and on the nearby avenues, storefronts have been spruced up, and new businesses have come in. The beautiful row houses, fashionable once again, are being bought up and renovated; some are resold at much higher prices. A new condominium complex at the fringe of Central Park North—Harlem's gateway—heralds a new middle class for Harlem.

RESTAURANTS AND BAKERIES

Sylvia Woods now describes her restaurant as "Queen of Soul Foods," but her **Sylvia's Restaurant** (328 Lenox Ave., Tel.: 212/534-9414 or 534-9348) was just a skinny luncheonette with a long counter and a few tables when it opened in the early 1960s. It was here that neighborhood residents came by for a breakfast of salmon cakes or eggs heaped with grits or hunks of sausage, and homemade corn bread or biscuits, or for a lunch or dinner of spicy ribs, smothered or fried chicken, pork chops, or baked ham. Side orders of collard greens, black-eyed peas, potato salad, or cole slaw were taken for granted. These staples are still to be had at Sylvia's—and in ample portions—along with such supersweet desserts as carrot cake with vanilla icing, sweet potato pie, or peach cobbler (Thursdays only), but the restaurant has tripled in size to include two dining rooms and a bar, including a party room for groups. A Sunday brunch, including a full meal and one drink, brings families to Sylvia's, and live music begins at 3:00 P.M.

Sylvia's daughters were still in school when the business opened, but daughter Bedelia manages the place now, and relatives and friends often help out. Always busy, noisy, and often teeming with children, the restaurant is both easygoing *and* frenetic, and service is very fast. Increased publicity has brought in many outside groups, and some Harlemites have criticized the restaurant's commercialization. In fact, if you want the feel of the "real" Sylvia's, you should sit at the original counter, where the neighborhood folks hang out.

Even older than Sylvia's, **La Famille** (2017 Fifth Ave., between 124th and 125th Sts., Tel.: 212/722-9806) is lower key and a bit fancier, occupying two floors of a four-story townhouse on a lovely block north of Marcus Garvey Memorial Park. Downstairs is a lively bar, which throbs at night with live music; the upstairs restaurant, with posters of Afro-American art decorating the walls and lacy curtains covering large picture windows, is more formal. The menu is continental style, with fish, veal, and chicken entrées. A filling chicken soup begins each meal, and servings come with two vegetables and homemade biscuits. La Famille offers a weekday lunch special that is irresistible: A full meal, including tax, is $4.01.

De de's Bakery (69 W. 125th St., Tel.: 212/410-2296), a down-home bakery that calls itself "better than good," sells coconut, pineapple, and spice cakes and pies by the slice—though "slab" is more like it. Specialties include bread pudding, bean pie, and a spectacular banana pudding. De de's welcomes special orders.

E&M Bakery Shop (53 East 125th St., Tel.: 212/722-9770), owned and operated by James Gaddist, has been in the neighborhood for 13 years. The specialties include three different kinds of sweet potato pie—plain, with coconut, or with raisins—sweet rolls, wedding cakes, and sandwiches. There are a few tables, so if you're in the area (it's down the street from the 125th Street Station of Metro North) come here for coffee and a piece of pie. Though it's a bit far from many of Harlem's tourist spots, the extra block-or-two walk is well worth it. You'll also find birthday cards and small gifts for sale. (E&M caters and bakes to order.)

SYLVIA WOODS
BARBECUED RIBS

For the sauce

1 can (8 ounce) tomato sauce
1 bottle (14 ounce) ketchup
2 cups water
1/2 cup Louisiana hot sauce
1/4 cup firmly packed brown sugar
1 onion, sliced thin
1 green pepper, diced
1 lemon, seeded and sliced

For the meat

2 slabs pork ribs (2 1/2 to 3 pounds each)
2 teaspoons salt
1 1/2 teaspoons red pepper flakes
1 teaspoon freshly ground pepper
1 1/2 cups cider vinegar

Combine all the sauce ingredients in a medium saucepan; cover and simmer over low heat, stirring occasionally for 45 minutes. Refrigerate covered for 24 hours.

Pat the ribs dry with paper towels. In a small bowl combine salt, red pepper flakes, and pepper. Rub well over both sides of the ribs. Cover loosely and refrigerate overnight.

Preheat the oven to 425° F. Place the ribs in a 16-by-11-inch roasting pan; pour in the cider vinegar. Bake for 1 to 1 1/2 hours, turning the ribs two or three times, until fork-tender and beginning to come away from the bone. Drain off pan juices. Bake 25 to 30 minutes more, until browned. Reheat the sauce over low heat. Spoon some sauce over the ribs before serving. Makes eight servings.

CANDIED YAMS

4 pounds fresh yams or sweet potatoes,
    unpeeled
or 6 cans (17 ounces each) yams or
    sweet potatoes, drained
6 tablespoons butter, cut up

3/4 cup sugar
1/2 teaspoon nutmeg
1 cup water
2 teaspoons vanilla extract

Peel fresh yams and cut into quarters, lengthwise. Boil fresh yams for 30 minutes in a large saucepan of boiling water. Preheat the oven to 350° F.

In a baking pan, combine fresh or canned yams with butter, sugar, and nutmeg. Toss gently. In a small bowl, combine water and vanilla and pour over yams. Bake for 1 1/2 hours or until tender, turning and basting occasionally. Makes eight servings. Note: If using canned yams, bake covered for 45 minutes, then bake uncovered for 45 minutes.

Turning the ribs at Sylvia's.

COLLARD GREENS WITH HAM

6 pounds collard greens, trimmed and
  coarsely chopped
1 meaty ham bone (about 1 ½ pounds)

5 cups water
salt and freshly ground pepper
2 tablespoons distilled white vinegar

Combine the greens, ham bone, water, 2½ teaspoons salt, and ½ teaspoon pepper in a 5-quart Dutch oven. Bring to a boil; reduce heat and simmer uncovered 1 ½ hours, adding more water if necessary. Remove the ham bone; shred the meat and return it to the Dutch oven, discarding bone and skin. Season with salt and pepper. Stir in vinegar. Makes eight servings.

PEACH COBBLER

1 cup plus 1 tablespoon sugar
3 tablespoons cornstarch
6 tablespoons butter, divided
6 cans (16 ounces each) peach halves,
  drained (reserve ¼ cup syrup)
2 tablespoons vanilla extract

2 teaspoons baking powder
½ teaspoon baking soda
½ teaspoon salt
1¾ cups all-purpose flour
⅓ cup cold shortening, cut up
¾ cup buttermilk

Combine 1 cup sugar and the cornstarch in a small bowl. In a large saucepan, melt 4 tablespoons of the butter with reserved syrup over medium heat; stir in the sugar mixture. Add the peaches and stir until well combined. Simmer over medium heat for 5 minutes. Remove from heat and stir in the vanilla. Transfer to a 3-quart baking dish, 2¼ inches deep; let cool. Cover and let stand at room temperature at least 6 hours or overnight.

Preheat the oven to 375° F. Combine the flour, remaining tablespoon of sugar, baking powder, baking soda, and salt in a medium bowl. With a pastry blender or two knives, cut in shortening until the mixture resembles coarse crumbs. With a wooden spoon, gradually stir in the buttermilk until just moistened. (The amount of liquid used may vary.) On a lightly floured surface, roll dough to ⅜ inch. Drape it over the peaches and trim if necessary. Bake for 25 minutes. In a small saucepan melt the remaining 2 tablespoons of butter; brush over crust. Bake until golden, about 5 to 8 minutes more. Serve hot or at room temperature. Makes eight servings.

WALKING TOUR

Note: On this and other walking tours of Harlem, bring a good guidebook to New York City. We've found the *AIA Guide to New York City* and *Blue Guide: New York* to be excellent resources; both are available in major bookstores.

Harlem's crossroads is 125th Street, and it remains a busy street clogged with fast-food shops, beauty salons, small businesses, an occasional sidewalk preacher, and even a Korean-owned "Seoul-food" restaurant. Begin at the corner of 125th Street and Lenox Avenue and head south on Lenox Avenue to 120th Street, part of the Mount Morris Historic District and location of some of Harlem's most majestic churches and residences. At 272 Lenox Avenue, the photographer James Van Der Zee (1886–1983) once had the studio where he took thousands of portraits that some call the definitive portrait of Harlem from the 1920s to the 1960s. Turn east at 120th or 122nd Streets and you'll find **Marcus Garvey Memorial Park,** with some of the area's most stunning homes. The **Ethiopian Hebrew Congregation** (1 W. 123rd St.) occupies an 1890 townhouse within the historic district. About 500 families in the New York metropolitan area are members of the Ethiopian Hebrew movement, which began in the 1920s. The synagogue is arranged with Orthodox Jewish seating; women sit in a separate section behind the men. If you visit during a Saturday service, expect to hear the Jewish liturgy combined with gospel-sounding melodies. Head back to 125th Street and Lenox Avenue. The so-called **African Market** (Lenox Ave., 125th to 126th Sts., west side) consists of outdoor stalls selling everything from blue jeans, incense, and "Gucci" T-shirts to African

jewelry, clothing, and textiles from the Ivory Coast, Liberia, and elsewhere in West Africa, as well as wood sculpture, heavy beads, and hand-crocheted hats. (Note: **Mart 1-2-5** on the south side of 125th Street between Adam Clayton Powell Boulevard and Frederick Douglass Boulevard, which opened in August 1986, now houses many stalls formerly in the outdoor market, but other vendors continue to sell goods on Lenox Avenue.)

Between Lenox Avenue and Adam Clayton Powell Boulevard are two important landmarks: The **Harlem State Office Building** (163 W. 125th St.), at an intersection also called "African Square," was built in 1973 to revitalize the area and bring more jobs to Harlem—it stands like a lighthouse in the area; the **Studio Museum in Harlem** (144 W. 125th St.) has rotating exhibits of fine arts, photography, and sculpture reflecting both historic Afro-American traditions and the continuing vitality of the black community. The modern facility also sponsors concerts and lectures, and has an attractive gift-and-book shop selling African jewelry and crafts, posters, and cards. **Theresa Towers** office complex (2090 Seventh Ave., corner of 125th St.) was originally a luxurious hotel built in 1910. One of its famous visitors before its conversion was Cuba's President Fidel Castro, who visited in 1960 when he came to the United Nations.

On the next block heading west is the **Apollo Theater** (253 W. 125th St.). For many years since it became a showcase for black talent in 1934, the Apollo was Harlem, and its famous amateur night gave aspiring unknowns Ella Fitzgerald and Sarah Vaughan, and, much later, Luther Vandross, their tickets to stardom. Opened in 1913 as a whites-only opera house, it hosted, as a black performers' showcase, legends-to-be Charlie Parker, Bessie Smith, Billie Holliday, Dinah Washington, and Harlem's own Duke Ellington, after whom a boulevard was named in 1976. (Duke Ellington Boulevard replaces West 106th Street from Riverside Drive to Central Park West.) Hard times in the mid-1970s led to the Apollo's shutting down, but it reopened in 1985 as part of an overall regeneration of West Harlem.

Walk back to Lenox Avenue and head uptown. **Astor Row** (130th St., Lenox to Fifth Aves.) contains along its south side unusual single-family homes with wooden porches and front lawns with rich shrubbery and trees almost surprisingly sylvan in Harlem's midst. Built as model housing in the 1890s, the homes today appear in conditions varying from adequate to dilapidated. **Liberation Bookstore** (421 Lenox Ave. at 131st St., Tel.: 212/281-4615) stocks a wide collection of Afro-American and third-world literature, including children's books, and doubles as a gathering place for local intellectuals. At 135th Street and Lenox Avenue is the stunning **Schomburg Center for Research in Black Culture**, which Arthur A. Schomburg, a Puerto Rican–born black, started as a private collection and which was donated, under the auspices of the Carnegie Foundation, to New York City in 1926. The current collection, occupying a new building that opened in 1980, contains more than 75,000 books, 60,000 photographs, and extensive oral history, videotape, film, artwork, and microfilm, plus an outdoor amphitheater and sculpture garden.

WEST HARLEM: HAMILTON HEIGHTS

To Get There:

By subway: Take the IRT 1 train to 137th or 145th St.

By bike: See the instructions for the "Harlem Sights & Soul" tour on page 247.

Located on a bluff overlooking the Harlem Valley are landmark sections with some of the area's lushest architecture and most important historic sights. Although much of West Harlem is still a black community, the Broadway area and its side streets are overwhelmingly occupied by Cuban and Dominican shops and residents.

RESTAURANTS AND BAKERIES

Calvin Copeland opened the elegant **Copeland's Restaurant** (549 W. 145th St., Tel.: 212/234-2356) in the early 1980s, and his success is clearly marked for anyone who looks by the photos of politicians and stars—Charles Rangel, Jesse Jackson, Richard Pryor—who've made their way there. Specialties include continental, Cajun, and southern dishes, including oxtails, peanut soup, corn fritters, and gumbo. You'll find the restaurant an abrupt change from the clutter and noise on nearby Broadway, and the service is as polished and attentive as the rest of the area is raucous and brusque. A small serving of gumbo is heaped with shellfish, while Copeland's Special Barbecue is piquant and ample. Dishes come with two vegetables, and you may find yourself too full to eat dessert.

Reliable Cafeteria (549 W. 145th St., Tel.: 212/234-2356) shares the same address and owners as Copeland's, although this next-door establishment is informal and very cheap. With an interior like that of a fast-food restaurant with crowded formica tables and plastic chairs, it nonetheless has a friendly, homey atmosphere. Portions of such specialties as smothered chicken, baked ham, and spiced ribs are whopping, including two vegetables and corn bread. You can also come early in the morning for breakfast.

Floridita Restaurant (3451 Broadway, near 141st St., Tel.: 212/926-0319) is the flagship, and by far the most attractive, of four Floridita restaurants in upper Manhattan specializing in Cuban cuisine. It has an enclosed café with artificial roses on each table, and although there's a dress code—no T-shirts allowed—the ambience is informal. Specialties include starchy Cuban breakfasts, with delicacies such as yucca, *mangu* and *tostones* (the latter are fried sweet plantains), and *queso frito* (fried cheese), and dinner entrées including steak, chicken, and seafood dishes with creole seasonings. Go as much for the animated atmosphere of this almost always busy place as for the very good, reasonably priced food.

La Rosa Bakery (3395 Broadway at 138th St., Tel.: 212/281-1500), an excellent Cuban bakery, features elaborate birthday cakes, flan, bread puddings, and Dominican specialties. Prices are much lower than in comparable bakeries elsewhere in Manhattan, and the service is friendly. If you don't speak Spanish, you'll surely find a customer (most likely a young student) who can explain what the different cakes are and help you order.

WALKING TOUR

Start at the campus of the **City College of New York** (130th to 141st Sts., Amsterdam Ave. to St. Nicholas Terrace) by following Convent Avenue at about 135th Street, roughly the center of campus. (Keep the *AIA Guide* handy for this tour.) Gothic and Neo-Renaissance architecture and Romanesque influences combine with modern academic buildings constructed as early as 1847 and as recently as 1976. The North Campus at Convent Avenue from 138th to 140th Streets has a lovely courtyard. CCNY, as it's better known, has traditionally been the ticket for immigrants and the poor to the American middle class, and although the tuition is no longer free, it's still very cheap and provides an excellent college education. CCNY is said to have more Nobel laureates as alumni than any other American university. Head north to 141st Street and make a right for a short downhill jaunt to Hamilton Terrace. Turn left onto Hamilton Terrace and follow it as it curves around to Convent Avenue. This area is known as the Hamilton Heights Historic District. Mrs. Lenon Holder Hoyte, who never had children of her own, instead became a compulsive collector of dolls and toys, and she turned her landmark residence on one of Harlem's loveliest streets into **Aunt Len's Doll and Toy Museum** (6 Hamilton Terrace, Tel.: 212/281-4143; call for an appointment). The house is packed with priceless dolls, some hundreds of years old, and exquisite dollhouses.

Alexander Hamilton's country home, built in 1801, is now a small federally run museum, the **Hamilton Grange National Monument** (287 Convent Ave., Tel.: 212/283-5154), with relics from the Colonial period. Walk east down 141st Street again, but this time go all the way downhill to Edgecombe Avenue, and turn right to 139th Street. Now turn left on 139th and continue until you are between Frederick Douglass Boulevard and Adam Clayton Powell Boulevard. **Strivers Row**, as mentioned earlier, is a two-block complex of some of Harlem's best homes. Built in 1891 as the King Model Houses for well-

to-do white Harlemites, they're luxurious and wider than most row houses. Note the lack of garbage cans in front of the houses. Rear alleys were set aside for the gathering of refuse—and to keep the horses which owners had, of course. Affluent residents in the 1920s and 1930s included musicians Noble Sissle, Eubie Blake, and W. C. Handy. Today Strivers Row is still home to many black physicians, lawyers, and other professionals.

You can trust me.

NORTHERN HARLEM/SOUTHERN WASHINGTON HEIGHTS

To Get There

By subway: Take the IRT 1 train to 157th St. and Broadway. Amsterdam Ave. is one block east.

By car: Take the West Side Highway to the 155th St. exit.

By bike: See "Harlem Sights & Soul" map on page 247. You can cycle directly there any number of ways. Broadway and Amsterdam Ave. go straight uptown but have lots of traffic. Riverside Dr. is a lovely alternative, and you can head east up many even-numbered streets to Broadway. From Central Park North, you can also take Lenox Ave., then bear left onto St. Nicholas Ave. at 111th St. and continue uptown. St. Nicholas gradually rises into Harlem Heights and gives you a sense of the changing architecture and economy of Harlem as you proceed north.

Geographically separated from the Harlem Valley by a bluff and rock formations along Edgecombe Avenue, this area contains elegant brownstone and granite homes, several grand, large apartment buildings, and the Audubon Terrace museum complex.

RESTAURANTS

Try **Wilson's Bakery and Restaurant** (1980 Amsterdam Ave. at 158th St., Tel.: 212/923-9821). Wilson's currently has a neighborhood monopoly as the area's most bustling, friendly eatery, with a sunny, enclosed café to boot. Baked specialties include sweet cakes, biscuits, and rolls, while the restaurant serves ample homestyle breakfasts heaped with grits and sausage, and full lunches including southern fried chicken and rib specialties. Informal and easygoing, the place is especially busy on weekends, but you won't be pressured to leave, even if others are waiting. As we were finishing a meal and wondering whether we ought to go, our waitress, poised with coffee urn, said, "Honey, this is my table and I don't want to work too hard today, so just keep sitting. Want a refill?" You can just have dessert here, too, including mouth-watering southern pecan or sweet potato pie, carrot cake, and peach cobbler with vanilla ice cream.

Not just ordinary cakes at Wilson's.

WALKING TOUR

Using Wilson's as a starting point, head north on Amsterdam Avenue to 160th Street and turn right for two blocks. On your left—you certainly can't miss it, although many people don't even know about it—is the **Morris-Jumel Mansion** and its lovely grounds. Built around 1765 and remodeled in 1810, the federally landmarked mansion sits in a park isolated from the rest of the area. Originally a summer residence for Roger Morris, a Revolutionary War officer, it briefly served as headquarters for George Washington. (Be prepared, when you visit, to hear more than you may want to know about the love life of Madame Jumel, who apparently got around.) A Federal-style home with a wood facade and shingled rear, the mansion has a colonial herb garden in the backyard. You are welcome to wander through the yard, and it's a delightful place to bring a book and a cup of coffee and corn bread from Wilson's. Sylvan Terrace, a short street parallel to 160th Street just west of the mansion, contains two rows of wooden houses built for workers in the 1880s. All but one were restored with federal funds. Head south on St. Nicholas Avenue to 152nd Street and turn left. At 466 West 152nd Street is the school of the **Dance Theater of Harlem,** which was founded in the late 1960s by Arthur Mitchell, the first black star of the New York City Ballet. Across the street you can't miss the quirky wooden house at 473 West 152nd Street, painted canary yellow, with a vast front yard and a widow's walk on its roof. The house was built around 1870 although it has a marker in front reading "1769: 9 miles from N. York." Walk two blocks west to Broadway and north to 155th Street. Now technically in Washington Heights, you'll come to the **Audubon Terrace** complex of museums and institutes that cover an entire city block: the best known is the **Museum of the American Indian.** Also located in the complex are the **Hispanic Society,** the **National Institute of Arts and Letters**, and a local educational program called **Boricua College**.

SOUTHWESTERN HARLEM

Sometimes known as "Cathedral Down Under" because it sits in the shadow of the Cathedral of St. John the Divine on the other side of Morningside Park, this section of Harlem is bordered by 110th Street, Morningside Avenue, 125th Street, and Lenox Avenue. More recently dubbed "Harlem's Gateway," it is lush with wonderful architecture—and rife with abandonment. Stick to 116th Street and Morningside Avenues, which are the busiest areas. There's not much to seek out right now, besides the **Graham Court** apartments at 116th Street and Seventh Avenue, which were built in 1901 by the architects who later designed the luxurious Apthorp at Broadway and 79th Street. However, there's much change due in this area, so keep your eyes open.

RESTAURANTS

Adele's Soul Food Kitchen (2003 Adam Clayton Powell Blvd. at 120th St., Tel.: 212/864-9196) is a neighborhood eatery whose reputation has spread far beyond Harlem's boundaries. The restaurant itself is small and unprepossessing and service is at crowded counters, or you can order takeout. Servings are generous and thoroughly soulful; dishes include fried and smothered chicken, ribs, collard greens, ample portions of potato or macaroni salad, and for dessert we especially recommend banana pudding.

At Lenox Avenue and 116th Street, you'll find a mosque, operated by the Nation of Islam, including a health-food store and the **Salaam Restaurant**.

SPANISH HARLEM

To Get There

By subway and bus: Take the IRT 6 train to 116th St. and Lexington Ave. Uptown buses along First, Third, and Madison Aves. stop at 116th St.

By bike: Travel north on uptown avenues, including First, Third, Park, or Madison. Lock your bike on 116th St. between Park and Third Aves. or on Lexington Ave., near the subway entrance for the IRT 4, 5, and 6.

Orientation: East Harlem's commercial hub runs along E. 116th St. from Madison Ave. to First Ave.; it also includes Park Ave. itself, underneath the Metro North tracks from 112th to 116th Sts. (La Marqueta); and portions of Lexington and Third Ave. a few blocks north and south of 116th St.

"Hey, *chica*, take a look at these earrings. Real cheap, real cheap." On a warm Saturday morning or afternoon, salesmen everywhere in East Harlem try to hawk a little this, a little that. The neighborhood is alive with *salsa* music, honking car horns, and families--little children trying to keep up with their parents—crowding into tiny *bodegas* (food markets) and clothing stores to do their weekly shopping. The stores explode with inventory, and racks, shelves, and boxes of goods are moved outdoors. All kinds of economies—legitimate, sidewalk, some a little fuzzy—go on almost everywhere. The aroma of *café con leche* and sizzling, deep-fried *cuchifritos* linger as you turn a corner or cross a street. A sidewalk astrologer offers to tell your future. Religious icons are sold side-by-side with "Mr. T"

dolls, pots and pans, pocketbooks, and bright jewelry. You're in *El Barrio*—the District; since World War II, it's been New York City's capital for Puerto Rican Americans.

These days *El Barrio* is both dreary and on an upswing. Blocks of old row houses are punctuated by boxy red brick housing projects built in the 1950s. There's lots of restoration going on, but plenty of abandonment, too. In its early days, East Harlem was a staunch immigrant working-class neighborhood, its reputation established as a revolving door for people on the way up and out. But the Puerto Ricans have stayed, even if new waves of immigrants from the island have displaced those who left for more space and greener

Catch of the day.

climes. Recently, however, a new kind of change has started filtering in: Gentrification from the Upper East Side of Manhattan has begun creeping uptown. On blocks like 103rd and 105th Streets near First Avenue, buildings have been renovated or turned into co-ops few local residents can afford. At the same time, East Harlem has some of New York City's deepest pockets of poverty.

One obvious feature of East Harlem, too, is its lack of real park area, of green space. But local residents have been creative. There are plenty of vacant lots, and many have been converted into local gathering places, furnished with all shapes and sizes of found objects—chairs, tables, planks of wood, odds and ends of metal piping, discarded toys. One lot had seats removed from old cars, which had been placed facing one another to resemble an outdoor restaurant. In other lots, small community gardens battle bricks and vandalism to flourish. Keep your eyes open for murals, too: A number of these—Lexington Avenue at 104th Street, Lexington Avenue at 116th Street, Pleasant Avenue at 119th Street—add extra beauty to Manhattan's Caribbean.

MARKETS

No visit to East Harlem can be complete without sampling the self-contained world of **La Marqueta**, the area's enclosed market at Park Avenue. The market complex is actually four separate arcades, erected in 1936 by the city administration headed by Mayor Fiorello LaGuardia (an

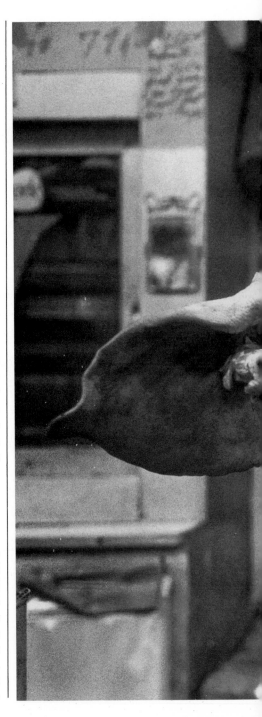

All right, all right, it's not *really* smoking a cigarette.

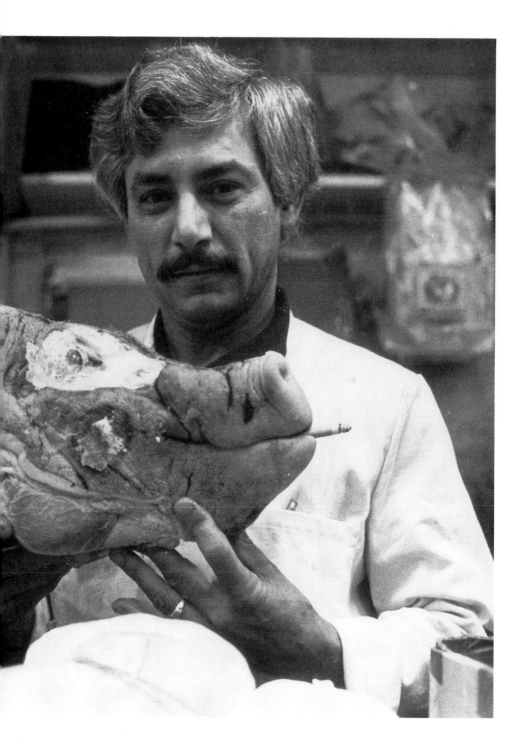

East Harlem native, by the way), to hustle dozens of Italian and Jewish street peddlers indoors. For modest rents, the merchants operated stalls that sold all kinds of foodstuffs and housewares to local residents, most of them as poor and struggling as the peddlers themselves. Lacking refrigerators at home (or enough money), they'd come daily to the market to buy small quantities of food for the day's meals. Since the neighborhood became Hispanic and black, the nature of the goods has changed. You'll find the produce stands crammed with Caribbean root vegetables, such as yams, batatas, yucca, and cassava used in stews or served alone (yucca with garlic sauce is delicious); fruits such as mangos, plantains, and coconut; tall stalks of sugarcane; banana leaves for wrapping, and the fragrant cilantro—coriander leaves—that give a strong flavoring to rice and paella dishes. Many stalls also sell collards, chitterlings, and catfish, essentials of "soul food" diets.

"Hey love, come here, come here," beckons George Ordonez, the young proprietor of the northernmost stall in the third arcade, the one that looks most like a general store. He knows everybody by name, but that's easy: Everybody is "love," "honey," or "baby." He is a gregarious and ready negotiator, and his customers are experienced hagglers. He is one of a handful of merchants in the

Botánicas provide nourishment for the soul.

market who offer hard-to-find imports along with bulk rice and dried beans and other household staples. His clientele includes Jamaicans and Africans as well as Puerto Ricans and other Latinos, so he stocks Jamaican ackee, syrups, and pepper sauces, and a modest selection of African goods, including red palm oil, *egusi* (melon seed), and *gari* from Nigeria, which is used for baking bread, plus huge cans of palm nut soup from Ghana. His specialty, however, is the ubiquitous *baccalao*—salted codfish, bought dried but ready to be boiled into a nutritious and inexpensive main dish.

As you wander through La Marqueta, don't be put off by the come-ons: Competition is what the place is all about, and you'll feel better if you just say no and smile—unless, of course, you decide to join the fray. Humor helps, and don't be shy about asking questions if you don't know what something is. You'll find other customers as well as shopkeepers willing to explain things to you, and even to help with the bargaining. By the way, if La Marqueta seems somewhat empty during your visit, that's because it's in the midst of change. The complex fell on hard times in the late seventies and early eighties, and in April 1986, the City of New York took it over from the merchant cooperative that had been running it. Plans include major renovation of arcade interiors and a proposed mall.

Knuckles and bones.

Say when.

Marqueta veteran.

No, *I'm* not for sale.

BAKERIES

Multilayered, elaborately decorated cakes are as much a folk art as comestibles in East Harlem, and we heartily recommend two bakeries that double as cake museums. **Valencia Bakery** (1869 Lexington Ave., Tel.: 212/991-6400) was founded more than 50 years ago by the Ripoll family from Valencia, Spain, and these days it is managed by countryman José Albos, who's worked here for more than 30 years. The store sells rich corn breads, bread pudding, and *pastillas* (patties) with guava and other fruit fillings, and its own brand of ice cream. But you should really go to see the spectacular wedding cakes, Valencia's specialties. Models are in display cases inside the bakery: An elaborate pagoda-shaped cake will leave you $275 poorer, and even more ornate "stairway" and "water fountain" cakes go for $300 and up. The cakes are populated with tiny plastic people, and the "fountain" cake has a miniature electric illuminated fountain. Other options include a cake cut in the shape of Puerto Rico, a baseball cake with its own diamond and two playing teams, and even a skiing cake with its own slope and skier. Service is friendly, and Valencia is often crowded.

    Capri Bakery (186 E. 116th St., Tel.: 212/410-1876) around the corner has bustled with customers since it opened in mid-1985. It offers a wide selection of *pan caliendo* (hot rolls), including garlic and egg; bread pudding; flan (custard); oozy iced pastries; rum-soaked cakes; *pastellillos* filled with guava, cream, meat, or cheese; Cuban sandwiches (ham, pork, pickle, and cheese toasted on a roll); and birthday cakes in as tantalizing a variety as Valencia's. Take a look at the samples in the store window: There's a Mickey Mouse cake, a football cake, and a wrestling cake with models of Hulk Hogan and a competitor ready to throw one another. Our favorite is the "hangover" cake: It features a drunken fellow flanked by tiny bottles of whiskey and gin.

RESTAURANTS

Fast-food stands and modest Spanish-American restaurants abound in East Harlem. One of our favorites is **El Farol**, "the lighthouse" (2261 Second Ave., Tel.: 212/831-4940), a colorful, busy eatery on the corner of 116th Street that Junior Diaz opened in May 1983. It has a counter and a few stools with a ledge along the window, is very bright and friendly, and has an excellent, inexpensive selection of typical Puerto Rican snacks and main dishes to eat in or take out. The specialty is cuchifritos, which are on display in the window. You specify which parts you want: pig ears, tongue, hog maw, or blood sausage. Other specialties include pork and steak dishes, *pastelles* (beef patties), *chicharron* (fried pork rind), *bacalitos*, and *rellenos de papa*. To complement these foods, there's a selection of sweet tropical drinks, including pineapple, coconut, *tamarindo*, and sesame seed, also known as *ajonjoli*, a cold thirst-quencher. There's also fried shrimp, shrimp salad, shrimp stew, and octopus. For less adventurous stomachs, the menu offers hamburgers, ham and cheese sandwiches, and other *norteamericano* dishes.

    For a fancier ambience and meal, visit the lovely **San Juan** (167 E. 116th St., Tel.: 212/860-2382). You'll pass through a long, dark bar in front to reach the ornate rear dining room, where murals of old San Juan and its modern beachfront evoke the land many of the restaurant's customers left behind. Dishes are ample and inexpensive; no main course is more than $13, and many are much less. Chef's specials include *paella* (seafood stew) and other spicy seafood combinations, stuffed beef, beef stew, and fried chick-peas with sausage. There are eight different yellow rice dishes, with such accompaniments as shrimp, lobster, crab meat, pigeon peas, chicken, and squid. Thick, filling soups (*asopaos*) offer similar combinations. Regular menu features include lobster creole in hot sauce, kingfish in vinegar (*escabeche*), and shrimp in garlic. Top these off with strong demitasse, and a dessert of flan or papaya with cream cheese.

EAST HARLEM'S *BOTÁNICAS:* BARGAINS FOR THE SOUL

Problems with love, work, or an annoying neighbor? Bad dreams? Do you need to earn more money fast or to tell a boyfriend (or girlfriend) to leave you alone? There's no doubt a candle to burn, a medal to wear, or a special incantation to chant at one of the many colorful and exotic *botánicas*—religious shops—throughout East Harlem that can help you find a solution. Enter one and you'll likely hear a customer seeking help for marital ills or fatigue. Before long, you might decide to spill out your woes, too. *Botánicas* sell huge inventories of incense, colored powders, candles, potions, roots, herbs, charms, statuettes, dream books, and assorted regalia to adherents of *Santería*, a religion that blends Christianity with African traditions that reached the United States via the Caribbean. The four **Otto Chicas Rendon** shops near La Marqueta (56 and 60 E. 116th St., 117 E. 115th St., and in La Mar-

queta) are among the area's oldest, having opened more than 50 years ago; inside you'll find a panoply of tropical "cures." In season, you can buy aloe leaves, advertised as a cure for dozens of ailments. We particularly recommend a *botánica* called **El Congo Real** (1789 Lexington Ave., between 110th and 111th Sts.). As the name suggests, the African influence is strong: The store is a jungle of wares and seems more like a huge outdoor market shoved indoors. Wood carvings, bamboo relics, dried leaves, and elaborate necklaces hang from the ceiling and on the walls. El Congo Real has a large selection of pamphlets and books in Spanish and English. For the uninitiated or merely curious, there's a full-length study of *Santería* and booklets explaining the Yoruba religion of Nigeria, which plays an important role in *Santería* rituals.

ITALIAN EAST HARLEM

Italian East Harlem is an area bounded approximately by 120th Street, the East River, 114th Street, and Second Avenue.

The building of the Second and Third Avenue elevated trains in the 1880s spurred the construction of tenements throughout East Harlem, and immigrants fleeing the overflowing Lower East Side found some breathing space there. It soon attracted masses of Italian settlers, among them many artisans, and during a period when piano playing was very popular, Italian East Harlem was the site of four of New York's piano factories.

From Italian East Harlem came the Italian-Jewish Mayor Fiorello LaGuardia and Congressman Vito Marcantonio. Educator-writer Leonard Covello grew up there, and, in his autobiography, vividly chronicled Italian East Harlem at its peak.

BAKERIES AND SHOPS

Only a remnant of the Italian community remains, but there's enough in East Harlem to merit a visit and a meal, and afterwards, perhaps a shave and a haircut over at **Claudio Caponigro's Barbershop** (360 E. 116 St.), where Claudio has cut hair for more than 40 years. Take a few minutes, if you can spare them, to visit the basement of **Ideal Pet Shop** at 356 East 116th Street. Pigeons are still kept as pets in East Harlem, and special breeds are cared for and sold here.

If you've been walking east along 116th Street in El Barrio and cross Second Avenue, you'll sense the change almost instantly: Bland low-rise buildings give way to more graceful brownstones that were elegant once and are still lovely, if a bit worn. A few Italian delis line Second and First Avenues. You might try **Mario's Deli** (2246 Second Ave. at 115th St., Tel.: 212/876-7280) for cheese, cold cuts, and Italian groceries. But you should make a bee-line for **Morrone & Sons Bakery** (324 E. 116th St., Tel.: 212/722-2972), which opened nearly 80 years ago and which Gabriel Morrone took over in 1959. These days, he, his wife, and some of his seven children keep it a close family operation, and the closeness is literal: The Morrones live in the building upstairs. The house specialties are *panella*, a round, flat bread with crispy dough; *calabrese*, a so-called "high bread" with very soft dough; loaves made with white flour or whole wheat; semolina loaves with or without sesame seeds; prosciutto and lard breads with spicy chunks of meat cooked into the bread; and French-style *baguettes*, which sell out early, warns daughter Maria Morrone. The secret to Morrone's bread—aside from Gabriel's recipes—is simple: an old-fashioned coal oven, one of about five left in New York City, says Maria. Early in the morning—about 4 A.M.—her father does the baking, kneading dough in a giant machine, shaping his loaves, and baking about 250 at a time. He also makes cookies and biscuits, some spiced with hot pepper. The selling area is small and austere, but business is brisk and friendly, and cars double-park as their owners, coming from all over, run in to make purchases. "It's the best bread in the city," says a husky, bearded man in a rush while his car's engine mutters in neutral. Morrone's doesn't depend only on store sales, and that's a good thing since the local population is down (many Italians left when housing projects went up in the area in the 1950s). It also supplies several restaurants around New York City, including **Rao's** on East 114th Street, as well as the Balducci family markets in Greenwich Village and on the Upper East Side.

Rex Italian Ices (2292 First Ave., Tel.: 212/427-5662) has been in the neighborhood for 30 years, offering up to 14 delectable flavors of this Italian specialty. Frank D'Agostino and his mother, Carmela (usually knitting), are the proprietors these days. The more unusual flavors—not always available—include almond, maraschino, cream, banana, and so-called "lily" (vanilla flavored with peanuts). While there, stroll around the corner along 118th Street between First and Pleasant Avenues, a tree-lined block with freshly painted brownstones that could easily be in the better part of the West Side or Brooklyn. "It's always been a special block," says Molly Lancieri Arles, who grew up nearby. She explains that the homes have always been in private hands and well cared for.

RESTAURANTS

Patsy's Pizzeria and Restaurant (2287 First Ave., Tel.: 212/722-5470), opened in 1932 by Patsy Lancieri, an immigrant from Melfi, is now owned and operated by his widow, Carmela, who turned 80 in 1986. The restaurant has a wide selection of meat and seafood specialties—daughter Molly Lancieri Arles recommends the baked clams—and homemade pastas and pickled vegetables. The restaurant used to draw people from the entertainment industry, especially as an after-theater hangout, but the prime days have passed, admits Molly (who long ago married and moved out of the neighborhood), although her mother continues to buy vegetables weekly at the **Bronx Terminal Market** and to prepare many of the dishes herself. A drawing of young Patsy Lancieri is on the wall above the jukebox, and the jukebox itself evokes the days when the restaurant bustled and jumped: Al Jolson singing "Mammy" and "Sonny Boy," Jimmy Dorsey, Perry Como, Dinah Washington, Tony Bennett, and Frank Sinatra. It bends to the new, too, with selections from Bruce Springsteen, Bette Midler, Willie Nelson, and Mr. Mister. There's a separate, small stand-up pizzeria two doors up the street, where one of the few coal ovens in New York City bakes a chewy, crust-just-right pizza to be taken out or eaten at a counter.

You can't just walk into **Rao's Restaurant** (455 E. 114th St. at Pleasant Ave., Tel.: 212/534-9625). Home cooking and hospitality have made this place a magnet for lovers of Italian food who want to spend their meal in an unhurried atmosphere. It's also attractive for the reasonable prices: Pasta dishes are $6.50 (including clam, risotto, marinara, and broccoli sauces), all chicken dishes are $9.50, and the most costly meat entrée is $18.00. Only 35 people fit into Rao's three tables-for-six and four booths, and that's how many people they'll serve in a night.

Once you're seated, relax, eat, and enjoy. But reserve way in advance: There's often several months' wait for tables. The restaurant opened in 1896 when brothers Giuseppe and Carmine Rao, from a small town near Naples, took over what had been a Dutch saloon. Vincent Rao, Carmine's son, owns it now, and he and his wife, Ann, who live right next door, create the menu and do most of the cooking. The kitchen is practically an open affair, and you can watch Ann slice tomatoes or sauté the veal that you'll soon be eating. "The secret," she says, "is that it's very *simple*." The pastas are cooked *al dente*, the olive oil isn't overbearing, and the roasted peppers and fish salad appetizers—two recommended specialties—are firm and tasty. Add to all this the welcome you'll get from the friendly and talkative manager, Frank Pellegrino, Vincent's nephew and a former entertainer, who also helps in the kitchen shucking clams or mixing salad dressing. A long bar, tended by Nick, a newcomer to Rao's with only eight years here, is a friendly hangout for locals who've been part of Italian East Harlem for decades. Although you may wait months to get in, the neighbors drop by anytime to while away the evening or gossip about the neighborhood. It's coming back, they all agree—why, look at the new TV studio being built at 117th Street and the East River, and all the brownstones being fixed up. "In ten years," Frank assures us, "this area will be very chic."

LOWER EAST SIDE & EAST VILLAGE: PUNK & PIROGEN

To Get There

By subway: The F train to Second Ave. (at Houston St.) or Delancey St. (at Essex St.) are the most centrally located. You can also take the F train to East Broadway if you want to be further downtown, on the edge of Chinatown; for the East Village, take the IRT 6 to Astor Place or the R train to 8th St. Walk east on St. Mark's Place.

By car: Take the FDR Dr. to Houston St. Travel west on Houston St. There is a public parking garage on Essex St., just north of Delancey St. There's generally parking on First Ave. if you plan to explore the East Village.

By bike: Take Broadway downtown, First Ave. uptown. This area is ideally suited to exploring by bike, since it's quite large and filled with dozens of surprising side streets. From downtown (Brooklyn Bridge), use Centre St., which turns into Lafayette St. Turn right anywhere between Kenmare St. (which becomes Delancey St.) and 14th St.

Airless tenements jammed with a dozen people in each dark apartment. Streets teeming with pushcarts and children. Small factories, filled with hat makers, piano makers, cigar rollers, and, of course, garment workers. By the East River were the docks, with ships from around the world snuggled into the harbor's shelter; the neighborhood's strapping Irishmen were the dockworkers. That was the Lower East Side of a century ago.

This is the section where Manhattan hangs out into the East River like a swollen belly, the place where hundreds of thousands of anxious immigrants first paced the streets of their adopted land. Once known simply as the Lower East Side, then as "Loisaida'' in the patois of the Puerto Ricans who came here, and now, thanks to real estate agents, as the East Village in its gentrifying northern section, this area is still home to one of New York's most diverse collections of nationalities.

An Italian family still lives above the store where it has been making cheese for half a century; wrinkle-suited Polish and Ukrainian men pass the warm months in their corner of Tompkins Square Park next to a day-glo daubed statue of nineteenth-century congressman Samuel Cox; shaved or spike-haired young punk music fans in black jackets lounge Saturday nights away across the street; peppery spices fill the air where a dozen Indian restaurants cluster on 6th Street. In this tumult are the hold-overs from the days when Second Avenue was the Jewish Rialto, when the Lower East Side was among the greatest centers of Yiddish culture in the world. There are still pickled tomatoes and beets and ears of baby corn in huge vats; fresh cream cheese and baked farmer cheese; long loaves of dark pumpernickel bread and chewy bagels fresh from the oven; knishes as good as you'll find anywhere; penny candies, roasted nuts, and smoked salmon at some of the best prices in the city.

We have divided this section into the Lower East Side (south of Houston Street) and the East Village (between East Houston and 14th Streets), which includes Little India on 6th Street. Third Avenue and the Bowery are the western limits of this area.

LOWER EAST SIDE

Shoppers wedge into the narrow kosher stores on Essex Street, buying cheese at one, felafel at another, knishes at a third, and stuffed cabbage at a fourth. There's a newsstand selling glatt kosher burgers, stores selling religious items and books, candy stores, and pickle stores. Although Essex Street is jammed with food stores, two blocks away on Orchard Street there is not a knish to be noshed. Instead, dozens of clothing stores spill into the streets with their baskets of socks and skivvies, pants, bras, girdles, dresses, and shoes.

MARKETS, BAKERIES, AND SHOPS

Economy Candy (131 Essex St., Tel.: 212/254-1531, and around the corner at 108 Rivington St.) offers a good selection of penny candies, nuts, and chocolates that is jammed into the original store—since 1937—on the corner of Essex Street. The newer shop a couple of doors down on Rivington Street is more of a gourmet store. Bins and barrels of nuts and candies—from bubble gum by the pound to pineapple spears to rum cashews—are in the Essex Street store, while in the Rivington shop you can choose between mint and balsamic vinegar and pick up a hand-dipped chocolate. The original store is one of the few survivors of a waning era; the newer one is a sign of changing tastes.

A sixteenth-century Portuguese spice trader would have thought he'd stumbled into heaven at **Kadouri Import Corp.** (51 Hester St., Tel.: 212/677-5441). There's a powerful smell of black pepper, cumin, bay leaves, and coffee in this charming store that offers a huge assortment of nuts, herbs, spices, and dried and glazed fruits.

Russ & Daughters (179 E. Houston St., Tel.: 212/475-4880) is one of the best stores of its kind in New York. This family business sells some of New York's finest smoked salmon, along with candies, coffees, bagels, cream cheese, and more.

J. Wolsk & Co. (81 Ludlow St. at Delancey St., Tel.: 212/475-7946) has been a "Gourmet Confectioners" since 1939. You'll find a staggering selection of imported chocolates and other candies, as well as nuts, and—believe it—kosher marshmallows and chocolate-covered pretzels (along with chocolate-covered apricots, orange peel, and candied figs).

Scotty Appetizers (132 Essex St., Tel.: 212/475-1284) offers a good selection of schmalz herring, shad, sturgeon, whitefish, gefilte fish, and lox at an outdoor stall.

Kossar's Bialy's (367 Grand St., Tel.: 212/473-4810) is primarily a large wholesale bakery; tucked into a front corner of the store is a retail counter. Known for its superb bialys, it also makes fine bagels.

New York City's only winery is on the Lower East Side, where the Schapiro family has been in business since 1899. What did **Schapiro's House of Kosher & Sacramental Wines** (126 Rivington St., Tel.:

212/475-7383) do during Prohibition? "They sold a lot of sacramental wine," says Lou Singer, a native of the Lower East Side who now leads tours of New York City. "Every Kelly and Signelli found a rabbi to give them a religious exemption." Today, huge wine vats hold a half-million gallons of wine in an underground cellar that sprawls across three-quarters of a city block. This is still a family operation: Grandson Norman Schapiro is now in charge, and his teenage sons are training for the day when they take over.

Gertel's (53 Hester St., Tel.: 212/982-3250) is perhaps the best bakery in the area—or, at least, the most comforting. Sit down and have a coffee and bagel or one of the dozens of kinds of pastries baked at the shop. You'll have plenty of company from the area's aging Jewish population.

The baking at **Moishe's Home Made Kosher Bakery** (181 East Houston St. or 115 Second Ave. at 7th St., Tel.: 212/475-9624) is actually done at the Second Avenue store, which is a more spacious, modern shop. But we still like to jam into the Houston Street shop, then walk next door to **Ben's Cheese Shop** (181 E. Houston St., Tel.: 212/254-8290) for cream cheese and Russ & Daughters for smoked salmon to layer on the bread and bagels from Moishe's.

The Sweet Life (63 Hester St., Tel.: 212/598-0092) offers some luscious dates, figs, and apricots, along with halvah, nuts, and other dried fruits, many imported from the Mideast. There are also (except during the summer) hand-dipped chocolates.

The Lower East Side's most famous knish shop is still in the store where Yonah Shimmel—a moonlighting rabbi—started out in

Ben's Cheese Shop.

1910. The dumbwaiter at **Yonah Shimmel Knishes Bakery** (137 E. Houston St., Tel.: 212/477-2858) still ferries the potato, kasha, and fruit knishes up from the cellar kitchen.

Leibel Bistritzky (27 ½ Essex St., Tel.: 212/254-0335) offers New York's best selection of kosher cheese. Jammed onto the shelves of this narrow grocery is a wide variety of other kosher products, many imported from Israel. You can buy everything from kosher toothpaste to soups to frozen broccoli.

The treat at **Miller's Cheese** (13 Essex St., Tel.: 212/475-3337) is baked farmer cheese: pineapple, blueberry, strawberry, and raisin walnut. There is also a good selection of other kosher cheeses. (They have another store at 78th Street and Broadway.)

Before Passover, the lines at **Guss Pickles** (35 Essex St., Tel.: 212/254-4477) stretch down the block from this extraordinary outdoor store. Customers are waiting to buy pickled cucumbers, tomatoes, beets, cauliflower, and hot peppers, and to pick up a little of Guss's fresh horseradish.

RESTAURANTS

Remember, if you go to a kosher restaurant, it will serve either meat or dairy products, but not both.

"We are the original glatt kosher Chinese restaurant," crows William Rosenfeld, who manages the 200-seat **Bernstein-on-Essex** (135 Essex St., Tel.: 212/473-3900). It might have a Chinese flavor, but this establishment is vintage

Inside Yonah Shimmel's: ''Sorry, we don't cut knishes.''

Lower East Side. "How long has the restaurant been here?" we ask one of the regulars. "Since it opened." "When was that?" "6:30 this morning." And so on. William Rosenfeld explains, "If somebody paid me $50 I wouldn't eat here—the shouting, the abuse, the lines of people." But the restaurant is popular especially among Orthodox Jews (frequently in groups), who make up about 90 percent of the restaurant's customers. "Wednesday nights it's a group from Monsey, New York, and Thursday night they come from yeshiva," says Mr. Rosenfeld.

You only have time for one meal in the Lower East Side? From the moment you walk through the doors at **Grand Dairy Restaurant** (341 Grand St. at Ludlow St., Tel.: 212/673-1904), you'll know this is the place. The warm, humid smell of home cooking, the middle-aged waiters in white shirts and black bow ties . . . it all harks back to a time when artists and political agitators, couples on a date, and families on a big evening out ate at restaurants like this one. Only one thing is different from the stereotype: The staff at Grand Dairy is actually friendly. From the rich Russian pumpernickel brought in from Brooklyn to the homemade soups, from the gefilte fish to the blintzes, this restaurant is a jewel.

A wonderful selection of takeout food awaits you at **Moskovic G & M Kosher Caterers** (41 Essex St., Tel.: 212/677-0090 or 254-5370), a Hungarian-style meat deli that has been in the neighborhood since 1956. Sample roast chicken, chicken soup, and chopped liver like mother used to make. There's much more: stuffed cabbage, soufflés (broccoli, spin-

Bernstein-on-Essex: originators of kosher Chinese food.

ach, cauliflower), pastrami, dumplings, *kasha* (buckwheat groats), potato or noodle kugel, rice pudding, and so on. In season, there is an Eastern European cold fruit soup.

Steinberg's Bake Shop & Dairy Restaurant (21 Essex St., Tel.: 212/254-7787) serves Middle Eastern food such as felafel in addition to the more typical soups and blintzes. **Ratner's Dairy Restaurant and Bakery** (138 Delancey St., Tel.: 212/674-9406) is a nice safe place where you can taste the Lower East Side experience. It is largely populated by people who grew up in the neighborhood—or had relatives who did—but now live out of town.

"Send a salami to your boy in the army," says the old news story in the window describing the war effort of **Katz's Delicatessen** (205 E. Houston St., Tel.: 212/254-2246). Letters from Presidents Carter and Reagan are also on display: This is a serious stop for ethnic politicking. But Katz's manages to keep the glory days alive—it was founded in 1888—rather than becoming a silly relic of the past. From the gruff white-capped gentleman who hands out a meal ticket to all who enter to the countermen who dish out the knishes and franks, you won't mistake this place for a museum. Walls are lined with hanging sausages, American flags, and neon signs advertising real American beers—Schaefer, Piels, Pabst, and Knickerbocker.

Sammy's Rumanian Jewish Restaurant (157 Christie St., Tel.: 212/673-0330) is a classic. Wedged into a narrow space one flight down from the street, Sammy's serves huge, well-prepared platters of food in a raucous atmosphere accented by Borscht Belt singers. The walls are covered with diners' business cards.

Send a salami . . .

After the plates heaped with chicken livers, chopped liver, and dumplings it's hard to plow through the broiled meats that are Sammy's specialty. Plenty of iced vodka makes it easier for many, judging by the bottles that grace many of the tables.

EAST VILLAGE

RESTAURANTS

A century ago, the East Village housed Germans and Irish. Since then Jews and Italians, as well as Ukrainians and Poles, hippies, punks, and, now, yuppies and mock bohemians, have come and stayed. The variety of restaurants is unmatched anywhere in New York City—from Afghan to Venezuelan, Cuban to kosher, Lebanese to vegetarian, as well as an assortment of sushi bars, Chinese and Indian restaurants, a trendy Dominican restaurant, and countless cafés and bars, from the sizzling to the somnolent. Most of the restaurants are on First and Second Avenues, Avenue A between 6th and 9th Streets, and St. Mark's Place. Sixth Street between First and Second Avenue is crowded with Indian restaurants.

Ukrainians and, to a lesser extent, Poles run many restaurants in the East Village. Meals are cheap and tasty. Specialties include blintzes, pirogen, and a variety of hearty soups, such as borscht and mushroom-barley soup, as well as heavier fare like veal cutlets, pork chops, and goulash. There are about a dozen similar restaurants in the neighborhood, and all have a devoted clientele. We've listed our favorites.

Veselka Coffee Shop (144 Second Ave., Tel.: 212/228-9682) has great soups, inexpensive dinner specials, and a dining room in the back that allows you to linger. Murals inside and out depict real East Village shop owners and residents. The original Café Metropole, one of the liveliest spots when Second Avenue was the Jewish Rialto, was located on this spot. Try the dill-flavored white borscht at **Jolanta** (119 First Ave., Tel.: 212/473-9936), a fine Polish restaurant.

Leshko Coffee Shop (11 Ave. A, Tel.: 212/473-9208) is a neighborhood institution on the corner of Tompkins Square Park. The sanitation men gather here on their morning coffee break, their white street cleaning machines and garbage trucks parked outside like giant beasts at a watering hole. **Odessa Coffee Shop** is three doors down, at 117 Avenue A (Tel.: 212/473-8916). Big dinner specials at mouth-watering prices are offered.

Kiev Restaurant (117 Second Ave., Tel.: 212/674-4040) and **Ukrainian Restaurant & Caterers** (132 Second Ave. at 8th St., Tel.: 212/533-6765) are popular among the outlanders who frequent the East Village. The food is comparable to that of the restaurants mentioned above, although the atmosphere doesn't have the same neighborhood feel.

Second Ave. Kosher Delicatessen & Restaurant (156 Second Ave., Tel.: 212/677-0606) is justifiably popular as a tourist magnet. Chopped liver and other deli specialties are still standouts, and the place is authentic down to the brusque staff.

B & H Dairy Restaurant (127 Second Ave., Tel.: 212/777-1930) is one of the only survivors of the era when Second Avenue was the center of Yiddish theater. Fine, inexpensive dairy food is still served. Don't miss the challah French toast if you're here for breakfast.

For a nice, simple Italian meal try **Focacceria** (128 First Ave.). This is a no-frills, fluorescent-lit place that serves up hearty, inexpensive food washed down with Italian jug wine. It's not the kind of place where you'll linger over your meal but is a favorite among people who live in the neighborhood.

Spaghetteria (126 E. 7th St., Tel.: 212/475-8180) is one of the survivors among the fancier restaurants that started opening in the area during the early 1980s. It offers an Italian menu, although the staff is decidedly East Village American.

Stromboli Pizza (83 St. Marks Place, Tel.: 212/673-3691) is the place in the neighborhood for pizza, as double-parked cabs and cars testify. A busy take-out window opening onto First Avenue proves that this is the best place for "a slice." Stromboli's pizza is thin-crusted and lathered with a spicy tomato sauce.

Sugar Reef (93 Second Ave., Tel.: 212/477-8427) is a sizzling Dominican restaurant that not only has been mobbed since the day it opened in 1985 but also happens to serve very good Caribbean food. It's loud and raucous, with trendies who've discovered the East Village frontier lined up three deep around the bar, where they guzzle fluorescent-colored drinks. It's not the sort of place we'd ordinarily mention, but the food includes tasty dishes like chicken mango salads, jerk (smoked) pork sandwiches, *calaloo* soup (kale with crabmeat and pork), and coconut shrimp.

Khyber Pass Restaurant (34 St. Mark's Place, Tel.: 212/777-9128) dishes up tasty Afghan food, including curries flavored with coriander and scallions; spiced pumpkin turnovers; soup with homemade noodles; and dumplings dipped in mint-flavored yogurt.

The Cloister Café (238 E. 9th St., Tel.: 212/674-9302) has a lovely outdoor garden that's the perfect place to sip iced coffee in the summer. The action moves to a cozy interior in cooler weather.

Yaffa Café is one of the older, friendlier cafés in the area (97 St. Mark's Place, Tel.: 212/674-9302).

McSorley's (15 E. 7th St., Tel.: 212/473-8800) is *the* oldest neighborhood hangout. In fact, it's the city's oldest tavern. Students line up here even on the coldest winter nights to soak up a bit of old New York and McSorley's own brew. Women weren't allowed in until the early 1970s; they still aren't entirely welcome, as the lack of separate bathrooms testifies.

Dojo Restaurant (24 St. Mark's Place, Tel.: 212/674-9821) is a survivor of the era when Japanese foods like teriyaki, tofu, and seafood were found only in avant-garde neighborhoods like the East Village. It still serves the freshest, most inexpensive food of this kind in the neighborhood.

Since 1980 the area around Tompkins Square Park has boomed. **The Life Café** (343 E. 10th St., Tel.: 212/477-8791) has expanded from a small, dark corner café decorated with little more than old copies of *Life* magazine to a glass-fronted hangout for the neighborhood. **Tompkins Park Restaurant**, also known as **The Pharmacy** (141 Ave. A, Tel.: 212/260-4798) was the first of the new restaurants to open in the area and today remains a comfortable, unpretentious place. Also on Avenue A is **Seven A Café** (109 Ave. A, Tel.: 212/477-8791).

MARKETS, BAKERIES, AND SHOPS

East Village Cheese Store (239 E. 9th St., Tel.: 212/477-2601) is one of the best places in the city to get inexpensively priced cheese. The quality and selection are not quite what you'd find at a boutique food store but good enough that there's always a crowd. East Village Cheese Store also has a good selection of jams, crackers, olives, and cured meats at bargain prices.

Do you like sausages? Some of New York's best Polish- and Ukrainian-style sausage shops are in the East Village, including **E. Kurowycky & Sons, Inc.** (124 First Ave., Tel.: 212/477-0344), **B & C Meat Market** (111 First Ave., Tel.: 212/677-1210), and **First Ave. Meat Market** (140 First Ave., Tel.: 212/777-4583).

There is a remnant of a small Italian community along First Avenue. Best known

is **Veniero Pasticceria** (342 E. 11th St., Tel.: 212/674-7264), a family-run pastry shop that's been around for nearly a century. Business has boomed in the last several years, and Veniero's has added a café next door, where there were only a few tables before. The selection of pastries is wide. Veniero's can be jammed on a weekend, since it's well known among out-of-towners.

DeRobertis Pastry Shop (176 First Ave., Tel.: 212/674-7137) is invariably half-empty, although it's only a half-block from Veniero's. This is puzzling, since the pastries are every bit as good and the atmosphere is more relaxed. Unlike Veniero's sleeker look, DeRobertis still has a black-and-white tile floor, large, comfortable booths, and superb walls that neighborhood connoisseur Lou Singer points out look strikingly like those used in the IRT subway station, which was constructed at the same time. "Probably a moonlighting Italian subway mason did the work." DeRobertis has remained a neighborhood place while Veniero's is the place where visitors invariably end up.

Russo & Son Dairy Products (344 E. 11th St., Tel.: 212/254-7452) is right between the two pastry shops. If there's a better place to get fresh mozzarella in New York City, we haven't found it. The Russo family has been making cheese here for three generations now, and they live above the small store, which also sells imported Italian cheeses, salami, pasta, and other Italian goods.

Need some lemon grass or star anise? Check out **Pete's Spice** (174 First Ave., Tel.: 212/254-8773) for a phenomenal selection of hard-to-get spices and flours, such as semolina and farina.

Sourdough, fine whole wheat, white

Italian, bread sticks—and even pizza dough—can be found at **New First Ave. Bakery** (121 First Ave., Tel.: 212/674-5699), a charming little neighborhood bakery.

If you ask for the **Ninth St. Bakery** (350 E. 9th St., Tel.: 212/777-0677) you'll probably get a puzzled look: Everyone seems to have his or her own name for this crammed bread store. Some call it the day-old bread store; some call it the Russian bread store (although there aren't any Russians there); and we even have some friends who call it Einstein's, because the owner's frizzled hair reminded them of the scientist's. No matter: What you'll find here is a good assortment of inexpensive breads and pastries—nothing fancy.

Fresh eggs, butter, honey, and cider trucked in from the country are sold inexpensively at **The Thursday Store** (72 E. 7th St., open Thursdays only). **Angelica's** (137 First Ave., Tel.: 212/677-1549) has one of New York's best selections of herbs (especially medicinal) and spices.

If you can't find the Middle Eastern spices you need at Pete's or Angelica's, head for Little India on Lexington Avenue in the upper twenties. Although the neighborhood stores are being squeezed by rising rents, there are still some good establishments left. Best known is **Tashjian & Kalustyan** (123 Lexington Ave., Tel.: 212/683-8458). You can also try **Foods of India** (120 Lexington Ave. at 28th St., Tel.: 212/683-4419), **Spice and Sweet Mahal** (135 Lexington Ave., Tel.: 212/683-0900), and **Annapurna** (127 E. 28th St., Tel.: 212/889-7540).

LITTLE INDIA ON 6TH STREET

A remarkable strip of Indian restaurants covers most of the south side of East 6th Street between First and Second Avenues, even spilling out around the corner onto the avenues. The enterprise began modestly enough a decade ago, when a group of Bengali students at New York University, unable to find any local restaurants that served their native food, began cooking large communal meals. First they opened one small restaurant, then another, and the block became a mecca for New Yorkers curious to try the northern Indian food the restaurants came to specialize in. Most Indians are Hindus and eat little or no meat. However, the Moslems in the north eat a good deal of beef and lamb, which you will find well represented at these restaurants.

Mixed appetizers are a good place to start if you aren't familiar with this type of food: samosas, fried banana, some *chapati* (crisp, wafer-thin bread), and dumplings filed with ground beef, potato, and green peas. Mulligatawny is a tomato-lentil soup, best when topped with coriander. The puffed-up poori (something like pita bread) is a good accompaniment to a meal, although there are a variety of other breads, including *pappadam* and *paratha*, which are good. (Paratha can be ordered as an appetizer stuffed with meat or vegetables.) The menus generally offer quite good explanations, but if you're completely unfamiliar with Indian food, you might want to try tandoori, traditionally chicken (although lamb and even seafood are now cooked tandoori style) that has been marinated in curds, ginger, garlic, and chilies. Biryani is a saffron-flavored rice dish with lamb, beef, or vegetables cooked with nuts and raisins.

RESTAURANTS

Best bets: **Mitali** (Tel.: 212/533-2508) is still the king of 6th Street. More expensive than most of the other restaurants, it boasts a full bar (you have to bring your own wine and beer at most others). Mitali's food is simply the most imaginative and well spiced.

Mitali faces competition from some newcomers, **Sonali** (Tel.: 212/505-7517) and **Calcutta** (Tel.: 212/982-8127), both of which are quite good and much less expensive. Other restaurants on 6th Street can be quite good; everyone who eats there has his or her favorite restaurants, but after dining extensively in virtually all of them, you may find they blur together in a haze of tandooris, *vindaloos*, kebabs, and pooris. They're all fine, and serve an adequate and inexpensive meal.

East 6th Street's Restaurant Row.

NINTH AVENUE NOSH

To Get There

By subway or bus: Take the A, AA, CC, or E train to 34th St. (Penn Station) or 42nd St. (Port Authority Bus Terminal) and walk one block west. If you get off at 42nd St., you can walk through Port Authority to the far (west) side of the station, which is bordered by Ninth Ave. By bus, take the 34th St. (M34) or 42nd St. (M42) crosstown buses toward Twelfth Ave.

By car: Ninth Ave. runs downtown, as the extension of Columbus Ave. If you come from downtown, it's best to come across 42nd St., and park near the intersection of Ninth Ave. If you come from New Jersey, the Holland Tunnel exits are one block west of Ninth Ave. Continue straight as you exit the tunnel.

By bike: There's no alternative but to brave the midtown traffic if you want to cycle to Ninth Ave. Try 43rd St. if you're coming from downtown (up Sixth Ave. or Eighth Ave.) or crosstown. From the Upper West Side, bear right off Broadway at Lincoln Center as Columbus Avenue becomes Ninth Ave.

Ninth Avenue has tripe and goat, fresh pasta and apricot strudel, French sausages and Thai fish. You can buy a simple meal of Latin-style rice and beans at a lunch counter or watch Argentinian tango dancers while feasting on a *parrillada* (mixed grill). On Ninth Avenue you can get a manicure and a pedicure or have your teeth pulled. You can pick up any kind of meat from quail to rabbit to pigs' knuckles—and take home a used sofa from a secondhand store.

Ninth Avenue is a microcosm of the city's kaleidoscope of cultures. The Ninth Avenue food fair, held every May, celebrates this ethnic diversity. The avenue's merchants come, of course, but they also invite others from around the city; Koreans, West Indians, and Japanese; Navajo Indians, Greeks, and Italians; Mexican, Spanish, and Ukrainians; Turks and Poles; Belgians and Indians all sell their native foods at the festival. It's become one of New York's great events, drawing some three-quarters of a million people between 37th and 57th Streets, for a gluttonous orgy. The amounts of food eaten are staggering. The *New York Times* reported that Bruno the King of Ravioli sold 200,000 ravioli in 1984; International Meat Market sold 10 suckling pigs, 18 baby lambs, more than 1,000 lambs' heads, and 1,000 quail.

"People were afraid to walk past Eighth Avenue because of the pornography," remembers Lili Fable, now president of the Ninth Avenue Association. "We decided to have a food festival in 1973 to let people know we were still here and to celebrate our ethnic diversity." Now, for those merchants who rent their shops, the problem is quite different: The development of the West Side threatens to force many out of business as rents rise.

Ninth Avenue was once in the midst of Hell's Kitchen, the notorious haven of mobsters, prostitutes, and gangs that clustered in the shadows of the New York Central rail yards. Railroad guards finally—and none too gently—broke the power of toughs like "Mallet" Murphy and "Goo Goo" Knox. The construction of the Lincoln Tunnel and the abandonment of the rail yards finished off the last vestiges of the gangs.

Paddy's Market, a crush of Jewish and Italian peddlers, thrived in the shadow of the Ninth Avenue El from the turn of the century until the late 1930s, when the approaches to the Lincoln Tunnel were built. The pushcart vendors were moved around the corner in one of those bureaucratic efficiencies that threatened their extinction. That the merchants survived and thrived back on Ninth Avenue is more remarkable because the Port Authority Bus Terminal was built smack on their old site in 1952. Some of today's shopkeepers had parents or grandparents who sold out of a pushcart under the el.

Ninth Avenue is about as unprepossessing as a street can get, but these few blocks contain one of the most stunning concentrations of different foods in the world.

MARKETS, BAKERIES, AND SHOPS

Poseidon Greek Bakery (629 Ninth Ave. at 44th St., Tel.: 212/757-6173) is a mecca for pastry lovers. First-timers will be satisfied if they venture no further than standards like baklava, *kantaifi* (shredded wheat), or *afali* (pistachio-wrapped pastry): The cognoscenti come for *flogera*, a fillo-wrapped custard that's not as sweet as many Greek pastries; other swear by the cheese and fruit strudel—apricot, cherry, pineapple, and apple-cheese. (You can also buy these frozen.) Those who aren't hungry for sweets eat the *spanakopita* (spinach pie) or the meat pie. This shop, run by the third generation of the Anagoustou family, makes such good fillo dough that they sell to Zabars, Quilted Giraffe, the Russian Tea Room, and other tony eateries. (You can also buy some fillo, fresh or frozen.) The rich buttery air that fills **Pozzo Pastry Shop** (690 Ninth Ave.,

Tel.: 212/265-7530) is a hint of what to expect: fine French and Italian breads and pastries.

Mazzella's Market (694 Ninth Ave. at 48th St., Tel.: 212/586-1448) is a wonderful wholesale/retail produce market that takes up much of the block. Two wonderful stores run by Peter and Sotiris Karamouzis comprise **International Grocery Store & Meat Market** (529 and 543 Ninth Ave., Tel.: 212/279-5514). The stores have a stunning variety of imported grains, beans, nuts, cheeses, and spices. You can find everything from Pakistani rice to Syrian apricot paste to oregano and mint from Greece. This is also a Greek butcher shop.

Empire Coffee & Tea (486 Ninth Ave. at 37th St., Tel.: 212/564-1460) has a good selection of inexpensively priced coffees and teas, which are jammed into this delightfully disorganized store. You'll also find chicory root, herb teas, and coffee-making equipment. Fear of a rent hike prompted the opening of a fancier store—but with the same low prices—at 592 Ninth Avenue at 43rd Street (Tel.: 212/586-1717).

Central Fish Co. (527 Ninth Ave. at 39th St., Tel.: 212/560-8163) and **Sea Breeze Fish Market** (541 Ninth Ave. at 40th St., Tel.: 212/563-7537) have a large selection of reasonably priced fish and shellfish.

A Ninth Avenue institution since 1904 (since 1921 at the same location), **Washington Beef Co.** (575 Ninth Ave. at 41st St., Tel.: 212/563-0200) does such a good business—both wholesale and retail—that owner Herbert Frank (whose German-born father started the store) says most meat comes directly from Midwestern packing plants, bypassing the Washington Street meat market. A good selection of meats at low prices is available. The Carnevale family has northern Italian blood, but in addition to specialties from the home region they also make some of New York's best French sausages at **P. Carnevale & Son** (631 Ninth Ave., Tel.: 212/765-0640). Their garlic sausage is a specialty.

Bruno the King of Ravioli (653 Ninth Ave. at 45th St., Tel.: 212/246-8456) is a charming family store that has been selling a tremendous assortment of fresh pasta on Ninth Avenue since 1905. The motto of **Manganaro's Hero Boy** (492 Ninth Ave., Tel.: 212/947-7325) is: "Heroes are Made, Not Born." This is the home of six-foot hero sandwiches and other Italian-American inventions. Jimmy Manganaro sells 360 hero-feet of sandwiches at the food festival, along with a half-ton of ziti and two tons of meatballs.

Ugo Lauritano makes a fine mozzarella in the back of **DiStasi Latticini** (484 Ninth Ave., Tel.: 212/563-2774). Up front the cases are stuffed with antipasto, sausage, cheeses, bread, and pasta at this tiny, very Italian deli.

RESTAURANTS
Manganaro Foods and Supreme Macaroni Co. (488 Ninth Ave., Tel.: 212/563-5331) is a delight. This spacious store/restaurant has an atmosphere that manages to be cool on a hot summer day and cozy in the winter. Unlike most delis, this one isn't crammed with goods. There is a luxurious sense of space, wooden floors, and cases filled with Italian cheeses and meats. Manganaro's has many hard-to-

find items, whether they be chocolates, candies, or olive oils. In the back, there's a unique luncheonette. Fettucine, gnocchi, and rice balls, along with a nice selection of antipasto, are dished up in the open kitchen. Have a glass of wine and eat by the deli counter or carry your food upstairs, where there are more tables.

Jim Crinion and Tim Scarola are partners in **Supreme Macaroni Co.** and **Guido's Restaurant** (511 Ninth Ave., Tel.: 212/564-8074 or 502-4842). They offer a nice selection of dried pastas in unusual shapes: *radiatori* shaped like radiators, cartwheels, spirals, jumbo shells, and the more usual fettucine, spaghetti, and so forth. The restaurant in the back of the macaroni shop is lit by a skylight; the walls are covered with pictures of family and friends. This is the kind of restaurant where you can come for lunch and lounge until dinner.

Mama Mia (629 Ninth Ave., Tel.: 212/974-9725) is a cozy Italian restaurant: There's no aluminum tubing, geometric patterns, or sleek glass. Red-and-white checked tablecloths, posters of "la bella Italia," and moderate food at moderate prices abound.

Adela and Jack Talanga run **La Milonga** (742 Ninth Ave. at 50th St., Tel.: 212/541-8382), a hopping Argentinian restaurant that is named after a hybrid of the waltz and the tango. They do a good job with typical Argentinian fare: grilled meats and pastas. (See "Argentinian Jackson Heights" on page 97 for a discussion of Argentinian food.) Their spicy meat pies are a big hit with Ninth Avenue food fair–goers.

La Tía Norma Peruvian Rest (365 W. 51st St.) is one of Manhattan's only Peruvian restaurants, and a new addition to the area.

AMBLIN' ON AMSTERDAM

To Get There

By subway: Take the IRT 1, 2, or 3 train to 96th St. Turn one block east to get to Amsterdam Ave.

By bike: If you're coming from downtown, ride north on Sixth Ave. and enter Central Park, following the Park Dr. (in the same direction as cars, or, on weekends, ride counterclockwise). After passing a wide stretch of ball fields beyond the E. 90th St. exit, turn left at a shortcut sign near 102nd St. (it's a paved road bisecting the park, and favored by joggers as well as cyclists). Exit at Central Park West and 100th St. You'll have to ride north or south on Central Park West since 100th St. is one way; we suggest riding south (left) to 91st St. and turning right toward Amsterdam Ave.

The 20-block stretch on Amsterdam Avenue from 90th to 110th Streets still has the diversity, rhythm, and funkiness that once typified the entire Upper West Side. Mostly Latinos, West Indians, and Haitians live in the area, but it is also home to long-time, now elderly, residents and to students at nearby Columbia University. On a summer evening, you're apt to find residents with folding chairs, stereos, and grills moved out onto the sidewalk. Radios or impromptu bands provide musical background. Occasional flea markets are set up in front of vacant storefronts. Dominoes or card games may be in full swing. Little girls play double-dutch jump rope or flaunt their "Cabbage Patch" dolls while the boys chase each other or weave on the street or sidewalk doing acrobatics on small-wheeled multicolored bicycles. It seems like an obsolete culture in Manhattan, and, in some ways, perhaps it is: Gentrification during the seventies and eighties of the West Side has already pushed out many long-time merchants and residents who are unable to pay luxury rents, and the Amsterdam Avenue area north of 90th Street may eventually be a casualty, too. In the meantime, this neighborhood is worth getting to know; it has many fine and friendly restaurants and markets.

RESTAURANTS

Opened in 1963, **Mi Tierra** (668 Amsterdam Ave. near 93rd St., Tel.: 874-9514) is the oldest Mexican restaurant on the

Upper West Side and one of the oldest in Manhattan. Marcola Santana, a native of the Dominican Republic, learned Venezuelan and Mexican cuisine as a cook at Mi Tierra for many years; she bought the restaurant from its Venezuelan owners in 1976. But you won't find it in the phone book; the phone number is that of Mi Tierra's pay phone. According to Gennero Santana, Marcola's husband, who also works here, they've just never gotten around to getting their own phone, and besides, a pay phone's cheaper! Among the specialties you'll find here are *nopalitos* (steamed cactus) and *queso Oaxaca* (a hot cheese-and-sausage appetizer), and Venezuelan entrées like *filetillo* (steak in tomato sauce) and *pernil* (leg of pork), as well as Mexican *chalupas*, *flautas*, enchiladas, and other typical dishes. Especially recommended, however, are the *mole poblano*, a homemade unsweetened chocolate sauce made with five different kinds of peppers, and the homeground tamales. There aren't any multicolored margaritas or Tex-Mex food; Mi Tierra's authentic cooking calls for subtle flavoring, and is matched by a quiet, never overcrowded or rushed dining ambience. There's a bar in one room (mostly for local folks) and a comfortable dim-lit dining area in the other. Be sure, by the way, to ask about some of the seafood specials—shrimp enchiladas and avocado-stuffed shrimp, and the Sunday brunch, which features *chimichangas*, deep-fried flour tortillas. Mi Tierra doesn't advertise much, and Gennero Santana explains why: "We have very loyal customers," he says, "and they bring their friends." You should go, too.

El Caribe (764 Amsterdam Ave. at 97th St., Tel.: 212/864-5648), a neighborhood Cuban restaurant, is modest to look at, but has a fine selection of specialties including bean soups made of garbanzos, black beans, or white beans, meat stews, codfish and creole beef and chicken entrées, and homemade desserts, including *flan con queso*—custard with cream cheese. A separate dining area allows for an easygoing meal, while the counter invites animated small talk between owners and customers. We asked a waitress to explain why an orange malted was called "Morir Soñando," which means "to die dreaming." "It's the Dominican name," she said, "and I don't know. But why do you have a *school* of fish? Can you explain that?"

Opened in 1983, **Caribbean Creole Cuisine Restaurant** (852 Amsterdam Ave. near 102nd St., Tel.: 212/316-4090) is one of only two Haitian eateries in Manhattan (the other, **Restaurant Soleil,** is at 875 10th Avenue), and the more attractive of the two. The walls are decorated with brightly colored paintings of Haitian scenes (they're for sale), and the cuisine features specialties such as goat stew, creole chicken, peppery steak, and fish entrées. Each main dish comes with a heaping portion of rice and beans, with fried plantains on the side and a small bowl of spicy sauce. We recommend a bottle of Haitian soda with your meal, especially the lime (*citron*) or banana flavors. These are bottled as Sékola brand (and, interestingly, are served in recycled Heineken beer bottles—look at the lettering near the bottom rim of the bottle) and are natural flavors—delicious. Bouncy Haitian music provides a delightful background for a simple but filling meal. No desserts are served here, so you might pop in at El Caribe for flan or fruit cup.

You won't hear the clatter of dishes or the clank of silverware in **Asmara African Restaurant** (951 Amsterdam Ave. near 107th St., Tel.: 212/662-1065), one of three Ethiopian restaurants north of 96th Street. Ethiopian food is eaten by hand, or actually scooped up with *injera*, a moist, thin pancakelike bread, which accompanies every meal. The cuisine includes mild and hot lamb, beef, chicken, and vegetarian (usually lentil or chick-pea) stews flavored with ginger, onions, peppers, and herbs, sometimes mixed with yogurt, and with an underlying taste of clarified butter which is an essential part of the cookery. The food is some of New York's most exotic, with names like *awaze*, *fitfit*, *yetsom beyanetu*, and *dorowat*. Each main course has generally just one dish, so to get the best from your visit to an Ethiopian restaurant, bring several friends.

Other Ethiopian restaurants are **Red Sea Restaurant** (3161 Broadway, two blocks south of 125th St., Tel.: 212/864-9101), and **Zula Café** (1260 Amsterdam Ave. at 122nd St., Tel.: 212/663-1610). Zula Café's entrées come with a small green salad. It also offers a combination platter, so if you're alone, you can sample different dishes. All except Red Sea serve Ethiopian honey wine. Red Sea features a savory Sudanese-influenced entrée called *full*, which owner Araia Isaac claims is usually eaten for breakfast! You'll find the three Ethiopian restaurants relaxing: Each often has the strains of recorded Ethiopian music in the background, and the walls are adorned with painted hangings, folk objects, or photographs of Ethiopia.

For many a returning Columbia alumnus, **V&T Pizzeria and Restaurant** (1024 Amsterdam Ave. between 110th and 111th Sts., Tel.: 212/663-1708) is the second stop in their pilgrimage—and it's one of the area's most popular hangouts for nonstudents, too. In the neighborhood since the 1940s, it offers a student-budget menu of formidable variety—about 30 pasta dishes, 9 veal selections, 20 seafood platters—not to mention an ample choice of appetizers, steaks, and chops. But most eyes head for the pizza: V&T doesn't skimp on its rich crusty pizza, and it's one of New York's best bargains.

A curiosity: We're told that the five Indian dishes at the bottom of the menu were added in the 1950s at the request of Indian students at Columbia. Apparently the recipe for pizza dough closely resembles the recipe for Indian breads, and with the right combination of ingredients, the chefs at V&T could whip up credible Indian platters.

Hungarian Pastry Shop (1030 Amsterdam Ave., Tel.: 212/866-4230) has been a neighborhood mainstay for more than two dozen years, and a place to relax over one of several different coffees (cappuccinos, Viennese, Russian, or Irish) or herb teas, or to indulge in political arguments, poetry, or your sweet tooth: There are rich, layered Hungarian pastries, as well as less fancy cookies and dunkable danishes.

Green Tree Hungarian Restaurant (1034 Amsterdam Ave., Tel.: 212/864-9106) has been in the neighborhood for decades, and offers traditional (and fairly simple) Hungarian cuisine, from the cold cherry or gooseberry soup in a sweet milky base as a starter, through entrées such as noodles stroganoff, goulash, stuffed cabbage, chicken *paprikash*, and spicy stuffed peppers, to apple strudel, napoleons, or *rigó jancsi*—chocolate mousse cake—for dessert. Plum dumplings are a specialty, but often unavailable, and *spaetzele*, tiny Hungarian flour-and-egg dumplings, are served on the side to absorb the gravy in many of the entrées.

MARKETS, BAKERIES, AND SHOPS

Patisserie Les Friandises (665 Amsterdam Ave., between 92nd and 93rd Sts., Tel.: 212/316-1515) opened on the West Side in early 1986. Though it would seem more in place, perhaps, in Montparnasse or on Madison Avenue, it's a welcome addition to the West Side for French pastry lovers. Early mornings—except Monday—you can come by for fresh croissants, brioches, or *pain au chocolat* (chocolate-filled pastry made of croissant dough), or later in the day for rich layer cakes with chocolate or fruit fillings such as the double chocolate truffle, *opéra maison* (almond layers filled with coffee butter cream and chocolate *ganache*), or passion fruit *miroir* (a tangy mousse of passion fruit with a touch of rum syrup). Simpler, but just as wonderful, are the seasonal fruit tarts. Les Friandises also fills special orders.

The popular **Vista Bakery** (926 Amsterdam Ave. near 105th St.) was forced out of a nearby Broadway location after many years because of a huge rent hike. But the move has proved worthwhile; now more directly serving its Hispanic clientele, Vista serves such specialties as flan (custard), marzipan pastries, guava cake, and bread pudding.

Quisqueya Grocery (932 Amsterdam Ave. at 106th St.) serves the particular culinary needs of the community which aren't met in large supermarkets. Outdoors, bins teem with produce—tropical root vegetables and melons, coconut, sugarcane, and different kinds of plantain. Inside is an icebox with frozen yucca, empanada or tamal dough, guava, and other specialties. A butcher in the rear sells the special poultry, pork, and beef cuts popular in Caribbean cookery, while the rest of the market covers the gamut of canned and other goods you won't find elsewhere: an oat drink, plantain soup mix, and bottled sodas from the Dominican Republic and Puerto Rico with flavors like passion fruit, banana, apple, and coconut. We wanted to know the flavor of "merengue" cola, and the counterman grinned and danced a few steps of the merengue, so we bought it: It is, appropriately, a spicy, bubbly cola.

WALKING TOUR

Head north, cross 110th Street, and enter Morningside Heights, another West Side altogether. Columbia University's campus begins at 114th Street, but for all intents and purposes, Columbia begins here: It's the area's major landlord. On the east side of Amsterdam Avenue are the gardens and buildings of the Cathedral of St. John the Divine, the largest Gothic-style cathedral in the world—and still under construction: Its towers are wrapped with scaffolding, and during the week you can visit the workshop adjacent to the church and watch stonecutters at work. The church's interior is awesome, yet not at all intimidating, with individual areas for contemplation. The gardens, especially around the Peace Fountain and its dramatic sculptural centerpiece, dedicated in 1985, are a peaceful refuge and lunch site. (You can also picnic on Columbia's beautiful campus; the gates are at 116th Street at Amsterdam Avenue and Broadway.)

WEST SIDE SAMPLER: ON (AND OFF) BROADWAY

After you amble up Amsterdam, you may want to amble down Broadway. Here are a few old favorites (and one newcomer) in the area.

RESTAURANTS

Opened in 1969, **Symposium Greek Restaurant** (544 W. 113th St., Tel.: 212/865-1011) is a comfortable, quirky Greek restaurant reflecting the creativity of owner-artist Yanni Posnikoff, who has painted almost every surface of his establishment with dreamy designs. The menu has both authentic and adapted Greek dishes, including avgolemono soup, Greek dips, Greek-spiced omelets and salads, entrées, and desserts.

Long-time Westsiders who frequent the Columbia area were used to seeing the restaurant site on the east side of Broadway just north of 111th Street change hands with about the same regularity as the change of semesters. For a long time in the early 1980s, the site was empty. **Caffè Pertutti** (2852 Broadway at 111th St., Tel.: 212/864-1143), which opened in 1985, seems to be a winner. It's both a real café (except for the busy dinner hours, you can linger for as long as you want over one of many espresso combinations) and a wonderful place for a pasta-and-salad dinner. About five different pastas and six or so sauces are available flavored with garlic, basil, cauliflower, or whatever the combination of the day. Cheeses and sweet pastry desserts are also available. The ambience is simple and pleasant, with soft peach walls and marble tables, and prices are reasonable (you can dine for about $10). All in all, this is a welcome addition to the West Side.

Frank Castro opened **Ideal Restaurant** (2825 Broadway at 109th St., Tel.: 212/866-3224), a Cuban eatery, in the mid-1960s, and it remains a dignified haven from the clutter and rush of Broadway. The interior is a mix of brickwork and dark wood paneling, and the red tablecloths give a warm feeling to the restaurant. You can eat alone at the counter, which doubles as a bar, or linger—you won't be rushed here—at one of Ideal's many tables. Specialties include a *paella Valenciana, arroz con pollo special* (rice with chicken cooked in white wine and beer), *pollo Ideal* (chicken cooked with sausage, ham, and vegetables), and steak sautéed in olive oil. The menu also includes a wide selection of shrimp, codfish, and lobster dishes and thick rice soups, as well as side servings of plantain, yucca (also called Indian potato), and red or black beans. Tropical desserts—flan, guava, papaya, and coconut—cap your meal.

Rosita (2799 Broadway at 108th St.) is a stark contrast to the staid Ideal, and is a favorite among students and neighborhood old-timers. It's a narrow luncheonette, really, but the kind where waitresses will engage in snappy banter with the customers. (Many are evidently regulars.) Come here for a Cuban sandwich, an omelet, a sip of espresso or *café con leche,* or the more filling beef, chicken, and shrimp dishes—Rosita serves them all. On a hot day, try a batido, a sweet milkshake flavored with tropical fruit, like guava, guanabana, papaya, or mamey, or wheat. (The latter tastes a bit like ground Sugar Pops cereal.) Watch the sugar: Batidos are sweetened with many spoonfuls, and you might ask in advance for just one or two.

A newcomer to the area—it opened in 1986—**Indian Café** (2791 Broadway near 108th St., Tel.: 212/749-9200) has already developed a loyal following, in part because of its 1985 antecedent, which still thrives at 201 West 95th Street near Amsterdam Avenue. The wide selection includes many vegetarian dishes, as well as tandoori and curried chicken, lamb muglai (with yogurt and almonds), and shrimp and goat entrées. Check for its daily specials; one vegetarian dish included a subtle blend of raisins and cashews with a vegetable mix, and the seafood biryani—a seafood rice stew—is subtle and luscious.

Grand Oriental (2707½ Broadway near 103rd St., Tel.: 212/866-7740) and **La Victoria China Restaurant** (2532 Broadway near 95th St., Tel.: 212/865-1810) are just two of the dozen or so Cuban-Chinese restaurants scattered around the Upper West Side.

Cuban-Chinese, you ask? You mean, wonton soup for a starter and longaniza frita—Dominican-style steak—for a main course? Or an egg roll on the side and papaya con queso for dessert? At either of these eateries, run by Chinese nationals who once settled in Cuba but migrated to the United States in the 1960s, you can enjoy an eclectic combination of comida china & criolla—literally, Chinese and creole food generally served in ample portions and at prices competitive with the area's many Chinese restaurants. La Victoria China is widely acknowledged to have the best selection and cooking, but its Chinese menu is Cantonese only, while Grand Oriental also serves spicy Szechuan dishes. Spanish specialties include chicharrón de pollo sin huesos—boneless fried chicken pieces; thick congee—a rich soup with shrimp, chicken, or beef; and broiled or stewed lobster.

MARKETS AND SHOPS
Mondel's Homemade Chocolates (2913 Broadway near 114th St., Tel.: 212/864-2111) is a Morningside Heights institution that has nothing to do with scholarship and research (though connoisseurs might argue otherwise). It has been churning out milk, bittersweet, white, and many other kinds of chocolate as well as other sweets since it opened in 1943. Among the specialties here are solid chocolate cups flavored with Amaretto, coffee, mint, or orange, chocolate bark, and whole chocolate pieces made from molds ranging from King Tut to a menagerie of animals.

Daniel and Delia Lopez, originally from Guadalajara, Mexico, opened **Lomore Delicatessen** (2746 Broadway near 105th St., Tel.: 212/222-3702) in the early 1970s. Its specialties are Mexican foodstuffs—a huge selection of imported sauces and other often hard-to-find ingredients from Mexico—plus Italian pastas and pastries, and beer, more than 140 brands, including about a half-dozen nonalcoholic beers. From 5 P.M. to 11 P.M., you can get fresh-made Mexican tacos, tostadas, tamales, enchiladas, or *burritos* to go, as well as *pozole* (Mexican soup), turkey or chicken in *mole* sauce, and, as daily specials, barbecue chicken, spare ribs, or chili. (It's wise to call in advance, even for the standard takeout fare, since it's not always available.) The beer tends to be slightly higher priced than elsewhere, explains Daniel Lopez, because he orders often, but in small quantities, in order to maintain the extraordinary selection of Australian, Indian, Peruvian, Texan, and other exotic brews.

AMZ Grocery Corp. (2652 Broadway between 101st and 102nd Sts., Tel.: 212/749-3053) is a friendly neighborhood market specializing in *productos tropicales*. It is the only one in the area that sells Haitian as well as Latino specialties: You can find Sékola or Lakaye soda here, Haitian coffee, and Haitian breads and cakes. There's also a comprehensive selection of spices, vegetables, and other foodstuffs oriented to the Caribbean diet.

Kalpana Indian and International Groceries and Spices (2528 Broadway between 94th and 95th Sts., Tel.: 212/663-4190) offers a surprising selection of groceries packed into a crowded, small space, and you'll get friendly help from owners Tony and Urmilla Maharaj if you're not sure what you want. The goods include everything you could possibly need for Indian cooking; Middle Eastern grains, tahini, and vegetables; Jamaican syrups and spices (the Maharajs were born of Indian parents but raised in Trinidad); hard-to-find African palm oil for cooking; ground cassava *(egusi)* from Liberia, used in baking; walnut and mustard oils; and huge bags full of dried beans, grains, and nuts. There are also vitamins, household sundries from India and the West Indies, and Indian-language videocassettes for rental. The freezer contains delicious Indian sweets and frozen parathas (Indian stuffed breads), and, on occasion, the store stocks cookbooks to tell you what to do with all the exotica for sale.

MANHATTAN MÉLANGE

LITTLE SPAIN

Manhattan's Little Spain—14th Street between Seventh and Eighth Avenues—is rarely called that anymore, but a stroll in the area reveals a Spanish benevolent society, a couple of Spanish-language bookstores, several restaurants, and **Casa Moneo** (210 W. 14th St., Tel.: 212/929-1644), a shop that effervesces with inventory from the Iberian peninsula and Latin America. Founded in 1929 by Carmen Moneo and now run by his grandson Santiago, Casa Moneo sells everything from tortillas to Latin records, and is worth a special trip. Whether you want *masa hari-na* (the fine corn flour used for tortillas), any of a dozen kinds of chilies, sausages, cheese, or almost anything else used in Latin cooking, it's a good bet you'll find it at Casa Moneo. (If you thought chilies were red, don't miss the purple California ones that look like baby eggplants!) There's an impressive array of imported canned and dry foods, plenty of olive oils and vinegars, and some unusual fresh items like aloe vera. Upstairs you'll find Latin records, cookware, magazines, clothing, and gifts.

BRAZILIAN CUISINE

Once you've navigated the steep stairs covered with eye-spinning, brightly colored murals at **Cabana Carioca** (123 W. 45th St., Tel.: 212/581-8088), you'll find a magical restaurant. Dark and small, the restaurant pulses with the zeal of its grimly efficient waiters, who are intent on overloading diners with food: Some national cooking can be characterized by its spices or its vegetables, but with Brazilian food the thread is the hearty simplicity of its dishes.

Brazilian food draws from the country's mixture of cultures: Portuguese colonizers, African slaves, and indigenous peoples. The ubiquitous *feojada* is Brazil's national dish: It's a steaming black bean stew filled with pork, beef, and sausage and served with rice, collard greens, and an orange. Other specialties at Cabana Carioca are shrimp, codfish, and broiled chicken.

Downstairs, at lunch there is a buffet, featuring all you can eat of close to a dozen dishes, ranging from rice and greens, through several varieties of squid, to feojada. Desserts, including flan and carrot cake, are also included. Upstairs, the best value is found at the bar, where inexpensive specials of the day are cooked up. What and how much you get can be whimsical, but a good dish to start off with is shrimp and garlic, served with a side dish of rice and beans and perhaps some home-fried potatoes. If you like a wee drop now and again, don't miss *caipirinha*, the Brazilian drink that seems like it was developed as a sidelight to the country's ethanol program. Pulverized fresh lime, sugar, and ice are fortified with *cachaca*, a sugarcane liquor. The glasses are small, but with caipirinha the effect is something like espresso: concentrated.

There is also good Brazilian food and great Latin and Brazilian music at **S.O.B. (Sounds of Brazil)** downtown at Varick and Houston Streets (204 Varick St., Tel.: 212/924-5221), although the cover charge for music pushes up the tab.

VIETNAMESE CUISINE

wrapped around sugarcane to spicy sausages. Often described as similar to Chinese cuisine, Vietnamese food is lighter, less fatty, and not as oily. "Almost all Vietnamese are skinny because you can eat lots of Vietnamese food and not put on weight," says Jan Khu, who runs Saigon Restaurant.

Vietnamese food is, with a few exceptions, not spicy hot, so aficionados of mouth-searing food will want to add some of the fiery chili sauce that is on every table. Two other sauces are on every table. One is a sweet *hoisin*-style sauce, similar to the one used in Korean cooking. It is usually spread on the inside of the paper-thin rice flour sheets used to wrap dishes such as pork balls. The other sauce is *nuoc nam*, a mild version of the fermented anchovy paste that is a staple of Vietnamese cuisine, and into which almost anything can be dipped.

Vietnamese food is unfettered by frills and frippery, characterized by a simplicity that lets the freshness of its ingredients and the tastes of its characteristic herbs—lemon grass, mint, and coriander—stand out. Perhaps the most surprising thing about Vietnamese food is how little of it there is in New York. Although there are perhaps 40,000 Vietnamese living in the city, there are only a handful of Vietnamese restaurants. That's unfortunate. Vietnamese cuisine is delightfully pungent, and ranges from blistering sauces to sweet ones, from delicate spring rolls to plump shrimp

RESTAURANTS

Saigon Restaurant (60 Mulberry St. near Mott St., Tel.: 212/277-8825 or 577-9763) is the best—and most enduring—Vietnamese family restaurant in Manhattan. You can make a meal out of appetizers. But if you only try a couple, start with the fried pork balls: Wrap them and the delicate vermicelli they're served with in lettuce leaves that you've dabbed with the hoisin-style sweet sauce. Or try the shrimp wrapped around skewered sugarcane that is a Vietnamese delicacy. Soups are good, although the hot and sour soup is something of a misnomer, since it's more like a sweet and sour soup.

If you like curries, try one of the *satay* dishes, a peanut-based curry sauce (similar to that found in Indonesian cooking). Saigon special beef, small pieces of marinated beef cooked in hot oil at the table, is also quite good. Vermicelli dishes are big tasty bowls filled with thin noodles and slivers of meat or fish in broth. By contrast, the fried rice dishes here don't stand out from others in Chinatown.

There are a variety of seafood dishes in the cooking, a legacy of Vietnam's coastal geography. Some of these—crab, shrimp, and lobster—are cooked in beer. As a novelty, the dish is worth a try; by the time you're finished, though, the beer broth smells a bit like last night's party.

Indochine (430 Lafayette at Astor Place, Tel.: 212/505-5111) is an elegant restaurant complete with the greenery and slow fans of a sultry hangout in a cinematic vision of old Saigon. The food (both Vietnamese and Thai) is quite refined—probably the best Vietnamese food in the city, and correspondingly priced. You're also paying for the scene—East Village/NoHo residents, and uptowners who are downtown for an evening.

It's one thing to buy all kinds of unusual vegetables, fruits, seafoods, and meats—and another to know what to do with them. Don't despair. A bookstore called **Kitchen Arts & Letters,** which opened in September 1983, can solve your problems. Its more than 3,000 titles cover the span of ethnic cookery as well as local or special-ingredient cuisines. You'll also find food catalogues plenty of titles on wines, desserts, culinary history, and gastronomic topics you didn't know existed. It's at 1435 Lexington Avenue, between 93rd and 94th Streets (Tel.: 212/876-5550).

SAIGON RESTAURANT
BARBECUED SHRIMP ON SUGARCANE

1 pound raw shrimp in shell
4 cloves garlic
1 teaspoon granulated sugar
2 egg whites, beaten until slightly frothy
freshly ground black pepper
2 tablespoons pork fat, boiled for 10
   minutes and diced finely

1 twelve-inch sugarcane
1/4 cup vegetable oil
shredded carrot
rice paper
hoisin sauce or *nam plah* (fish sauce)

Shell and rinse the shrimp. Use a blender or food processor to reduce the garlic and shrimp to a smooth paste. Add the granulated sugar and egg whites until well blended. Add the black pepper and pork fat and mix well.

Slice the sugarcane in half lengthwise, then chop into 4-inch sections. Dip your fingers into oil and pick up about 2 tablespoons of shrimp paste, molding it around the sugarcane.

Preheat the oven to 350° F; put the sugarcane on an oiled baking sheet and bake until brown. Serve with shredded carrot wrapped in rice paper and hoisin (or nam plah) sauce. Serves six as an appetizer.

BARBECUED PORK BALLS

1 pound trimmed fresh ham
2 cloves garlic, chopped
2 shallots (or substitute white part of
   scallions), chopped
1/2 teaspoon salt
1/2 teaspoon granulated sugar

black pepper
2 ounces pork fat, boiled 10 minutes and
   diced
shredded carrot
rice paper
hoisin sauce or nam plah

Coarsely dice the ham. Combine with garlic, shallots, salt, sugar, and pepper and marinate at least 2 hours.

Blend in a food processor until the mixture is reduced to a paste. Transfer to a bowl and mix in the pork fat. Shape into balls and bake in a 300° F oven for 15 minutes on each side. Serve with shredded carrot wrapped in rice paper that has hoisin or nam plah sauce on it.

THE BRONX

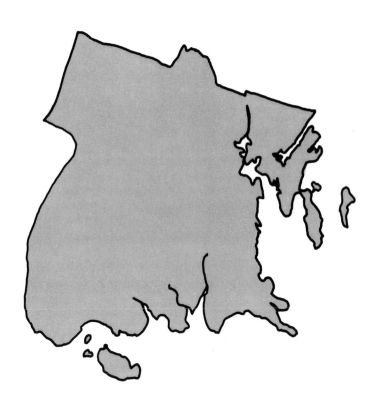

It's hard to say whether Jonas Bronck, were he alive today, would be more baffled by the borough that bears his name—or by the "Bronx cheer." In 1641, when the native of Denmark bought 500 acres of farmland from the Dutch West India Company along what is now the Bronx River, the area was an expanse of undeveloped land occupied mainly by indigenous peoples and Dutch farmers. The Bronx would remain almost as rural as Bronck found it until the 1840s, when Irish and German immigrants helped build new railroad lines and the Croton Aqueduct, and then settled nearby. By the end of the nineteenth century, New York City's only mainland borough was a country of small villages. Among these was Mott Haven, with its iron foundries and factories, which was almost entirely Irish (a landmark portion of Alexander Avenue is a remnant of those early days). To its east was Melrose, whose main street, Melrose Avenue, was nicknamed "Dutch Broadway" because of the many Germans in the area.

Village life changed with the construction of public transportation in the 1890s and early 1900s. Now more accessible, the Bronx attracted upwardly mobile immigrants from crowded slums in Manhattan, who spurred rapid apartment development. From 1890 to 1920, the borough was still villagelike, an innocent area set off from the rest of the city; the 1920s signaled the Bronx's rise as a political and intellectual center. From the 1920s to the 1950s, the Bronx had its Golden Age: Its spacious apartment houses attracted workers, many of whose children attended the tuition-free city colleges or New York University's fine campus on Uni-versity Heights overlooking the Harlem River, with palatial buildings designed by McKim, Mead & White. Later, Hispanic settlers to the South Bronx turned parts of the borough into a *barrio* even larger than that of East Harlem.

Italian settlers, arriving in the early 1900s, created communities in Belmont and on Morris Park and Allerton Avenues. The Irish from Mott Haven moved north, to the Fordham area and Gun Hill Road. For Jews, the Bronx was a release from the close quarters of the Lower East Side, and they once occupied many of the large buildings along the Concourse. Along Pelham Parkway, Yiddish is as apt to be heard as English: After World War II, refugees from Europe, including many concentration camp survivors, found a welcome place in the Bronx. Even today, the Bronx continues to attract immigrants, from areas as diverse as Albania, Russia, and Cambodia. And for some of these newcomers, the Bronx has enabled them literally to own a piece of the American dream. The Albanians have become successful real estate owners; the Cambodians have opened a temple.

For all the bad press of the past two decades, the Bronx is on the rebound, and it offers a rich assortment of sights, wonderful bicycling, and a wealth of social and architectural history. We've only profiled three areas—Belmont, City Island, and a small shopping enclave near Pelham Parkway along Lydig Avenue—but for additional exploring, keep the following areas in mind:

Longwood Historical District (see "City Island Odyssey" map on page 235 for location): More than 100 mostly owner-occupied brownstone homes, packed together within about a dozen

square blocks, make Longwood an example of what much of the South Bronx once looked like and how neighborhood activism helped preserve the area when adjacent areas fell apart. Generations of families living together have kept Longwood cohesive and optimistic, and in 1982 their efforts were rewarded with designation as a Federal Historic District. There has been a spillover effect: The so-called "Banana Kelly" project nearby (named for the banana-shaped blocks on Kelly Street) came together as a result of residents wanting to save their neighborhood, and now has a community garden and solar heating in some buildings. Between Longwood and Banana Kelly, a new complex of attached single-family homes was completed in 1986. About a half-mile away, at Charlotte Gardens near Crotona Park (see "Little Italy of the Bronx" map, on page 241), several dozen detached single-family homes signal the birth of a minisuburb in the South Bronx. Built with a combination of federal and state funds, the homes may be sold only to middle-class families who weathered the South Bronx during its worst years. When presidential candidates Carter and Reagan visited Charlotte Street during their campaigns, the area resembled a bombed-out city.

Grand Concourse Boulevard: First opened as a "speedway" in 1892, the wide, majestic Concourse ran north-south the length of the borough with separate carriage and bicycle lanes leading to Van Cortlandt Park. The opening of public transportation spurred apartment construction, and by the 1920s and 1930s, the Concourse was a luxurious residential boulevard with much of the best Art Deco architecture around. The Concourse fell on hard times in the 1960s, and by the mid-

1970s fell prey to neglect and abandonment; even the trees seemed to be dying or had been vandalized. The 1980s has become an era of new vigor and restoration—you'll see many apartments with new windows and sandblasted facades—and of the hope that the rebirth of the Concourse is the beginning of a broader neighborhood revival. Landmarks include the **Bronx County Courthouse** at 161st Street (built in 1934), the **Andrew Freedman Home** at 168th Street (completed in 1908 by a wealthy subway contractor as a home for rich people who'd fallen on hard times; it's now a home for the elderly poor), and the **Poe Cottage** in Poe Park near Kingsbridge Road. Edgar Allan Poe moved with his ailing wife to the Bronx in 1846, hoping the "country air" might soothe her tuberculosis. It didn't, but the cottage survives as a memento of his residence there.

The Bronx Zoo and the **New York Botanical Garden:** The largest urban zoo in the United States and one of the world's leading botanical research institutions are centrally located and within walking distance of both Belmont and Lydig Avenues. The 252-acre zoo, opened in 1899, is roughly half animal houses and half zoological park, with its 40-acre "Wild Asia" display allowing 14 species of animals to roam free while zoo visitors are confined to a monorail. The 240-acre New York Botanical Garden, north of the zoo across Fordham Road, opened in 1895 and was patterned after the Royal Botanical Gardens in Kew, England. The stunning Enid A. Haupt Conservatory is a greenhouse complex including gardens from the past, a medieval herb garden, tropical flora, Renaissance-inspired galleries, and an exhibit of cacti. An adjacent

rose garden explodes into color in spring and summer. The park combines wilderness areas with planned garden beds, and has wonderful groves for picnicking. The museum building offers lectures and exhibits, and has a lovely gift shop and frequent plant sales.

Pelham Parkway: Laid out in the 1890s, Pelham Parkway remains a luxuriant roadway connecting Bronx Park with the northeast Bronx, leading to Pelham Bay Park, City Island, and Orchard Beach. Separate bike lanes make it one of the finest bike paths in New York.

Riverdale: A combination of posh estates, private neighborhoods such as Fieldston, and middle-class apartments, this area in the western Bronx (although some folks in Riverdale refuse to acknowledge it's in the Bronx at all) sits in a picturesque hilly area with some spectacular views of the Hudson River. **The Wave Hill Center for Environmental Studies** (252nd Street and Independence Avenue), a former estate overlooking the Hudson and now owned by the City of New York, has hiking trails, lovely gardens, concerts, and nature programs—but no picnicking. Bicycling is one of the best ways to reach Wave Hill—but you must pedal up steep Riverdale Avenue to get there.

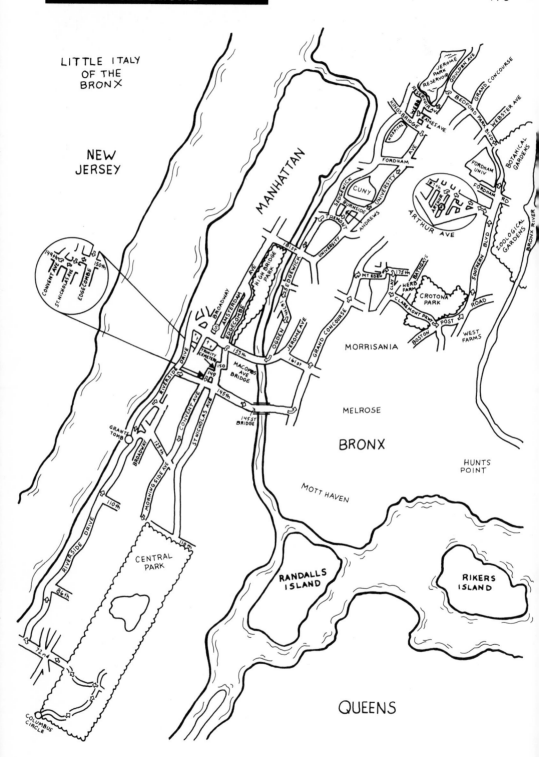

LITTLE ITALY
OF THE
BRONX

NEW
JERSEY

MANHATTAN

JEROME
PARK
RESERVOIR

GOULDEN AVE

GRAND CONCOURSE

KINGS BRIDGE

JEROME AVE

BEDFORD PARK BLVD

WEBSTER AVE

BOTANICAL
GARDENS

HOSPITAL
AVE

FORDHAM

FORDHAM
UNIV

FORDHAM RD

SEDGWICK

CUNY

UNIVERSITY

ARTHUR AVE

ZOOLOGICAL
GARDENS

SOUTHERN BLVD

BRONX RIVER

BURNSIDE

TREMONT

ANDREWS

CONVENT AVE

ST NICHOLAS AVE

EDGECOMBE

150th

149th

MT EDEN

175th

BATHGATE

CUNY

HERB
FARM

CROTONA
PARK

ROAD

CLAREMONT PKWY

BOSTON

POST

WEST
FARMS

BROADWAY

AMSTERDAM AVE

EDGECOMBE AVE

HIGH BRIDGE PARK

SEDGWICK

OGDEN

JEROME AVE

GRAND CONCOURSE

MORRISANIA

RIVERSIDE DRIVE

TRINITY CEMETERY

150

155th

161st

MACOMBS
AVE
BRIDGE

149

145th

145 ST
BRIDGE

MELROSE

BRONX

GRANTS
TOMB

CONVENT AVE

ST NICHOLAS AVE

BROADWAY

125th

MORNING SIDE AVE

HUNTS
POINT

110th

MOTT HAVEN

CENTRAL
PARK

86th

RANDALLS
ISLAND

RIKERS
ISLAND

72nd

COLUMBUS
CIRCLE

QUEENS

LITTLE ITALY ON ARTHUR AVENUE

To Get There

By subway and bus: Take the D train to Fordham Rd., walk east on Fordham Rd. or E. 188th St. for about 12 blocks (15 minutes) to Arthur Ave., and turn right to E. 187th St. Or take the IRT 2 or 5 train to White Plains Rd., and the Bx-12 bus on Pelham Pkwy., destination 207th St. Ask the driver to leave you at Arthur Ave. and Fordham Rd. (in front of Fordham University).

By car: From Manhattan, cross the 145th St. Bridge, and turn left onto the Grand Concourse, continuing north to E. 188th St. Turn right to Arthur Ave. and turn right again. You'll see a sign for a municipal parking lot two blocks down on your right.

By bike: See the instructions for the "Little Italy of the Bronx," tour on page 241. For a quicker route than on the map, ride north on the Grand Concourse from the Bronx County Courthouse to E. 188th St.; turn right for 12 blocks to Arthur Ave.

Orientation: E. 187th St. and Arthur Ave., which meet at right angles (see map on page 241), are the main shopping streets. You'll soon realize that the area is a clutter of delightful shops, as well as perhaps two dozen private "social clubs" that cater to Italian men in the community. (A couple of these—the Ballkan on E. 187th St., for example—are meeting places for Yugoslav and Albanian men, who make up a smaller component of the neighborhood.)

I grew up in Brooklyn and live on Long Island," says Lou Izzo, owner of **Modern Foods** at 2385 Arthur Avenue and **Rigoletto's Café** at 2355 Hughes Avenue. "But when I tell my kids I'm going to the neighborhood, they know I'm talking about here."

"Here," where Lou Izzo's father grew up, is Belmont, an Italian enclave in the

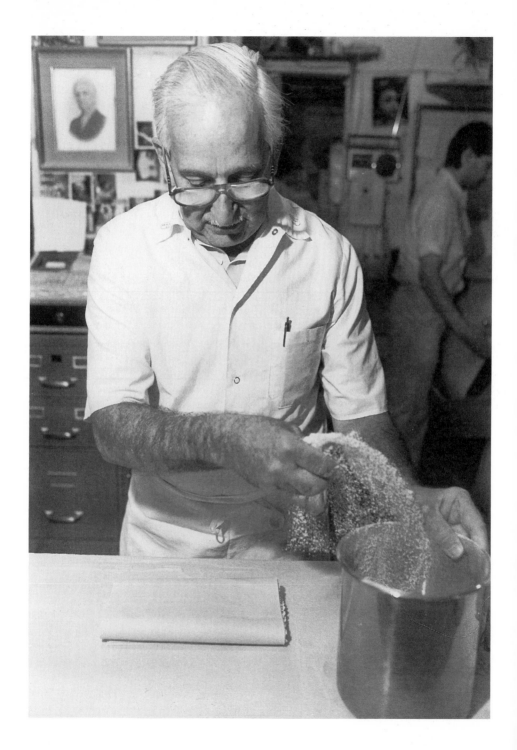

south-central Bronx. Most people know it just as Arthur Avenue, whose four blocks from East 183rd to East 187th Streets form the core of this nearly century-old community. Settled by Italian immigrants who came as construction workers at the Bronx Zoo and Jerome Park Reservoir, it has grown into a vibrant agglomeration of cafés, latticini, salumeria, fish markets, and general-purpose stores serving a close-knit population. Although the neighborhood remains working class, it is rich in family ties and community pride, which become quickly evident to the first-time visitor. That's because so many stores are passed on from father to son (or, in some cases, to daughter). And when shops are sold, they still often stay in the "family": When Rose DeLillo Smith sold **DeLillo Pastry Shop** at 606 East 187th Street in 1985 after more than 30 years in the business, the buyer was Louis Florio, the head baker for 28 years.

MARKETS AND SHOPS

Arthur Avenue once teemed with outdoor pushcarts, but in 1941, citing health reasons, Mayor Fiorello LaGuardia brought them into an enclosed city-built retail market in which space was divided into individual stalls. These days the market is the centerpiece of the community, a symbol of its European past, its present viability, and, most likely, the neighborhood's future as a haven for the hard-working, individualistic merchant who likes to be his own boss. There are still some merchants left over from the old days, like Joe Libertore, who loves to talk about how he spent five

Sprinkling cornmeal on sheets of fresh pasta.

years with a pushcart before the market opened. You don't have to nudge him before he points to the articles on the wall about him from *Il Progresso*—the Italian-American newspaper—and the *Daily News*. Arthur Avenue is a magnet for journalists, and in almost every bakery, or at Dominick's and Mario's, the neighborhood's flagship restaurants, you'll see news clippings celebrating the area's vitality. And it's no hype, for this community is unique. On three sides it's surrounded by some of the most desolate sections of the South Bronx. (Fordham Road and Fordham University form a buffer on the north.) There were tough times for Arthur Avenue during the recession of the mid-1970s, when some stores closed and merchants and residents feared widespread abandonment. No longer. "They're coming back now," says an optimistic Mr. Izzo, whose work with a local merchants' organization has attracted funding for new housing and other civic amenities. C's Pastry Shop got a major facelift in 1984, and Mr. Izzo's own café, opened in late 1985, has added new sparkle and color to Hughes Avenue, one block east of Arthur Avenue. You can get everything you want in Belmont, from fresh ricotta and mozzarella to Italian syrups and soft drinks, from cappuccino and calorie-laden *cannolis* to fresh-roasted espresso beans and espresso makers. There's stand-up eating for those on the go and fancier sit-down dining for lingerers. There are endless quantities, it seems, of everything an Italian food lover could want. There's also something that makes people want to come back again and again, some intangible, which those in the neighborhood call *amore*.

Arthur Avenue Retail Market (2344 Arthur Ave., Tel.: 212/367-5686) is a fairly authentic model of the sprawling indoor markets that can be found throughout towns and cities in Europe. As is the custom overseas, the service is quite personalized and in some cases prices are negotiable. Joe Libertore, first on your left as you enter, sells plants and produce, including baby vegetables and hard-to-find spaghetti beans. Theresa Marchese, a woman in her mid-thirties whose children

With a little help from above . . .

"I think I can slice you a sausage or two."

and relatives often help out, is proprietress of **Marchese Grocery** (Tel.: 212/933-2295), an extensive concession occupying much of the market on the far left of the main entrance, specializing in imported goods, including tubes of garlic, anchovy, and tomato pastes; cooking wines and vinegars; nuts, dried beans, and loose spices; pastas (including whole wheat pasta with bran); and dozens of

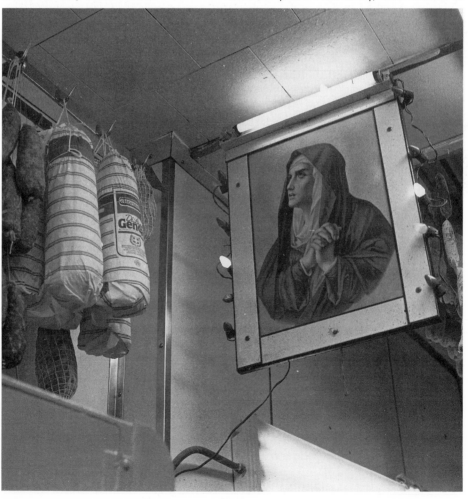

fruit drinks, including tiny bottles of fruit-flavored Italian bitters. For weary visitors, there's a sit-down café next to Marchese's, where you can buy pastries and cappuccino. At **Mike Greco's Deli,** sausages and cheese of various sorts can be bought—with a line or two of opera thrown in free by a singing counterman as you make your purchase. **Isidore Berenstein Housewares** is found on the right-hand aisle near the Arthur Avenue entrance. A Polish Jew who spent much of World War II in Italy, Mr. Berenstein organized the market merchants to get the City of New York in 1982 to renovate the decaying building sheltering the stands; the new structure is almost *too* neat, but it has appealing skylights to keep the place sunny. Mr. Berenstein, by the way, sells all sorts of pizza cutters and pasta molds, garlic presses, espresso makers, rolling pins, and other devices a good Italian cook needs.

Up the street at **Teitel Brothers** (2372 Arthur Ave., Tel.: 212/733-9400) you have almost the entire Arthur Avenue market compressed into a cluttered corner store. Outdoors, crates of dried beans and stacks of olive oil cans are the come-ons. Come in—and wait; it's almost always crowded. But service is friendly and helpful, and you'll no doubt leave with what you came looking for—and more.

Several fruit and vegetable stands, including **Vitale's Fruits** (2350 Arthur Ave.), **Gambino's Fruits & Vegetables** (2376 Arthur Ave.), and **Little Italy Fruits and Vegetables** (2380 Arthur Ave.), crowded almost on top of one another, have clogged the sidewalks for years, especially on Saturday, the busiest shopping day. Pedestrians are often forced to squeeze around crates and into the street,

where cars are always double-, and sometimes triple-, parked. (A modest municipal parking lot opened a block from Arthur Avenue and East 186th Street in 1983, but the Saturday gridlock seems as enduring as the pizza and provolone.) Produce here is cheaper than in many neighborhoods, and often of superior quality. Italian specialties that you'll find (in season, of course) include zucchini flowers, dandelion greens, fava beans in the pod, baby eggplants and artichokes, and broccoli rapé. You'll also find several clam bars on Arthur Avenue, adjuncts to fish stores, such as **Cosenza's** (1254 Arthur Ave., Tel.: 212/364-8510) and **Randazzo's** (2340 Arthur Ave., Tel.: 212/367-4139), where you can buy plates of clams, mussels, and oysters. Don't miss the snails and fresh sea urchins, round prickly critters from which you scoop a pulpy meat and eat it plain or with lemon.

Bread can be a very personal issue, and many locals profess loyalty to **Addeo's** (2372 Hughes Ave.), which has been in the neighborhood for 30 years. The specialty—often sold out by noon—is *pane di casa,* a round soft-dough bread. Also popular in the neighborhood, at Addeo's and other bakeries, including **Madonia's** (2348 Arthur Ave.) and **Terranova** (691 E. 187th St.), are lard breads, shaped like big bagels, which are cooked with chunks of sausage and lots of pepper, and semolina loaves and long Italian breads.

Many local shops sell fresh pasta, but the acknowledged patriarch of pasta makers is **Borgatti's** (632 E. 187th St., Tel.: 212/367-3799), which opened its doors more than 50 years ago. Fresh pastas of many shapes and sizes are avail-

Olives at Teitel Brothers.

able, including varieties enriched with tomato, spinach, carrot, and broccoli. Huge sheets of fettuccine can be cut to order, and Mario Borgatti has a handout ready with recipes and instructions on pasta storage.

For cheese, we recommend **S. Calandra & Sons Cheese** (2314 Arthur Ave., Tel.: 212/365-7572). It's just a bit farther from the busy intersection, and the prices are just a bit lower. The owners, Jo and Fred, will slice for you half-pounds of buttery, melt-in-your mouth smoked mozzarella (many other stores won't cut it). Ricotta is driven in daily from the family factory in Nazareth, Pennsylvania, and the mozzarella is prepared on the premises. Other homemade cheeses include fresh Romano and Parmesan.

In your wanderings, you'll stumble upon a dozen or so delis that sell prepared salads and imported Italian foods. We can't decide if any one is better than another, but a good example is **Joe's Deli** (685 E. 187th St., Tel.: 212/367-7979). As you enter, savor the aroma of the olive oil and tomatoes. You have a splendid choice of oils and sauces, specialty sugars and flavorings for baking, and broccoli or spinach breads, baked with mozzarella, that can be heated up for a marvelous snack.

Wander off the main streets we've listed and you won't find too much. But we stumbled happily on **The Coffee Store** (611 E. 188th St., Tel.: 212/584-6952), a tiny shop selling about a dozen different types of coffee beans. Fred Harrison's grandfather, a Hungarian Jewish immigrant, founded a wholesale coffee outlet more than 40 years ago to supply restaurants and hotels. The business grew and moved, but Fred's a sentimental fellow and has kept this store almost as a hobby. (He only

comes by on Saturdays; the rest of the time he's a pension planner in Westchester.) Frances (who declined to give her last name) has lived in Belmont for more than 50 years and is in charge of day-to-day operations. If you want to stay closer to the area's hub, you can buy excellent coffee beans for far less than you'd pay almost anywhere else in places such as **Marie's Roasted Coffee Beans and Gifts** (2378 Arthur Ave., Tel.: 212/295-0514), **Costanza's Gifts** (624 E. 187th St., Tel.: 212/933-7709), and **Cerini's Gifts** (660 E. 187th St., Tel.: 212/534-3449). Coffee beans are the most popular commodity in these stores, but you'll almost have to search for them among the ceramic and glass knickknacks, clocks, giant spaghetti bowls, chandeliers, vases, and other housewares and gifts. A sign in Marie's in Slavic and Italian warns customers to keep their hands off the china.

CAFÉS

Tired and want to sit down? We love **Caffè Margherita** (673 E. 187th St., Tel.: 212/364-8910). Owner Ralph de Fuccia, who came here from Naples in 1964, opened the café in 1976, and put his very personal, if delightfully eccentric, stamp on it. Inside are gaudy murals of an ancient Roman scene depicting the mythical Diana, surrounded by nude maidens, near the deer-headed god Neptune, flanked by doggy followers. A giant photo of Sylvester Stallone (in *Rocky II*) hangs nearby, and next to that is a giant photo of Ralph de Fuccia smoking a cigar. The café is full of hanging plants and plants in elaborate floor vases, which Ralph, who is also an artisan, made and decorated with dozens of seashells. He also set the marble floor himself. In warm weather, he brings umbrella-covered tables and chairs onto the sidewalk, along with a jukebox filled with mostly Italian records. Sip espresso here and watch the world of Belmont go by.

For a richer snack, a number of pastry shops have indoor café service so you can nosh on a cannoli squishy with sweet ricotta or a rum-soaked *baba* with your cappuccino. **Egidio's** (622 E. 187th St., Tel.: 212/295-6077) has been in the neighborhood for nearly 80 years. On the fringe of the neighborhood—you'll have to walk about five short blocks east from Arthur Avenue toward the Bronx Zoo to get there—is **C's Pastry Shop** (2373 Prospect Ave., Tel.: 212/367-5737). Tastefully renovated in wood and tile, with large, sun-filled picture windows, it has a huge selection of pastries and cookies, including spectacular napoleons and fruit tarts, cheesecakes, and giant cream pastries, a lovely espresso bar, and a comfortable seating area that transports the visitor to a small *villaggio* in southern Italy.

RESTAURANTS

For more than a pastry but less than a big meal, there is, of course, pizza. **Ann & Tony's** (2407 Arthur Ave., Tel.: 212/364-8250) and **Full Moon Pizzeria** (602 E. 187th St., Tel.: 212/584-3451) are old standbys, popular with tourists, comfortable but plain, and with good food. You're less likely to be tempted by the outside of **Maria & Joe's** (712 E. 187th St., Tel.: 212/584-3911), but you won't be disappointed if you go in, and we think it's special. Maria Salvaggi and her family,

originally from Palermo, Sicily, offer fresh pasta dishes, five kinds of *calzone* (stuffed dough), including ricotta and eggplant, luscious vegetable dishes, and a crusty potato pie that we especially recommend. You can eat in at one of the four Formica tables, or order food to go. You're not apt to see **Roma Luncheonette** (636 E. 187th St., on the corner of Belmont Ave.) in any guidebook, but it's a place that seems to have been transported intact from overseas. Its chubby red-and-white awnings are a bit fancy for the cube of an eatery that's inside, but there's an Italian villagelike atmosphere here that you won't find elsewhere. While a TV clatters away in the background, sometimes in Italian, sometimes in English, the proprietress, Signora Cerini, chats with customers in Italian, taking orders at her espresso bar or for sandwiches or *soup del giorno*, or sharing gossip and giving advice. On a cold day, a bowl of lentil, *ceci* (chick-pea), *piselli*, or *fagioli* soup is warm and filling, and there's a modest selection of pasta dishes and sandwiches. There's also a delicious homemade brandy-soaked ricotta cake. And there's anisette on the counter to add to your *caffè*.

For the family in for a visit to the city, **Mario's** (2342 Arthur Ave., Tel.: 212/584-1188) is the place to go, and people have been going since 1919. It's plush, big, noisy, and happily gaudy, but not formal, and don't be surprised if the waiter and the family sitting next to you are on a first-name basis. The menu selection is large, including such Neapolitan specialties as *spiedini alla romana* (a deep-fried mozzarella sandwich in anchovy sauce), octopus salad, and potato gnocchi (dumplings) in tomato sauce. **Dominick's,** across the street (2335 Arthur

Ave., Tel.: 212/733-2807), makes life just a bit easier for customers by its lack of a menu. Plain, small, and crowded, it is known for being able to serve just about any fish, meat, or pasta specialty a customer requests.

It's hard to keep yourself away from Arthur Avenue; even the barber shops and local shoe stores have a special neighborhood charm that seems to have vanished a generation or more ago from New York's other neighborhoods. You'll look forward to second or third visits as soon as possible, accompanied, perhaps, by trips to the

Counter folks at Egidio's.

nearby Bronx Zoo or New York Botanical Garden. Arthur Avenue is proof that a caring community can keep a neighborhood flourishing and lively even as adjacent areas decline.

Note: Don't leave Arthur Avenue without visiting the **Enrico Fermi Cultural Center** at 610 East 186th Street (corner of Hughes Avenue), which is the local branch of the New York Public Library. Opened in 1982, it has become a major resource for Italian-American studies with more than 35,000 books, hundreds of record albums, Italian-language periodicals, and extensive clip files on Italian-American history. The reading room is spacious and relaxing, and the center doubles as a community meeting place (Tel.: 212/933-6410).

S. CALANDRA & SONS CHEESE
JOSEPHINE CALANDRA'S RICOTTA CHEESECAKE

3 pounds ricotta cheese—"preferably
  ours"
8 eggs
1 cup sugar

2 tablespoons flour
2 teaspoons vanilla
one 3½-ounce jar orange
  marmalade

"Throw first five ingredients together," then stir in marmalade. Pour it all into a 10-inch greased spring pan and bake for one hour in a 350° F oven. Shut off the oven, but leave the cake in the *closed* oven for another hour. Eat.

BORGATTI'S
MARINARA SAUCE

two 28-ounce cans crushed plum
  tomatoes
⅓ cup salad oil
2 cloves of garlic, thinly sliced
10 chopped basil leaves (or 1
  tablespoon dried basil)

1 tablespoon chopped parsley (or 1
  teaspoon dried parsley)
salt to taste
freshly milled pepper to taste

Heat the oil in a saucepan and add the garlic, salt, and pepper. Cook slowly for 5 minutes. Add the remaining ingredients, and bring to a simmer, stirring often. Cook for 30 minutes.

FETTUCCINE ALFREDO

For each pound of fettuccine

6 ounces butter
½ cup heavy cream

1 egg yolk
½ cup grated Parmesan cheese
black pepper

While fettuccine are boiling in 6 to 8 quarts of salted water (Borgatti's fresh fettuccine cook in 4 to 5 minutes), carefully melt the butter (preferably in double-boiler top). Add the heavy cream and half of the Parmesan cheese while whisking the mixture together. Drain the noodles quickly to prevent overdrying. Toss them in a bowl with the hot sauce and the egg yolk and mix rapidly. Serve piping hot. Add grated cheese and freshly milled black pepper to individual portions as desired.

BOLOGNESE-STYLE MEAT SAUCE

1/3 cup oil
2 ounces salt pork, diced
1 clove garlic, finely chopped
1/2 cup chopped onion
1 cup chopped carrot
1 cup chopped celery
1 pound ground lean beef
1/2 cup white wine
1/2 cup light cream

2 cups broth (one 28-ounce can of
    peeled, crushed tomatoes and 1 cup
    of broth may be substituted)
1 tablespoon tomato paste
1 cup peas
2 ounces butter
salt and pepper to taste
1/2 teaspoon nutmeg

In a saucepan, heat the diced salt pork in the oil until the pork is light brown in color. Remove the salt pork. Add the finely chopped garlic to the oil and brown to taste. Add the onion and cook until translucent. Add the carrot and celery and cook until they soften and begin to change color. Add the ground beef; stir and cook until it turns brown in color. Pour in the wine and increase the heat to get a boiling action while stirring. Pour in the light cream and bring to a boil for 3 minutes. Dilute the tomato paste in the broth and add to the saucepan. Add the peas to the saucepan, cover, and allow to simmer for 45 minutes. Add the butter, salt and pepper, and nutmeg. Stir well and allow to cook at a simmer for 15 minutes.

FETTUCCINE CARBONARA

1 pound fettuccine
8 strips bacon
6 ounces unsalted butter
2 tablespoons finely chopped onion
6 ounces thickly sliced prosciutto
1 tablespoon finely chopped parsley

black pepper
1/3 cup white wine
1/2 cup heavy cream
1/2 cup milk
1/2 cup grated Parmesan cheese
1 egg yolk

While the water is set up to boil, cook the bacon and drain it thoroughly. Cut the prosciutto and bacon into half-inch squares. Melt the butter in a saucepan, add the minced onion, and sauté over a low flame until the onion is translucent. Add the cut-up bacon and prosciutto and stir over a low flame for 3 to 4 minutes.

Pour the wine into the saucepan and raise the flame to bring the mixture to a low boil for 5 minutes while stirring. Add the cream and milk and bring to a low boil again for 5 minutes. Lower the flame, and add the parsley and approximately half of the grated cheese. Pour the mixture over the boiled, drained pasta. Add the egg yolk and toss the pasta and sauce together thoroughly. Add grated cheese and freshly milled black pepper to individual portions.

PASTA TIPS FROM BORGATTI'S

Fresh-cut noodles may be kept in the refrigerator, in a paper bag, for several days. If a plastic bag is used, they may be kept for up to ten days under proper refrigeration. To keep them for a longer period of time, freeze them after wrapping properly (freezer wrap, foil, etc.). Dough for lasagne and manicotti may be kept in the same manner as fresh-cut noodles. Do not defrost frozen pasta prior to boiling. Cooking pasta: Put noodles into an ample quantity of boiling, salted water. As the water resumes boiling cook the noodles 4 to 5 minutes. (Spaghetti cut will require 8 minutes due to the greater thickness of the dough.) Extremely fine cuts, such as capellini and fedelini, cook in 3 to 4 minutes.

Manicotti and lasagne require only 1 minute of boiling time. (They are boiled only to make them soft enough to work with). Instead of draining them in a colander, where they may adhere to each other, it is advisable to run cold water into the pot (after the 1-minute boil) and to continue running the cold water until you can "fish" the lasagne strips or manicotti "squares" from the water with your fingers. Shake off the excess water as you remove the pieces of dough from the pot. It is usually best to place six or eight pieces on a clean cloth to further blot them and then work them into your baking pan. In the case of lasagne, alternate the strips with layers of sauce and filling.

In preparing manicotti, lay the "squares" flat on a cloth, placing filling across the center of the dough, not quite reaching the edges on each side. Turn up the edge nearest to you so that it lies on top of the filling. Then turn the back edge forward so that it lies on top of, and partially overlaps, the first edge. You now have a "cannoli-like" tube that you turn over and place seam down into a baking pan on a layer or bed of sauce. Continue until the pan has a complete layer of filled manicotti. Spoon more sauce over the top of them and bake.

The recommended baking time for lasagne and manicotti is 40 to 45 minutes at 375° F. After removing the pan from the oven, allow it to set about 10 minutes before serving. Additional sauce may be added to individual portions as desired.

A good basic filling for lasagne and manicotti is a mixture of 1 pound ricotta, 1 whole egg, ¼ cup grated cheese, and salt and pepper to taste. If desired, add parsley and mozzarella, and, for lasagne, precooked sausage and/or meatballs.

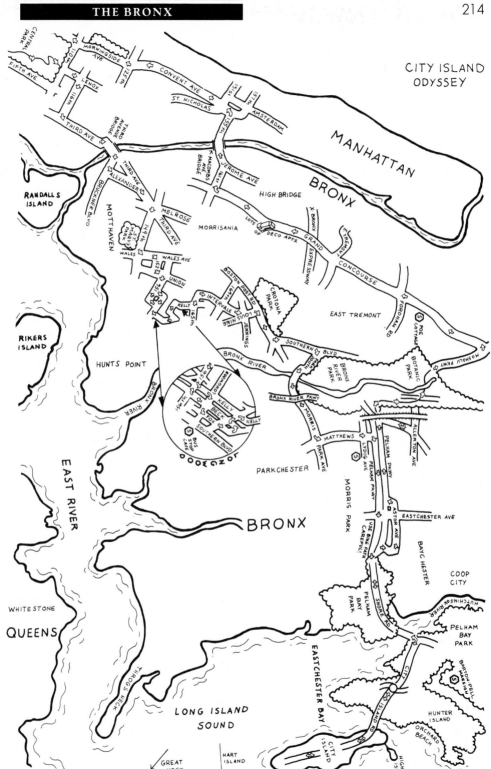

CITY ISLAND
ODYSSEY

CENTRAL PARK

MORNINGSIDE AVE

FIFTH AVE

LENOX

CONVENT AVE

125th

145th

ST. NICHOLAS

AMSTERDAM

151st

155th

THIRD AVENUE BRIDGE

THIRD AVE

ALEXANDER

BRUCKNER BLVD

THIRD AVE

JEROME AVE

MACOMBS AVE BRIDGE

161st

HIGH BRIDGE

MANHATTAN

BRONX

RANDALLS ISLAND

MOTTHAVEN

MELROSE

ST. MARY'S PARK

THIRD AVE

WALES

149th

WALES AVE

151st

163rd

UNION

MORRISANIA

LOTS OF DECO APTS.

X. BRONX EXPRESSWAY

GRAND CONCOURSE

E. TREMONT

FORDHAM RD

POE COTTAGE

INTERVALE

151st

BOSTON POST RD

LOUIS NINE

JENNINGS

KELLY

165th

CROTONA PARK

EAST TREMONT

SOUTHERN BLVD

BOTANIC GARDEN

MOSHOLU PKWY

RIKERS ISLAND

HUNTS POINT

BRONX RIVER

BRONX RIVER

156th

LONGWOOD

KELLY

BECK

FOX

SOUTHERN BLVD

BUS STOP CAFE

KELLY

KELLY

BRONX RIVER

BRONX RIVER PKWY

BRONX RIVER PARK

MADISON

MORRIS'S

ALLERTON AVE

MATTHEWS

PARK AVE

LYDIG AVE

PELHAM PKWY

BOTANIC GARDEN

PARKCHESTER

MORRIS PARK

PELHAM PKWY

ASTOR AVE

EASTCHESTER AVE

BAYCHESTER

COOP CITY

EAST RIVER

USE BIKE PATH CAREFUL!

SHORE RD

HUTCHINSON RIVER

BRONX

PELHAM BAY PARK

PELHAM BAY PARK

WHITE STONE

QUEENS

THROGS NECK

CITY ISLAND RD

BARTOW-PELL MANSION

EASTCHESTER BAY

HUNTER ISLAND

ORCHARD BEACH

LONG ISLAND SOUND

CITY ISLAND

HIGH ISLAND

GREAT NECK

HART ISLAND

CITY ISLAND SAIL

To Get There

By bus: Take the Bx12 bus toward City Island/Rochelle St. The bus run begins at 207th St. and Broadway in Manhattan, at the northern terminus of the A train and near the IRT 1 Broadway local. It runs across the Bronx along Fordham Rd. and Pelham Pkwy., connecting with every subway in the Bronx.

By car: Take the Hutchinson River Pkwy. to Pelham Park. Follow the signs to City Island.

By bike: See "City Island Odyssey" tour on page 235.

City Island, attached to New York City only by name and a narrow causeway, first witnessed development in the form of a solar salt works in the 1830s. Before that it changed hands rather frequently, serving variously as collateral for loans; home to, alternately, British and American troops during the Revolutionary War; and the site of an abortive seaside entertainment spot for city folk. From the mid-nineteenth century on, City Island prospered on the strength of its oystermen's efforts. It later gained fame for its shipbuilders, who constructed several America's Cup winners on the island. Today, although it is actually on Long Island Sound, it survives as one of the city's most tangible links to the sea, where urban fishermen, bicyclists, sunbathers, and water-gazers alike can live the fiction of an oceanside existence.

For some, though, the salty seaside life is more than a Sunday-afternoon fantasy. Several sailmaking operations thrive, and there are fishermen who still ply Long Island Sound. There are hundreds of boats, many of them inhabited year round by people who commute to Manhattan during the week. Everywhere on the island, for visitors and old-timers alike, there's always the tangy taste of salt on the tongue, and the sparkle of sun on the sea is never more than a fair-weather day away.

The strip of City Island Avenue is lined with marine tackle shops, sailboats that have pulled up onto the edge of the main street, a couple of picturesque churches, and far too many restaurants. The eateries wear names like Johnny's Reef, Tony's Pier, Lobster Box, Neptune Inn, and so on. For the most part, they serve relatively pricey, standard fare. Not surprisingly, there's lots of seafood.

RESTAURANTS

Restaurants on City Island tend to be expensive. The two most prominent exceptions are at the far end of the island: **Tony's Pier** (1 City Island Ave., Tel.: 212/885-1424) and **Jimmy's Reef Restaurant** (2 City Island Ave., Tel.: 212/885-9732, an outdoor pay phone).

Anna's Harbor (565 City Island Ave., Tel.: 212/885-1373) bills itself as City Island's most elegant restaurant, and it's true. It's a long, cavernous place, so make sure you get a waterfront seat. Entrées are in the $12 to $21 range, and you're paying for the view of the marina and, off in the distance, the Manhattan skyline.

Twilly's (272 City Island Ave., Tel.: 212/885-9781) has a fine backyard garden that provides a nice respite on a summer day. The extremely limited menu has light Mexican appetizers and, of course, a seafood salad. There is a good selection of tasty ice cream concoctions, starting with sundaes and becoming progressively more elaborate.

For a change, you might check out the Offshore Sailing Club's **Café Offshore** (190 E. Schofield St., one block east of Main St., Tel.: 212/885-3200). This small, pleasant hideaway has a small outdoor deck, an authentic yachting atmosphere, and a view of plenty of sailboats. It's open during the summer only. If you're smitten, you can sign up for sailing lessons.

WALKING TOUR

No matter what you do, make sure you wander off City Island Avenue onto some of the side streets. There are two parallel streets at the northeastern end of the island, Minnieford and King Avenues, which are worth exploring. Some very small streets in the area, almost alleys, are even nicer. Turn sharply left, almost doubling back, as soon as you get over the City Island Bridge for the best tour of this northeastern part of the island. (You can also take any of several streets to the left off City Island Avenue.) If you like graveyards, Pelham Cemetery, at King and Reville Streets, is a nice spot to relax. It's on the eastern side of the island with a nice view over the water. If you're more adventurous, walk over to Orchard Beach (especially in the off-season), part of Pelham Bay Park, one of the largest parks in the Bronx.

LYDIG AVENUE: A RICH ETHNIC STEW

To Get There

By subway: Take the IRT 2 or 5 train to White Plains Rd. Lydig Ave. is parallel to Pelham Pkwy., one block south.

By car: From Manhattan, cross the 145th St. Bridge and follow 149th St. to Third Ave.; fork right when it meets Boston Rd. Continue north on Boston Rd. and turn right onto E. Tremont Ave. to White Plains Rd. Turn left to the Pelham Pkwy./Lydig Ave. area.

By bike: See "City Island Odyssey" tour on page 235.

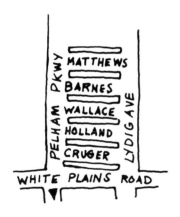

▲ = #2,5 IRT TRAIN

MARKETS, BAKERIES, AND SHOPS

Once a virtually all-Jewish area, including many World War II refugees, the Pelham Parkway neighborhood is now a rich ethnic stew combining the older community with young Oriental families, Russian immigrants, Albanians, Italians, and others. The Bronx Municipal Hospital complex at Pelham Parkway and Morris Park Avenue attracts many people in the medical professions. The result is a mix of old-fashioned kosher and Jewish (though not kosher) bakeries and markets, Israeli felafel restaurants, and newer food shops and produce stores that offer a huge variety of foods. On both Saturdays—when the kosher stores are shut—and Sundays, the area is clogged with shoppers, often out on family excursions. White Plains Road has several large delicatessens and restaurants, while Lydig Avenue is dense with smaller neighborhood-type markets. One of the most interesting, newest additions to the area is **Luba's Deli-Dairy & Grocery** (745 Lydig Ave., Tel.: 212/822-3505). Luba Konkin, originally from Odessa, moved to the Bronx in the late 1970s and opened her shop in 1985. Its stock is huge but particularly reflects her Russian tastes: herring, prunes, several types of caviar (among them sevruga, beluga, and sturgeon), baked milk-and-kvas (kvas is a Russian malt-barley drink), and East European specialties, such as pickled watermelon and apples. There are also several kinds of farmer cheeses, including a homemade plain cheese and flavored cheeses like nut-raisin, peach, pineapple, and blueberry. There are sausages from all over Europe, as well as luscious tub butter and fancy Italian chocolates. You'll also find cans of Russian and Georgian black teas. Nearby, **Gruenebaum's Bakery** (741 Lydig Ave., Tel.: 212/828-7265) is one of a small chain of kosher bakeries in New York City. Its warm, old-fashioned ambience—the counter folks are on a first-name basis with many of the bakery's mostly elderly customers—is matched by the high quality of its strudels, coffee *babkas*, chocolate cakes, and varieties of nut, fruit-flavored, and chocolate-dipped cookies. **Helen's Bake Shop** (757 Lydig Ave., Tel.: 212/822-9013) is a crowded, friendly place with a Jewish ambience, although it's not kosher. It doubles as a community meeting place and the walls are crowded with notices of local events. **Jack's Dairy** (733 Lydig Ave., Tel.: 212/792-0455) is a small grocery specializing in dairy products. **International Food and Appetizers** (709 Lydig Ave., Tel.: 212/822-7413) is a Russian-owned market with a good range of gourmet-type offerings, including Bulgarian eggplant, pomegranate juice, and fish specialties.

Lydig Avenue is a great place to shop when you're visiting the nearby Bronx Zoo or New York Botanical Garden.

CAMBODIA IN THE BRONX

To Get There

 By subway: Take the IRT 2 to Bronx Park East; follow Morris Park Ave. (you'll be at its beginning) for 10 minutes until you reach the market near White Plains Road. (If you're tired, there are plenty of small Italian cafés where you can sip espresso and rest your feet.)

 By car: From the Cross Bronx Expressway, exit onto White Plains Road. The market is on Morris Park Ave. just off White Plains Road.

 By bike: Follow the "City Island Odyssey" tour on page 235 to Morris Park Ave., and look for the market at the Morris Park Ave. and White Plains Rd. intersection, five blocks before the turnoff onto Matthews Ave.

Morris Park Avenue, stretching from the edge of the South Bronx to the edge of Pelham Parkway, is dotted with Italian social clubs, dairies, espresso cafés, bakeries, meat shops, and delicatessens—and the **Angkor Market** (689A Morris Park Ave., Tel.: 212/822-6078), possibly New York City's only Cambodian grocery. Owner Luy Yuthy opened Angkor to serve a small but growing Southeast Asian community in the Bronx, including newcomers from Laos, Thailand, and Vietnam, and most of the stock is from Thailand, China, and the Philippines. The Cambodian refugee community also has a temple in the Bronx, located at 2748 Marion Avenue near Fordham University.

STATEN ISLAND

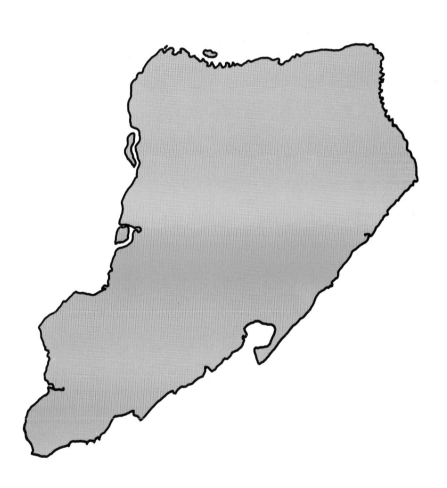

Staten Island is much more than one end of the world's most spectacular ferry ride. Between its spiny hills and its hidden coves are some of the wildest areas in New York City. There are marshes hiding tumbledown shacks that could be from a rural backwater, a quiet, gleaming boardwalk that looks out on the Atlantic, and vast wooded parks that snake among the hills. From its heights are spectacular views of Brooklyn, Manhattan, and New York Harbor.

Staten Island never had the crush of immigrants that the other boroughs felt, so there are no ethnic neighborhoods that stake out their claim against a surrounding cityscape. There are, however, separate towns that have not been overpowered by the pace of development and in them are traces of the island's Dutch and, more recently, Italian inhabitants. Because Staten Island has been less developed there is also a sense of history that survives as nowhere else in the city. **Richmondtown Restoration** is an ambitious attempt to recreate a colonial village, while the **Conference House** in Tottenville, at the southern tip of the island, stands much as it did when Benjamin Franklin and John Adams rejected the British offer of amnesty for American rebels there in 1776.

Staten Island attracted wealthy vacationers in search of rustic pleasures for a time during the second half of the nineteenth century. (Among the less wealthy visitors were Henry David Thoreau and Ralph Waldo Emerson.) The country's first lawn tennis court and first canoe club were both on Staten Island to entertain this crowd. Of course, Staten Island was always much more than a playground for the rich. Most of the people who lived there were fishermen and farmers. There was no flood of immigration, because there was little industrial development. Some of the most interesting immigrants were Italian patriots, many of whom, including Giuseppe Garibaldi, came to Staten Island after one or another of the abortive uprisings against Austrian rule in Italy during the early part of the nineteenth century. Even today, there's a remnant of a settlement of freed blacks who had been oyster fishers in Staten Island beginning in the mid-nineteenth century. Known as **Sandy Ground** and located in Arthur Kill, this area is now a Federal Historic District. It is a collection of old wood houses and a church surrounded by the condominiums of the new Staten Island.

Staten Island has shaken off its sleepy past since the completion of the Verrazano Narrows Bridge in 1964. Unfortunately, much of the development has been an unplanned sprawl. But with a little bit of persistence you can discover some of the city's most unexpected pleasures in what remains the least developed borough.

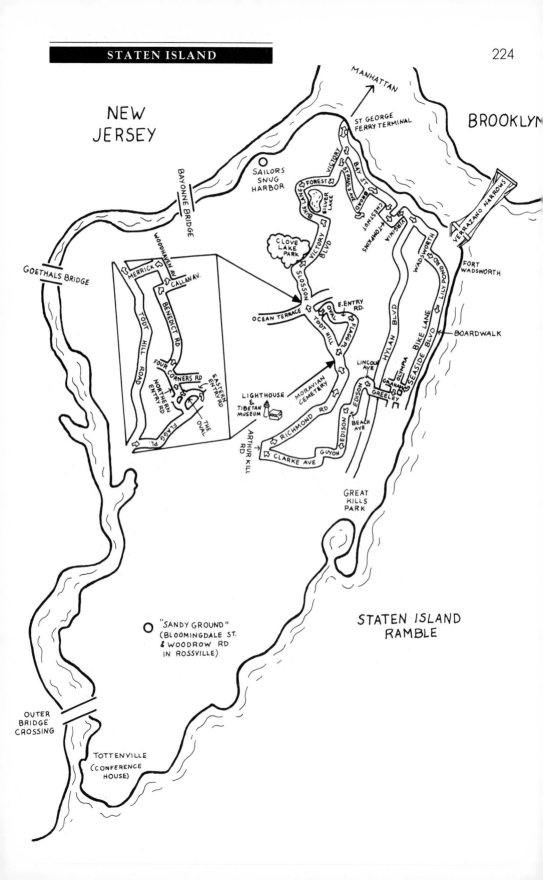

SURF & TURF: NEW YORK'S COUNTRY BOROUGH

To Get There

By ferry: New York's most stunning travel bargain is the 25-cent (round trip) ride from Battery Park, Manhattan, to St. George, Staten Island.

By subway: Take the R train from Manhattan to 95th St., Brooklyn, the last stop. The #7 bus runs from there to Staten Island.

By bike: See tour directions for the "Staten Island Ramble" on page 256 to come from Manhattan.

Orientation: There is a Rapid Transit line and bus service on Staten Island, but to really explore you need either a bicycle or a car. (If you drive, you may want to take the Verrazano Narrows Bridge at least one way.)

RESTAURANTS

If there's a native cuisine in Staten Island, it's probably fast food, since there seem to be more franchise food outlets per inhabitant than anywhere else in the city. Staten Islanders take an almost perverse pleasure in extolling the lack of good eateries in the borough. "It's terrible, just terrible," said one Staten Islander we found eating pizza in Brooklyn. When the *Staten Island Advance* recently listed its pick of the top ten restaurants, two of them were in Brooklyn! Confesses an *Advance* reporter: "I go to Manhattan when I want to go out to eat." As always, persistence rewards the urban adventurer. **Richmondtown Restoration** serves authentic early American dinners during the summer. **Basilio** offers dining that is closer to the Italian countryside than anywhere in Manhattan. And, of course, running through the alphabet from **Angela's Pizza** to **Villa Capri,** there are scores of Italian restaurants. Here's a sampling of some of the more endearing eateries.

Reason enough to visit Staten Island, **Basilio** (2 Galesville Court, between the Verrazano Narrows Bridge and South Beach in Arrochar, Tel.: 718/447-9292), is a charming, moderately priced Italian restaurant set in a nineteenth-century carriage house. There's a grape arbor on one side of the house, a boccie court in the back, and, of course, opera music in the background. The Asperti family runs the restaurant as a bit of the old country: On a balmy summer evening it's not hard to imagine that you're dining in an Italian villa. Basilio is only open from April through the first week in January. (Good news for nondrivers: Basilio is easily accessible by the #7 bus from the end of the R line in Brooklyn or the #2 bus from the ferry: Both let you off at McLean Avenue and Lily Pond Avenue; Basilio is two short blocks ahead on Lily Pond Avenue—turn right on Galesville Court.)

To reach **Brown & Ferri** (396 Van Duzer St., Stapleton, Tel.: 718/273-6890), take Staten Island Rapid Transit to Stapleton. Walk up Prospect Street two blocks, and make a left on Van Duzer St. The restaurant is two blocks ahead, between Beach and Wright Streets. Return via Wright Street and you'll walk through a restored square that was once the center of a thriving Tomkinsville. A renovated mid-nineteenth-century house, it contains a formal dining room downstairs serving hearty American food—rack of lamb, duck, swordfish—with a light nouvelle touch (entrées are priced from $10 to $18). Upstairs there's a bar, marble tables, and light café food—pizzas, oysters, salads, pastas, and burgers (mostly under $5). "People think we're a French restaurant because we use brown sauce or a fruit sauce," says Mary Anne Malzone, "but I'm Italian and my partner Kathy Maher is Irish." There are also outstanding homemade desserts.

"Paella and an Ocean View" is the slogan at **Carmen's** (750 Barclay Ave., off Hyland Blvd., Tel.: 718/948-9786). The food—Spanish and Mexican—is uneven, but the view from this charming *hacienda*-style restaurant overlooking Raritan Bay is always stunning.

DeNino's Tavern (524 Port Richmond Ave., near the Bayonne Bridge, Tel.: 718/442-9401) is a popular Italian pizzeria with a front section that doubles as a poolroom and bar; its dining room is often packed.

Forest Inn Restaurant (834 Forest Ave. near Broadway, Tel.: 718/727-6060) is Staten Island's answer to Tavern on the Green—glassy, flowery, and lit up at night like a birthday cake.

La Candela Española (3932 Amboy Rd., Great Kills, Tel.: 718/356-8798) is a 5-minute walk from the Great Kills Rapid Transit Station. Get off at the back of the train if you're coming from the ferry. Turn right on Gifford Lane and, a half-block later, turn left on Amboy Road. The restaurant is one-and-a-half short blocks ahead. It serves good Spanish and Mexican food in an unprepossessing atmosphere.

Lido (37 Victory Blvd., St. George's, Tel.: 718/447-9247) has a nice wood-paneled bar ringed with prints by Staten Island artist John Noble. It has the character of an old-style place, which it is, and offers moderate prices for unpretentious food.

Marina Café (154 Mansion Ave., Great Kills, Tel.: 718/967-3077) is at the foot of Hillside Terrace, about a 20-minute walk from Great Kills Rapid Transit Station. Follow the directions given above for La Candela Española; take the first right off of Amboy Road onto Hillside Terrace and follow it down to the water. This marina restaurant offers a nice glassed-in view of Great Kills Harbor. There's a continental menu, complete with *chateaubriand*, and a heavy emphasis on seafood, but you're mainly paying for the view.

If you make it to Richmondtown Restoration, **M. Bennet Refreshments** (3730 Richmond Rd., Tel.: 718/979-5258) will sustain you for the long trek back with a snack or light meal.

Montezuma's Revenge is now **Montezuma La Fosse Aux Loups** (11 Schuyler St., St. George, Tel.: 718/442-9111). Perhaps Staten Island's best restaurant, Montezuma specializes in new American cooking. The only problem: It's so good and so near the ferry that it's in danger of being overrun by non-Islanders. Notoriety has already prompted the owners to gussy up the restaurant with cool colors and, of course, to raise the prices.

Sports Bar at the Caves (742 Van Duzer St. at Broad St., Tel.: 718/442-1396) is a sports lover's paradise or a mediaphobe's nightmare: This former brewery has giant video screens and smaller monitors strung around the room. You can watch up to eight games at once and catch up on the others with a computerized sports ticker. In addition to a full bar, there is sports food: burgers, steaks, and thick sandwiches.

A newly opened bar/restaurant with a light, cheery atmosphere, **R.H. Tugs** (1115 Richmond Terrace, one long block south of Sailors Snug Harbor, Tel.: 718/447-6369) is replete with a big wooden bar, ceiling fans, and a view out over the water—to New Jersey's nearby refineries. Reasonably priced food runs the gamut from light fare like salads to more substantial victuals like steaks. There are some imaginative pizzas, such as broccoli, shrimp, and Texas beef, and a well-chosen sensibly priced wine list.

Road House Restaurant (1402 Clove Rd., between Victory Blvd. and the Staten Island Expressway, Tel.: 718/447-0033) is a hopping pizzeria with a nice wood bar out front that's famed for its clam pies (the pizzas aren't served until 5 P.M.). The hero sandwiches—try the fried eggplant, pepper, and salami combo—are also quite good.

There's lots of garlic at **Spain Restaurant** (502 Jewett Ave., Tel.: 718/816-8237), which specializes in seafood dishes, including paella and lobster.

The Staten Island Historical Society (441 Clarke Ave., Tel.: 718/351-9414) has a series of authentic early American dinners every July and August. The evening dinners feature meats like roast beef or turkey cooked on an open spit; seasonal vegetables; home-baked bread and home-churned butter; pies with seasonal fruit; and much more. Call the Society for more information; if you'd like to be fully apprised of events you can become a member.

The Society also sponsors occasional tours for groups with special interests. For the Culinary Restoration Society, Society members arranged a visit highlighting cooking implements, food preparation, and the like in colonial times.

"A typical trendy place," is how the waiter describes **Waterfront Café** (809 Father Capodanno Blvd. near Slater Blvd., Midland Beach, Tel.: 718/979-1888), right across from the South Beach boardwalk. Yes, but almost all the salads, pastas, and other light fare served in this glassy, angular restaurant are under $5. If you want a break from the beach, or you're just cycling by, this is a great find.

MARKETS

Open since 1887, **Montalbano's** (1134 Bay St., Rosebank, Tel.: 718/448-8077) stands with the best delis in Little Italy—except its prices are so much cheaper. "It's not Balducci's," avers a Staten Islander—no, not at all. But the store is straining at the seams, ready to burst with dried mushrooms, bags of oregano and chili pepper, carob pods, dozens of kinds of pasta, meats, cheeses, and the house specialties: breads filled with vegetables (broccoli or cauliflower) or meat and cheese (salami, sausage, and provolone). There is also a good selection of inexpensive olive oils.

There are a number of other good small markets farther along Bay Street in Rosebank, as well as scattered around Staten Island, but with the exception of Montalbano's we haven't found any worth going out of your way for.

Appendix:
Hungry Pedalers
Gourmet Bicycle Tours

TIPS ON CITY CYCLING AND THE HUNGRY PEDALERS TOURS

Cycling in New York City isn't much different from cycling anywhere else: You need common sense, some experience, and careful preparation. The city has many great bike lanes, including shoreline routes and park paths, but it's inevitable that you'll find yourself from time to time on high-traffic streets or on roads with almost no shoulder. So just follow these guidelines, and you'll find your cycle touring a breeze.

1. *Make sure your bike's in good shape.* If you haven't ridden in a while, check the following: Are your brakes properly adjusted? (If your fingers touch the handlebars when you squeeze the brake levers, the cables may be loose. Have them tightened, or replaced.) Do your gears switch easily? If your bike has three or more speeds, can you switch gears to each one? Is the frame clean? Are your tire treads so worn down that the tires are almost bald? Are the tires fresh or are the walls dried and cracked? Does your bike have any nasty squeaks that make everyone around you grimace? If you don't do your own repairs, it's time for an overhaul at your local bike shop. An overhaul can be anything from a quick once-over to a thorough cleaning and greasing of your bike hubs and bottom bracket and replacement of cables. It's wise to shop around to get estimates of the cost and to ask precisely what will be done. A good overhaul is worth the cost—you'll come out with an almost new bike.

2. *Wear a helmet.* A hard-shell helmet is an excellent investment, whether you're cycling in the city or countryside. The latest models cost between $30 and $50, are lightweight and well ventilated, and provide good protection in case of rain. White and bright-colored helmets also make you more visible in traffic.

3. *Be prepared* . . . with a pump, patch kit, spare inner tube, good lock—and a subway token. If you don't know how to change flats and you're not near a bike shop, you can take your bike on the subway—except during rush hours. Better yet, take a basic bike repair course before you start long touring. American Youth Hostels, local Y's, and many adult night schools offer classes, and several illustrated guides offer step-by-step how-to's. Do-it-yourself bike maintenance sounds intimidating until you find out how easy it really is. Keep a good Swiss army knife on hand, too; it's great for picnics and handy in aiding with repairs. Find out in advance where the nearest bike stores are on your route (the *Yellow Pages* is a good reference), and invest in a few basic tools: three tire irons, pliers, and a 6-inch adjustable wrench. A patch kit is handy in case you need to repair your inner tube. (If you use your spare, save the damaged one and repair it at home. It's great in emergencies.) Oh yes—bring tissue, waterless hand cleaner, or Handiwipes. It's no fun cycling with greasy fingers, and these are convenient for after-meal riding.

Also . . . keep a rain poncho on hand, and bring a pair of panniers (saddlebags). You just might find yourself tempted to do shopping, and you'll be glad to have the storage space. Extra stretch cords (also known as "bungies") are useful to attach things to your rack. (Do you have a rack? If not, get one!) In warm weather, you might want to bring a plastic water bottle made for bikes: These are inexpensive and handy—most fit in cages that go on the frame, and in hot weather it's very important to drink frequently and not get dehydrated. (Water bottles are less important in the city, since in a pinch you can almost always find a deli where you can buy bottled water or juice.)

4. *Locks.* A good U-shaped lock costs $25 to $35 (Citadel and Kryptonite are the best-known brands). That may sound expensive, but these locks are extremely hard to break and include insurance policies if your bike is stolen due to lock failure. If your front wheel has a quick-release lever, remove the wheel and lock it with your rear wheel, and make sure your frame is locked, too.

5. *What about traffic?* Most of our routes stay away from major traffic roads, but we couldn't avoid all of them. So . . . (1) be sure to ride in the same direction as traffic; (2) use the proper hand signals to indicate turns; (3) observe traffic lights and stop signs; and (4) don't ride too close to parked cars in case a passenger suddenly opens the door on the street side. If you're with friends, ride single file when you hit traffic—and then don't ride too close together. If the person in front stops short, you could have a rear-end collision and lose a friend as well as, perhaps, a good wheel! Always be alert for glass and potholes: These are an unfortunate fact of city life, although we've noticed substantial repaving in recent years, and the New York State bottle bill has left the streets noticeably cleaner.

6. *A final tip.* Our maps and written instructions are as thorough as we could make them, but it's a good idea to take along a complete city map in case you want to change your route or take a shortcut home. (Square-bracketed numbers in the tour directions refer to miles completed.) Of course, we can't account for street repairs or construction, so be alert for possible detours.

BRIGHTON BEACH K'NISH K'NOSH

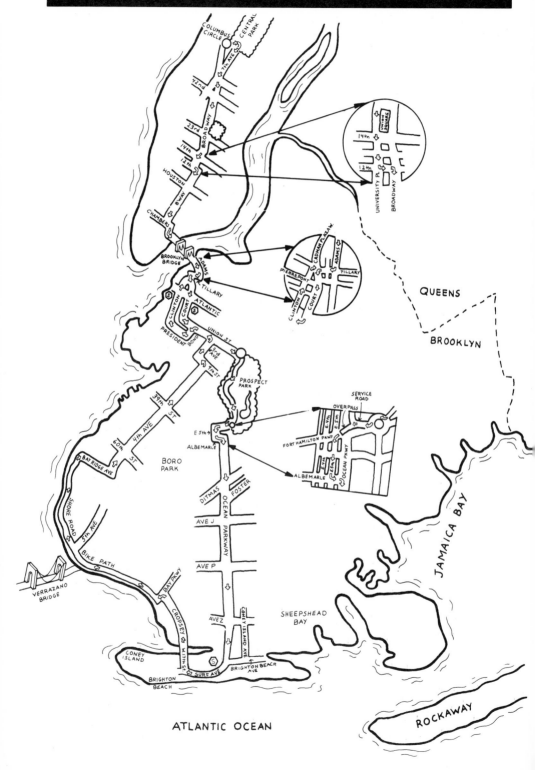

Pedal through Brooklyn's Prospect Park and along Ocean Parkway to "Little Odessa," nosh a knish at the famous Mrs. Stahl's, stroll along the Boardwalk or explore the neighborhood, then head home with a shoreline ride followed by a stop for hummus, babaganouj, and other Middle Eastern delights on Atlantic Avenue. Bring a bathing suit if it's summertime!

TOTAL DISTANCE: **38 Miles.**

[0.0 Miles] Start at Columbus Circle (59th St. and Eighth Ave.). Ride into Central Park and take the first exit onto Seventh Ave. Go downtown on Seventh Ave., bearing left on Broadway at Times Square (44th St.). Continue on Broadway through Herald Square (34th St.) and Madison Square (23rd St.). Bear right at 17th St. onto Union Square West, which becomes University Place south of 14th St.

[2.7] Turn left on 12th St. Make a right back onto Broadway. Follow Broadway all the way downtown to City Hall Park. Turn left on Chambers St. On your right is the back of the Tammany Hall Courthouse. One block later turn right on Centre St.

[4.6] Get onto the Brooklyn Bridge walkway, which begins just south of the corner of Centre St., and follow the bridge walkway all the way to the end (don't take the first set of stairs).

[6.1] Turn right onto Tillary St. for two blocks. Turn left onto Cadman Plaza West, which turns into Court St. (Brooklyn Heights is to your right.)

[6.7] Continue on Court St. across Atlantic Ave. Brooklyn's Arab section (see page 6) is to the right.

[7.3] Turn left on Union St. in Carroll Gardens (see page 44). Union St. descends, crosses the Gowanus Canal, and then climbs through Park Slope, home of some of New York's most distinctive and finely crafted brownstones.

[8.9] At the top of Union St. is Grand Army Plaza (modeled after L'Étoile in Paris) and the entrance to Prospect Park. The park was built by Frederick Law Olmsted and Calvert Vaux, who considered this a finer work than Central Park, which they had previously designed. Enter the park and bear right on the park drive.

[10.5] Exit at Ocean Pkwy./Coney Island Ave. Go straight through the intersection and take the first right off the traffic circle. (The street is marked Fort Hamilton Pkwy., although this is actually a small road parallel to the main road.) Take the pedestrian/bike overpass a couple of hundred feet down the road, opposite E. 7th St. Turn left at the end of the overpass onto E. 5th St. and continue three blocks.

[11.2] Turn left on Albemarle Rd. One short block later turn right onto Ocean Pkwy. The bicycle path along the parkway, between the service road and the main road, begins two blocks later. Follow this all the way to Brighton Beach Ave., just as cyclists have done for nearly a century, since Ocean Pkwy. was constructed in 1894. Ten thousand people rode out to Coney Island on opening day. One disadvantage today: Cars turn on and off the parkway. Be especially careful near the end, where there's an entrance to the Shore Pkwy.

[16.2] Turn left under the el onto Brighton Beach Ave. to explore the Russian area or to get to the less crowded beach. (See page 16 for more information. To continue on to Coney Island follow the directions below.)

To get home: The fastest way back is to retrace your route out. Here's a nicer alternative that will take you along the waterfront:

[16.2] Turn left back onto Ocean Pkwy., so that you're continuing in the same direction you were on the way out. Bear right as Ocean Pkwy. curves around to Coney Island and becomes Surf Ave. It's all here: the New York Aquarium (moved to Coney Island from lower Manhattan in 1955 in a fit of spite by Robert Moses), the Astroland Amusement Park, Nathan's Hot Dogs, sideshows, used furniture joints, 4-feet-tall pink rabbits, and other brightly colored, larger-than-life stuffed animals.

[17.2] Turn right onto West 17th St., which turns into Cropsey Ave. and leads over the sluggish Coney Island Creek—all that's left of the waters that separated the island from the rest of Long Island—and the Belt Pkwy.

[19.0] Turn left onto the Bay Pkwy. (not well marked: just past Bay 31) and pass under the Belt Pkwy., through the right-hand side of a shopping center parking lot and out onto a stunning view of the Lower New York Bay, Staten Island, and northern New Jersey.

[19.3] Make a right onto the bicycle/pedestrian path that begins by the ball field. (Cycling is prohibited for the first hundred yards.) The path hugs the shore for more than four glorious miles, winding underneath the Verrazano Narrows Bridge and along the Narrows, and finishes with a stunning view of lower Manhattan.

[23.7] A pier marks the end of the shore path. Turn right, once again passing under the Belt Pkwy., and pedal uphill on Bay Ridge Ave. to Fourth Ave.

[24.5] Turn left on Fourth Ave., a well-traveled street, and follow it all the way to Union St. (four blocks past 1st St.).

[28.2] Turn left on Union St., cross the Gowanus Canal, and immediately bear left onto Bond St. Take the first right onto President St. One block later, you'll take a short jog left onto Hoyt and an immediate right onto President. Follow President St. for three blocks through Carroll Gardens (see page 44).

[29.2] Turn right onto Clinton St., a lovely street that passes through Cobble Hill, crosses Atlantic Ave., and then goes through Brooklyn Heights. Clinton St. bears right and dumps you back onto Tillary St. at Borough Plaza.

[30.2] Continue straight; the bike path over the Brooklyn Bridge is two blocks ahead.

[30.4] Turn left at Adams St. to get back onto the Brooklyn Bridge.

[31.9] To return uptown in Manhattan: Continue straight, on Centre St., at the end of the bike path. Centre St. becomes Lafayette St.

[33.3] At Astor Place (8th St.) you can turn right onto St. Mark's Place and continue east to First Ave. A left on First Ave. will take you up the east side. Or continue straight, as Lafayette St. becomes Fourth Ave., which becomes Park Ave. at 14th St. Turn left on 9th St. to get to the west side. On weekends both Sixth Ave. (which has a bike lane of sorts) and Eighth Ave. are tolerable.

CITY ISLAND ODYSSEY

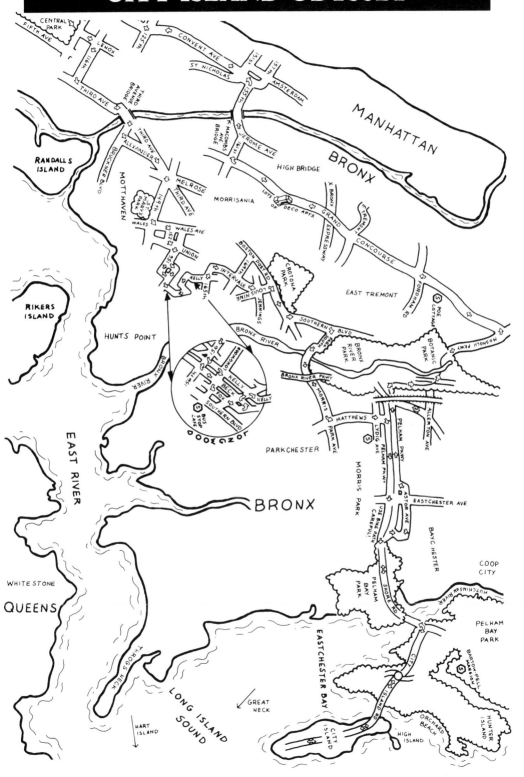

This tour to New York's salty fishing village in the Bronx includes the Mott Haven and Longwood Historic Districts, and leisurely cycling along Pelham Parkway. Return via the Grand Concourse, one of New York's grandest boulevards.

TOTAL DISTANCE: **38 miles.**

[0.0 miles] Begin at the Maine Monument, 59th St. and Central Park West. Enter Central Park and ride with the traffic (counterclockwise) until you reach the north end.

[3.4] Exit at Lenox Ave. (and 110th St.) and ride north on Lenox Ave. Turn right on 116th St. Turn left on Third Ave. (For more information on this area see the "Spanish Harlem" section on page 142.) Third Ave. ends at 128th St. Cross the Harlem River using the sidewalk directly across 128th St., which leads to the pedestrian walkway on the Third Ave. Bridge.

[5.4] Turn right on Bruckner Blvd. immediately after the bridge. Make a left on Alexander Ave. (two blocks later). The Mott Haven Historic District is centered on Alexander Ave. between 137th and 141st Sts. Two churches, a police station, and a library anchor a neighborhood of row houses and apartment buildings that has weathered the abandonment of the South Bronx surprisingly well.

[5.9] Make a left onto 141st St. and make an immediate right onto Third Ave.

[6.3] Make a right on 149th St. (center of a bustling shopping area known as "The Hub").

[6.9] Make a left on Wales Ave. A series of quick turns follows: right on 152nd St.; left on Union St.; right on 156th St. Bear right on Leggett Ave. at Dawson St., where 156th St. becomes one way. Next is a left on Beck St.; then a right on Longwood Ave. (Note the bas-relief wall sculpture of neighborhood residents high on a wall one block to your left.) Take the next left onto Fox St. (The Bus Stop Café, a nice neighborhood bakery, is one block further, at the corner of Longwood Ave. and Southern Blvd.)

Longwood is both an historic district and a dynamic neighborhood. Along with the surrounding areas, it is home to some of the most dynamic revitalization efforts in the Bronx. Check out Tiffany Plaza, one block north of Fox St. and Intervale Ave. Also note the new housing recently constructed; the Banana Kelly group has been particularly successful with its development on Kelly St. north of Intervale Ave.

[7.9] Make a left on Intervale Ave. Continue to the end and bear left on Louis Nine Ave.

[9.2] Make a right on Boston Rd. (For more information on the single-family houses here, see page 196)

[9.6] Bear left onto Southern Blvd. where Boston Rd. crosses under the el.

[10.4] Make a right onto Bronx Park South (at the edge of the zoo); then right on Boston Rd. (for one block) and left on 180th St. Make a left on Morris Park Ave. (under the el). (Morris Park boasts dozens of Italian stores; you may want to pick up some picnic supplies here.)

[11.9] Make a left on Matthews Ave., five blocks after White Plains Rd. (One block before Pelham Pkwy. is Lydig Ave., which has a nice selection of largely Jewish stores strung along the five blocks to your left. For more information, see page 217)

[12.7] Make a right onto the parkway service road. At the first intersection, turn left to cross the parkway and pick up the bicycle path that runs through the greenery on the north side of the road. Turn right and follow the bike path to the end. Cross to the other side of the parkway and pick up the path on the south side. The path winds around a bit when it crosses the Hutchinson River Pkwy. and the Bruckner Expressway/New England Throughway (be careful of entering and exiting traffic), but it's much nicer than riding on the street. The bike path ends shortly after the Bruckner. Continue on the road, following signs for City Island (or take a side trip to Orchard Beach).

Once you cross the causeway you can ride straight down City Island Ave., the mile-long main street, to the end. On weekends it's clogged with traffic. We suggest making an immediate left when you get off the bridge and doubling back onto Sutherland St. Turn right on King Ave. You'll have to make a short right turn to get onto Minnieford Ave., and several short turns to work your way down the island. There are only a few streets, so you really can't get lost. You'll eventually be forced back onto City Island Ave. at Carroll St., but you'll have a feel for the life of the island.

[19.0] At the end of the island, enjoy lunch, dinner, or a snack at any of the restaurants, clam bars, or fish-and-chips joints. (For more information, see page 215)

To get home: Take City Island Ave. off the island and continue back through Pelham Bay Park. Turn left onto Shore Rd. and rejoin the bicycle path, taking it to the end, just past White Plains Rd., where the IRT train crosses overhead at White Plains Rd. (There is a map of Bronx bike paths on the west side of White Plains Rd.) Continue on the bike path. Turn right, and just north of the corner of Bronx Park East and Pelham Pkwy. North you can pick up the continuation of the bike path.

[25.6] Make a left at the first cross street (Theodore Kazmiroff Blvd.) and cross under the Bronx River Pkwy. Get onto the sidewalk where it begins just after the parkway exit.

[26.8] Make a right on Mosholu Pkwy.

[27.7] Turn left on Van Cortlandt Ave. and take a left onto the Grand Concourse, two blocks further. Follow the Grand Concourse (best to ride on the service road) all the way back to the Bronx County Courthouse at E. 161st St. On Grand Concourse at Kingsbridge Road (near 193rd St.) is a small park called Poe Park. There is an old cottage there that in the 1840s was briefly inhabited by Edgar Allan Poe. It's worth a visit.

[31.2] Make a right at E. 161st St. and descend the hill by Yankee Stadium. Turn left at the T-intersection and cross the Macombs Bridge. (You may want to walk your bike here.) Bear right as you exit the bridge, onto W. 155th St. This is a steep uphill; turn left on Amsterdam Ave., near the top.

[33.0] Bear right onto Hamilton Place at 144th St.; then right on 138th St. and left on Broadway. (See the Harlem sections on pages 135–140 for more information on suggested stops, such as Wilson's Bakery at Amsterdam Ave. and 158th St.; Floridita Restaurant at Broadway and 140th St.; and La Rosa Bakery at Broadway and 138th St.) Continue south on Broadway (or you may want to take Riverside Dr. if it's open). Turn right on Tiemann Place, one block south of 125th St. Take the next left onto Claremont Ave. Make a right on 120th St. and left onto Riverside Dr. to return downtown. Turn left at 72nd St. and take it to Central Park. Take the park drive back to Columbus Circle.

KOSHER SPECIAL

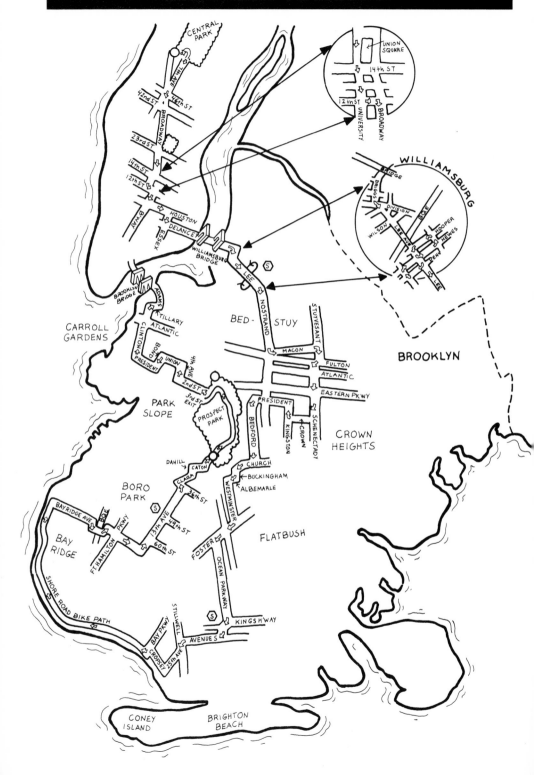

You don't have to be kosher to enjoy this trip, an urban "archaeological expedition" through four very different neighborhoods in Brooklyn. Highlights include a light nosh in Hassidic Williamsburg, lunch in a Sephardic neighborhood, and dessert in sprawling Borough Park.

TOTAL DISTANCE: **44 miles.**

[0.0 miles] Begin at Columbus Circle. Follow directions for Brighton Beach K'nish K'nosh to Houston St. and Broadway.

[3.5] Make a left on Houston St. to Essex St.; then a right on Essex St. to Delancey St. Make a left on Delancey St. to the Williamsburg Bridge.

[4.5] Use the stairs that are located on the traffic island in the center of Delancey St. to enter the bridge. You'll probably want to walk your bike for the first part of the bridge, since there's usually an obscene amount of glass on the pathway. (See page 161 for information on the Lower East Side.)

[5.9] Exit the bridge and turn right onto Driggs Ave., then left on Division Ave. Bear right on Lee Ave., one block later. Park your bike anywhere on Lee Ave. (See page 51 for more information on Williamsburg) To continue the tour, follow the instructions in the two-borough "Moveable Feast Tour" on page 244, until you get to Schenectady Ave. Continue on Schenectady Ave. past Eastern Pkwy. Make a right on Carroll St., then right on Kingston Ave. (For information about Crown Heights, see page 56.)

[12.4] To leave Crown Heights, turn left on President St. Ride west until you come to Bedford Ave.

[13.1] Make a left on Bedford Ave. As you descend Bedford Ave., you'll notice Ebbets Field Housing on your right—a sad fate for what was once the proud home of the Brooklyn Dodgers.

[14.5] Make a right on Church Ave., busy even on Sundays, then left onto Buckingham Rd., just where the commercial strip ends. (Note: On your right is 16th St.) This neighborhood of large, well-maintained homes is Prospect Park South (marked by a monogrammed "PPS" on columns at the neighborhood's edge), a tribute to farsighted urban design by developer Dean Alvord. Make a right on Albemarle Rd. at the end of the block; make a left on Westminster Rd. four blocks later.

[16.2] Make a right on Foster, then left on Ocean Pkwy. Follow the Ocean Pkwy. bicycle path or service road.

[18.3] Make a right on Kings Hwy. (between Quentin Rd. and Ave. R), a legacy of the British presence in Brooklyn (Kings County). Even earlier, the way was an Indian trail. Park your bicycle between E. 2nd and 3rd Sts. (For more information on the Kings Highway area, see page 59).

[18.6] Make a left on E. 2nd St. and a right on Ave. S (passing through an Italian neighborhood) until it ends.

[19.6] Make a left on Stillwell Ave., then quickly bear right onto 25th Ave.

[20.3] Go right on Cropsey Ave. (badly marked), one block before 25th Ave. ends.

[20.7] Make a left on Bay Pkwy., underneath the Shore (Belt) Pkwy. and toward a shopping mall. Keep the playing fields on your right and ride through the parking lot out to the edge of the water. Turn right onto the bike path (you'll have to walk for the first hundred yards) for a spectacular four miles along the Narrows. This ride has stunning views south to New Jersey and, eventually, Manhattan.

[25.4] At the end of the promenade, turn right onto Bay Ridge Ave. to 13th Ave. (You'll have to jog around the Brooklyn Queens Expressway at Seventh Ave.)

[26.6] When Bay Ridge Ave. deadends, take a right, then the next left over the Expressway, and another left immediately after the overpass and a right back onto Bay Ridge Ave.

[27.6] Make a left on 13th Ave., passing through an Italian neighborhood before entering the Jewish section of Borough Park, which begins around the intersection of 13th Ave. and New Utrecht Ave. (For more information, see page 62.) Continue north on 13th Ave. to its end.

[29.3] Make a left on 36th St., then an immediate right onto Clara St. Turn left at Dahill Rd. (two blocks later), and right onto Caton Ave.

[30.2] Make a left onto the service road on the far side of Ocean Pkwy. (You'll cross Ocean Pkwy. on an overpass.) Follow the service road as it loops around and dumps you onto a traffic circle.

[30.5] Enter Prospect Park, on the far side of the traffic circle. Follow traffic around the park (counterclockwise) to the 3rd St. exit (after Grand Army Plaza).

[32.7] Exit at 3rd St. and Prospect Park West. To return to Manhattan see the instructions in the "Moveable Feast Tour" on page 244. Alternatively, you might return by turning left on Prospect Park West, right on 4th St., and right on Seventh Ave. Turn left on Union St. Follow the instructions in "Brighton Beach K'nish K'nosh" (page 232) once you reach the Gowanus Canal.

LITTLE ITALY OF THE BRONX

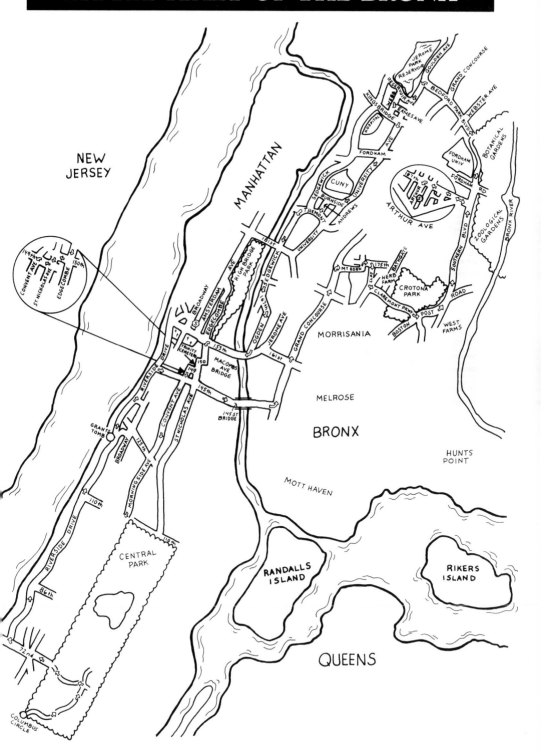

Dozens of bakeries, cheese shops, espresso bars, pork stores, and an indoor retail market are found in this four-generations-old Italian community. Cap off the visit with a picnic in the nearby New York Botanical Garden.

TOTAL DISTANCE: **29 miles.**

[0.0 miles] Start at Columbus Circle (Central Park South and Eighth Ave.). Ride into Central Park, following traffic. Follow signs for W. 72nd St. Exit the park at W. 72 St. and Central Park West. Turn right on Riverside Dr. At this writing, Riverside Dr. is under repair: you'll have to detour to Broadway just after you pass Riverside Church and Grant's Tomb, near 120th St. Follow detour signs and rejoin Riverside Dr. at 135th St.

[6.2] Make a right (uphill) on W. 145th St. You might want to stop in this area for Cuban coffee—try Floridita on Broadway at W. 141st. or Mama Lila further up on 145th St. near Amsterdam Ave. Continue on W. 145th St.—watch for traffic on the north-south cross streets—and cross the 145th St. Bridge into the Bronx. Continue

straight (you're now on E. 149th St.) to the Grand Concourse.

[8.2] Make a left onto the Grand Concourse, one of New York's most remarkable boulevards and one whose solid apartment buildings are helping it make a comeback. Note the impressive Bronx County Courthouse on your left at 161st St., one of the city's greatest Art Deco structures.

[10.2] Turn right on Mt. Eden Pkwy., and left (at the end) on Topping Ave. (unmarked). Take the next right on E. 173rd St.; then the next right onto Clay Ave., which runs into Webster Ave. Next turn left on Claremont Pkwy. (Take Bathgate Ave., the third block on your left, for a side trip to GLIE Farms, New York City's only commercial herb farm, located in the Bathgate Industrial Complex.) Continue on Claremont Pkwy. through Crotona Park: On the far side of the park are the Charlotte Gardens homes, built on the site where presidential candidates Carter and Reagan both campaigned— a surreal mushrooming of single-family homes sprouting from the wreckage of abandoned housing that characterizes much of the surrounding area.

[11.6] Turn left on Boston Rd.

[12.0] Make a left on Southern Blvd. (This is where Boston Rd. passes underneath the el.)

[13.2] Turn left on E. 187th St. to Arthur Ave. and park your bike here. (See page 199 for more information about Arthur Ave.)

[13.6] Return to Southern Blvd. on E. 187th St. Turn left on Southern Blvd. The main entrance to the Botanical Garden is on your right **[14.5],** past Fordham Rd. (You can't bring bikes into the Garden; lock your bicycle here or at the entrance a bit further along Southern Blvd.)

[15.0] Turn left on Bedford Park Blvd. Turn left at the end onto Goulden Ave. Turn right onto Reservoir Ave. and enjoy the fantastic reservoir view. Make a left onto Webb Ave. Three blocks later, turn left onto Eames Ave., and right onto University Ave. for a mile-long stretch. (You'll pass Bronx Community College campus, with buildings by McKim, Mead & White.) Turn right on Burnside Ave., then left on Andrews Ave. Make a right on W. Tremont Ave. down the hill to Sedgewick Ave., then left on Sedgewick Ave. Turn left up the 167th St. hill, after passing under a series of bridges, to Ogden Ave., then right on Ogden Ave. uphill, then (careful!) a steep downhill to where it ends at Macombs Dam Park. Walk your bike across the street (Jerome Ave.) and cycle up the sidewalk leading to the north side of Macombs Bridge.

In Manhattan, turn sharply left onto Edgecombe Ave. to 150th St. Turn right, then make a quick left on St. Nicholas Ave. and then right on 149th St. to Convent Ave. Turn left on Convent, which sweeps through lovely landmarked sections of Harlem and then through the City College campus (see "Harlem Sights & Soul" on page 247). Continue south past 125th St., where the road becomes Morningside Ave. and then Manhattan Ave. You may turn left at 110th St. and follow the Central Park roadway south to Columbus Circle.

MOVEABLE FEAST TOUR

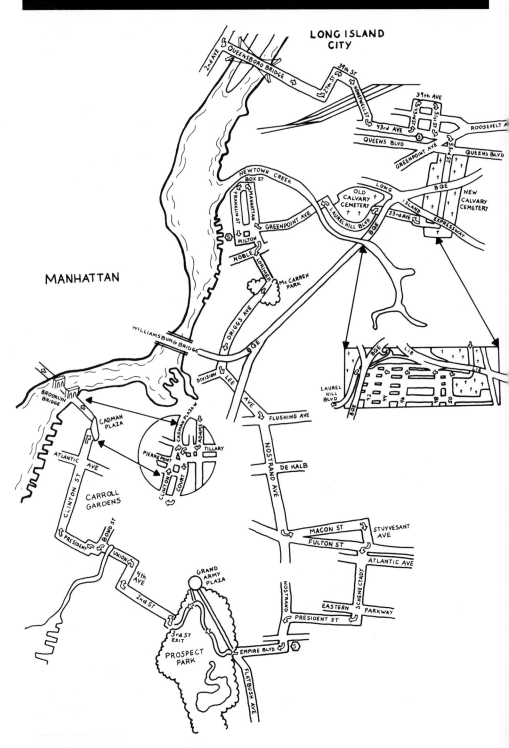

This trip sails through Queens and Brooklyn on a gluttonous voyage. Stops include an Armenian bakery in Sunnyside, Polish Greenpoint, and a roti shop in Crown Heights. The tour also passes through Bedford-Stuyvesant, Prospect Park, and Park Slope.

TOTAL DISTANCE: **27 miles.**

[0.0 miles] Begin this tour at 59th St. and Second Ave., at the Queensborough Bridge. Bear left off 59th St. up the bridge ramp. Toward the top of the ramp bear right to get onto the outer roadway, which is usually closed to cars. (Even if autos are on it, it is legal—though not pleasurable—to ride on it.) The views back to Manhattan and on to Long Island are stunning. On the Queens side, continue straight one block. Turn left onto 27th St., crossing Queens Blvd., and continue three blocks. Turn right on 39th St. and continue for four blocks to Northern Blvd. Cross Northern Blvd. (you're now on Honeywell St., which is closed to cars). You'll do best to ride on the sidewalk because the road is cobbled. Continue straight one block past the end of the bridge. Make a left on 43rd Ave. Pedal to 43rd St.

[3.0] Park here to explore Sunnyside (see page 113). Continue on 43rd Ave. and turn right on 52nd St., across Queens Blvd., and through New Calvary Cemetery. Continue straight through, and cross Laurel Hill Blvd. Go right at the T-intersection just after you've crossed under the Long Island Expressway (note: this is the second underpass, near the southern end of the cemetery) and exit the cemetery. Go straight on 54th Ave.

[5.0] Make a left on Laurel Hill Blvd., at the edge of New Calvary Cemetery. (There's a classic view of midtown beyond the gravestones here.) Follow the perimeter of the cemetery as Laurel Hill Blvd. becomes Review Ave.

[5.9] Turn left onto Greenpoint Ave. to cross Newtown Creek into Brooklyn. Follow Greenpoint Ave. to Manhattan Ave. This is a good place to lock your bike and explore the neighborhood. (For information on Greenpoint, see page 34.) A nice way to get an overview: Turn right on Manhattan Ave. and follow almost to the end; turn left on Commercial St. and left on Franklin St. (note the Astral apartments by India St.). Make a left on Milton St. Lock your bike at Manhattan Ave., at the top of Milton St.

[6.9] Turn left (as you face Manhattan) on Manhattan Ave. and right on Noble St. two blocks later. Take the first left on Lorimer St. and continue to Driggs Ave.

[7.5] Turn right on Driggs Ave. through McCarren Park. Continue on Driggs Ave. under the Williamsburg Bridge **[8.6]**. (Take this to return to Manhattan.)

[8.8] Turn left on Division Ave., where Driggs Ave. dead-ends. One block later, bear right on Lee Ave. through Williams-

burg (see "Kosher Special" on page 238). Lee Ave. becomes Nostrand Ave. at Flushing Ave. Continue on Nostrand Ave.

[10.9] Turn left on Macon St.

[11.8] Turn right on Stuyvesant Ave., then right on Fulton St. The next left is onto Schenectady Ave.

[13.0] Turn right on President St., just after Eastern Pkwy., a broad boulevard with fast traffic.

[13.5] Kingston Ave. is the commercial spine of the Lubavitcher community in Crown Heights. (For more information, see page 56.)

[13.9] Turn left on Nostrand Ave., then right on Empire Blvd., at the bottom of the hill. (Gloria's, our favorite roti shop, is on the corner.)

[14.9] Enter Prospect Park at Flatbush Ave. Bear right on the park drive. Continue around past Grand Army Plaza to 3rd St.

[16.2] Exit at 3rd St. and Prospect Park West. Turn right and walk your bike one block to 2nd St. A bike path takes you through Park Slope ("the Slope").

[16.9] Turn right on Fourth Ave.

[17.2] Make a left on Union St. and follow the instructions in "Brighton Beach K'nish K'nosh" on page 232 to return to Manhattan. Alternatively, continue on Fourth Ave. and turn left on Bergen St. or Pacific St. Continue to Clinton St. Turn right on Clinton St. and then follow the "Brighton Beach K'nish K'nosh" instructions on page 232.

HARLEM SIGHTS & SOUL

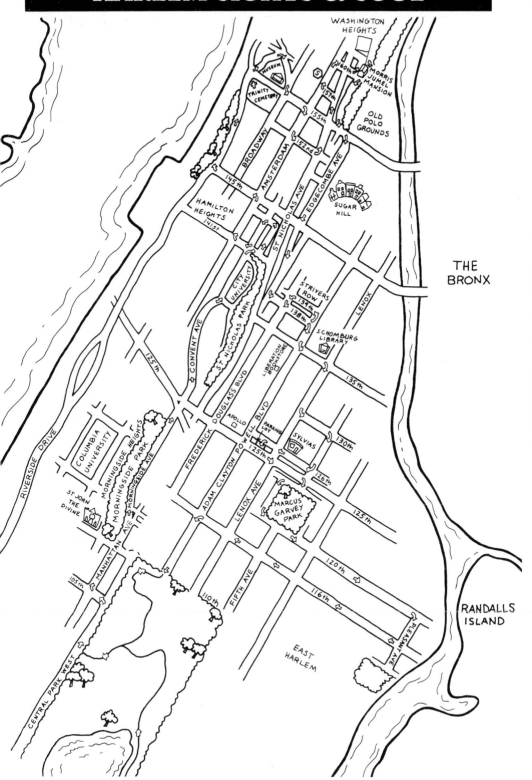

This is a spirited ride through Hamilton Heights, part of Washington Heights, and the Harlem Valley. Stops include City College, Hamilton Heights Historic District, the Morris-Jumel Mansion, Strivers Row, and Italian East Harlem.

TOTAL DISTANCE: **19 miles.**

[0.0 miles] Start from Columbus Circle at 59th St. and Central Park West. Enter Central Park and ride with the traffic (counterclockwise) around the park. Take the cut-off on the left shortly after the E. 102nd St. exit. Turn left when you rejoin the park drive on the West Side. Take the next right and exit at W. 100th St.

[2.9] Turn right on Central Park West. Turn left onto W. 105th St. Take the next right onto Manhattan Ave. Bear left onto Morningside Ave. (at the bottom of Morningside Park) at 113th St. On the Heights you can see the huge back side of the Cathedral of St. John the Divine, the world's largest Gothic-style cathedral. Continue straight across 125th St., where Morningside Ave. becomes Convent Ave. Take Convent Ave. up to Hamilton Heights and the campus of the City College of New York. (You can get a good view of Harlem by taking a right onto St. Nicholas Terrace, at the north end of the CCNY campus **[5.3]** and following the street as it loops back, skirting the edge of the Heights. Take your next right and then another right back onto Convent Ave. and you will be back in the middle of the campus again. For more information, see page 135.)

Continue on Convent Ave. Turn right on W. 140th St. Take the next left onto Hamilton Terrace, a beautiful landmark district, justly lauded for its brownstones. Follow the street as it turns left. Turn left onto Convent Ave. You'll see Hamilton Grange

(summer home of Alexander Hamilton). Turn right on W. 141st St. and continue to Riverside Dr. Turn right on Riverside Dr.

[7.2] Turn right at W. 155th St. on the north side of Trinity Cemetery. Follow 155th Street for about 200 feet, then bear left (this is still Riverside Dr.). Turn right at the second intersection and make an immediate right, which brings you to Broadway. Turn right on Broadway, passing the Audubon Terrace museum complex on your right. Turn left on W. 152nd St. (Note the old wood-frame house, across from the Dance Theater of Harlem on the block between Amsterdam and St. Nicholas Aves., and the old Post Rd. marker "1769: 9 miles from N. York" in the front yard.)

Turn left on St. Nicholas Ave., then left on W. 157th St. Turn right on Amsterdam Ave. Wilson's is at the corner of W. 158th St. and Amsterdam Ave. This is a great place to get a cup of coffee or a sweet to take to the grounds of the Morris-Jumel Mansion.

[8.4] Continue on Amsterdam Ave. Turn right on W. 160th St., then left on Jumel Terrace, and enter the grounds of the Morris-Jumel Mansion, Manhattan's sole surviving mansion from the Revolutionary War–era. Now a city-maintained museum, the building and its grounds are a fascinating oasis.

Turn right onto Jumel Terrace as you exit. Turn right again at the corner (W. 162nd St.) and right onto Edgecombe Ave. Follow Edgecombe Ave. and cross 155th St. (the Polo Grounds, where the New York Giants baseball team played, was just down the hill). Continue catty-corner across the intersection, remaining on Edgecombe Ave. (It's the smaller street to the left; make sure you don't get on the busier St. Nicholas Ave.)

Turn left onto W. 138th St. Between Frederick Douglass Blvd. (Eighth Ave.) and Adam Clayton Powell Blvd. (Seventh Ave.) is Strivers Row, a landmark district where some of Harlem's most prominent residents have lived. Turn left onto Adam Clayton Powell Blvd. and left onto 139th St. to see the other block of this extraordinary development. Turn left onto Frederick Douglass Blvd. and left onto W. 138th St. to complete the loop. Make a right onto Adam Clayton Powell Blvd. and left onto W. 135th St., past the Harlem YMCA and the Schomburg Center for Research in Black Culture, which houses one of the country's best collections of black American history. Turn right onto Lenox Ave. (Sixth Ave.) and left onto W. 130th St., past a row of wood-frame houses on your right fronted by what must once have been lovely wooden porches.

[12.0] Turn right on W. 126th St. Sylvia's (see page 129) is at 328 Lenox Ave., between 126th and 127th Sts. You can park your bicycle at the municipal garage on 126th St. between Lenox Ave. and Adam Clayton Powell Blvd.

Turn left on Lenox Ave., then left on W. 125th St., then right on Fifth Ave. Follow the road around Mount Morris (Marcus Garvey) Park. On the south side of the park continue straight east on E. 120th St. to Pleasant Ave., one block past First Ave. Turn right on Pleasant Ave. and right again on E. 116th St.

[13.6] This area has what remains of Italian East Harlem, as you'll notice from some of the shops. Continue east on 116th St., passing La Marqueta. (For more information, see page 144.) Turn left on Adam Clayton Powell Blvd. and return to Central Park. Turn right and return downtown on the park drive.

QUEENS CORNUCOPIA

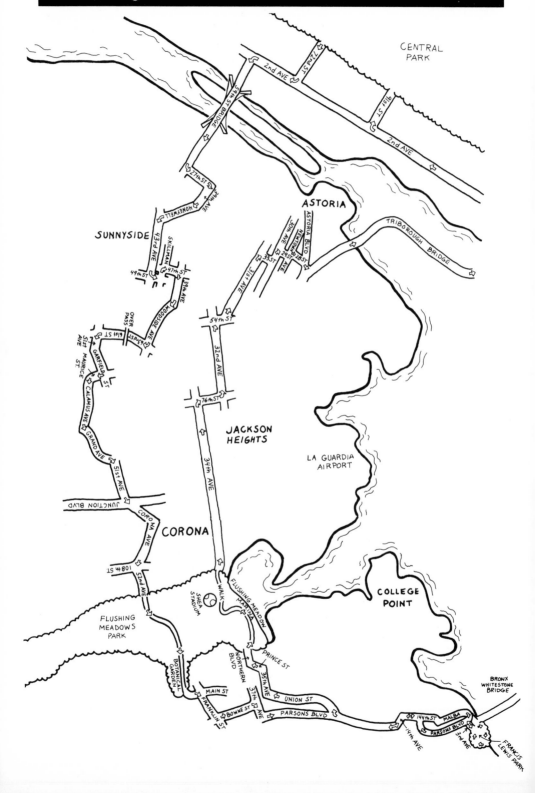

See New York's real melting pot on this tour, including Latin American, Indian, Japanese, Korean, and Greek neighborhoods, as well as a picnic spot on Long Island Sound.

TOTAL DISTANCE: **30 miles.**

[0.0 miles] Begin at 59th St. and Second Ave. Follow instructions for the "Moveable Feast Tour" on page 244 to Pyramid Bakery in Sunnyside. (For more information on Sunnyside see page 113.)

[3.0] Continue on 43rd Ave. Turn left onto 49th St., then left on Skillman Ave. and right on 45th St. Turn right onto 39th Ave. Turn right on Woodside Ave. (where 39th Ave. ends) and take it to Roosevelt Ave.

[4.6] Cross Roosevelt Ave. and continue on Woodside Ave.: You'll have to jog right on 58th St. for a few feet; turn left on Roosevelt Ave. and turn right back onto Woodside Ave.

[4.9] Turn right onto 63rd St. Cross Queens Blvd. and (jogging left) under the Brooklyn Queens Expressway. You'll end up on 61st St.: Keep going straight.

[5.5] Turn left on 51st Ave., then right on 66th St., then left on Maurice Ave.

[6.0] Bear right onto Calamus Ave. at 69th St.

[6.7] Turn left onto Grand Ave. (the next major intersection). Wind around a bit before recrossing Queens Blvd.

[7.2] Two blocks later, turn right onto 51st Ave. Turn left onto Junction Blvd. at the end of 51st Ave.

[7.9] Turn right onto Corona Ave. two blocks further on. Corona Ave. weaves around a bit: Stick with it!

[8.7] Turn left on 52nd Ave., where Corona Ave. runs into 108th St. (This is the heart of Italian Corona. The Lemon Ice King—home of some of New York's best

ices—is at this corner. Ringed around what could be a town square is a VFW post, a salumeria, an espresso bar, Italian restaurants, a pasta shop, and so on. It's worth a stop.) Turn right on 111th St. Go through the parking lot on the left and into Flushing Meadow Park. It's easy to get across the park if you've done it before, but easy to get turned around if you haven't.

[9.0] The goal is to go across the park in a straight line as if 52nd Ave. continued. Bear left toward the carousel after you enter the park, then right, and over the Grand Central Pkwy. (A big sign for Taystee bread is on the far side of the park, ahead and to your left.) Go to the Unisphere (the huge globe on your left) built for the 1964 World's Fair. Turn right at the globe and ride along the series of reflecting pools. (You'll probably see a lively game of soccer on your right.) On the far side of the last reflecting pool, take the paved path under the Van Wyck Expressway, up a steep ramp over College Ave. and through a grassy area.

[10.6] The Queens Botanical Garden entrance is on your left. Walk your bike in. Fittingly, this charming little oasis is soon to be the site of an extensive Asian botanical garden. Exit through the front of the garden. Turn left on Main St. and ride to Franklin St. (Park here to explore the area.)

[11.0] Turn right onto Franklin St., then left on Bowne St. At 37th Ave., go right (walk your bike) through Weeping Beech Park, home to one of the city's most extraordinary trees, a giant weeping beech. (The Bowne House, a museum on the edge of this small park, was the meeting place for some of this country's first Quakers.)

[11.9] Turn left on Parsons Blvd. Follow Parsons Blvd. all the way out to 14th Ave.

[13.6] Turn left on 14th Ave. Go over the Whitestone Expressway and right onto 143rd Place. Turn right at the bottom of the hill onto 11th Ave. Turn left on Malba Drive, named after this posh waterfront neighborhood. Follow it all the way as it swings around to Parsons Blvd. Make a left on Parsons Blvd. and under the Bronx-Whitestone Bridge to **[14.7]** Francis Lewis Park, directly east of the bridge. (If you explore the neighborhood and lose your way, just look for the bridge.)

Return, turning right as you leave the park, then left on the Whitestone Expressway (actually a small service road), which dumps you out onto Parsons Blvd.; turn left on Parsons Blvd., then left onto 14th Ave. **[15.5]**, then right on Parsons Blvd.

[16.2] Bear right where Willets Point Blvd. splits from Parsons Blvd. (25th Ave.). Willets Point Blvd. turns into Union St.

[17.1] Turn right on 35th Ave., then left on Prince St. to Northern Blvd. Turn right onto the bike/pedestrian path over Flushing Creek. Follow traffic as you exit and follow a shore path, bearing right to stay off the highway.

[18.5] Turn left when you see the back of Shea Stadium directly through an underpass (sign says ''Theater in the Park'') and head toward Shea. Take the paved path on your right directly past the underpass. Walk your bike across a highway entrance ramp, then along an interchange and across a service road. As long as you keep heading west, toward Manhattan, you're on the right track: It's only a couple of hundred yards.

[19.0] You'll come out on 34th Ave. at 114th St. Take 34th Ave. to 75th St.

[21.0] Turn right on 75th St., then left on 32nd Ave.

[22.1] Turn right on 54th St. Take the next left onto 31st Ave., all the way to 29th St., just past the el. Make a right on 29th St. to 30th Ave. (Park on this block if you'd like to eat pastries at HBH European Café. For more information on Greek Astoria, see page 74.)

To return to Manhattan: Continue on 29th St. Turn left onto Newtown Ave. and make a quick right onto 28th St. Turn left onto Astoria Blvd., and the next right (onto 27th St.) will take you to the Triborough Bridge **[23.9]**. The bicycle path is accessible by the stairs at 27th St. and Hoyt Ave. South.

[25.9] When you exit the Triborough Bridge onto Randalls Island, the ramp to Manhattan is on your right, by the toll booths for Manhattan traffic. (See the alternate return to Manhattan given below.) Turn right after coming off the ramp. Turn right again just after you've passed the pair of flagpoles, and you'll soon be at the base of the ramp to Manhattan.

[26.8] You'll come out on Second Ave. You can take this downtown, heading west where it is convenient. The Queensborough Bridge is at mile 30.4.

Note: Second Ave. traffic is very fast. Here's an alternate route to get back: On Randalls Island follow the road south on the overpass to Wards Island. At the end of the road there is a gate with a roadway at your right. Turn onto that roadway and ride past several institutional buildings. At the end, turn left and ride to the lavender-painted bridge leading to Manhattan. Cross the bridge. On the far side take the bridge over the FDR overpass. Turn right on First Ave. to 106th St., then left on 106th St. to Fifth Ave. You can head south here or enter Central Park at 102nd St.

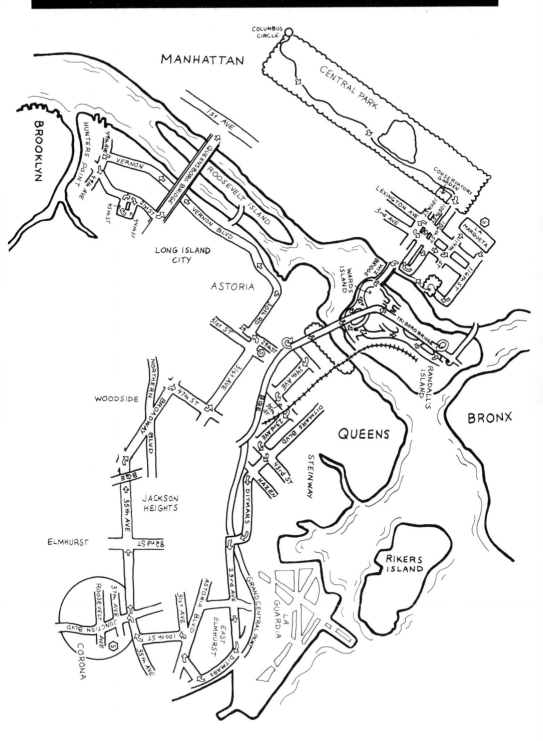

SALSA & SPANAKOPITA

Start with Spanish Harlem and its bustling La Marqueta, before a spate of country cycling on Wards Island. Head over the Triborough Bridge with its stunning view of Manhattan's skyline before pedaling to the Latin American neighborhoods of Jackson Heights and Corona. Return via Greek Astoria. The starting point is the Maine Monument at Columbus Circle.

TOTAL DISTANCE: **25 miles.**

[0.0 miles] Enter Central Park and follow traffic counterclockwise (toward the East Side) until you pass the exit marked 102nd St.

[2.9] At the traffic lights (before the park drive drops steeply), walk your bike to, and then follow, the path on your right that drops down to the north side of the Central Park Conservatory Garden, a magnificent set of three formal gardens that is one of the park's great treasures. (Cycling inside the gardens is prohibited.) Exit at Fifth Ave. and 106th St. Ride along 106th St. to the end.

[3.9] Turn right and right again on 105th St. Turn left at Lexington Ave. (Note the community garden on your left and the mural on the corner of Lexington Ave. and 104th St.) Turn left on 104th St., left again on Third Ave., left again on 111th St., and right on Park Ave. Lock your bike at 115th St. and Park Ave. (For more information, see the section on La Marqueta on page 144.) Continue up Park Ave.

[5.4] Turn right on 116th St. to Pleasant Ave., near the East River. Turn right on Pleasant Ave., which ends at 114th St. Continue straight (south) through Jefferson Park (around a playing field) toward the ramp over the FDR Dr. at approximately 112th St. Take this overpass to the East River walkway, and ride downtown (the same direction) along the river.

[6.8] Take the foot bridge at 103rd St. across the river to Wards Island. (This is known as the "Wiz Bridge" because a scene from the movie *The Wiz* was shot here.) As you exit the bridge onto Wards Island, follow the path on your right, which skirts the island. Keep bearing right along the water. Take a left after you pass under the Triborough Bridge and go up a small hill. Continue in the direction of a red smokestack. Turn right just before the smokestack and follow a road between the Triborough Bridge and the Hell Gate railroad bridge north to Randalls Island. As you come off the bridge onto Randalls Island there is a traffic circle. Get off your bike and walk to the left, crossing underneath the Triborough Bridge.

[8.9] The ramp to Queens is ahead of you, just north of the stadium. The ride over the Triborough Bridge to Queens has stunning views. It also has three sets of stairs.

[10.9] When you exit the bridge turn right on 27th St. and cross under the bridge approach. Turn left onto Hoyt Ave. North and make an immediate right onto 26th St.

[11.3] Turn right onto 23rd Ave., then left on 43rd St.

[12.4] Turn right on Ditmars Blvd. Ditmars Blvd. curves right just before LaGuardia Airport and then turns sharply left at 82nd St. **[13.3]**, just after crossing the Grand Central Pkwy. (If you reach Astoria Blvd. you've gone too far. Turn back.) Continue straight (you'll find yourself on 23rd Ave. for a while before picking up Ditmars Blvd. again just past 102nd St.).

[14.2] Turn right on Ditmars Blvd., then right on 27th Ave., then left on 100th St. (Walk your bike a half-block to avoid a one-way street.) Make a quick right onto Astoria Blvd. Turn left onto 98th St. Continue four long blocks to 34th Ave.

[15.5] Turn right on 34th Ave., then left on Junction Blvd., which is a busy commercial street. Turn right onto 37th Ave. (You can park your bike here if you want to explore the neighborhood.) Turn right on 83rd St.

[16.6] Turn left on 35th Ave. (Turn onto 35th Ave., a residential street, sooner if you want to avoid the congestion on 37th Ave.)

[17.6] Turn right on Broadway, where 35th Ave. ends.

[18.5] Turn right on 47th St. Three blocks later, turn left on 30th Ave. (See page 74 for more information on Greek Astoria.)

Alternate route: For a bit of New York eccentricity, turn right off Broadway at 55th St. A tiny eighteenth-century graveyard on your left between 31st and 32nd Aves. is maintained here by students from a local school and a neighborhood resident. Turn left on 31st Ave. to 47th St., where you can retrieve the route.

[19.7] Turn left on 29th St., just after crossing under the el. Turn right on 30th Dr. to the water.

[20.4] Make a left on Vernon Blvd. (stunning views of Manhattan).

[21.9] Turn left on Queens Plaza South, immediately after the bridge. Continue to the bike path, which is on the south outer roadway.

[22.4] The path begins at Crescent St., where traffic exits the bridge. (The bike path is sometimes closed because of construction on the bridge. You can either take the subway, which is about one hundred yards east or, as many cyclists do, share the outer northern roadway with the cars.)

[23.8] On the Manhattan side, walk to Second Ave. If you want to return to Columbus Circle, walk to 60th St. and cycle west. Loop through Grand Army Plaza at Fifth Ave. Turn right on Central Park South to Columbus Circle.

STATEN ISLAND RAMBLE

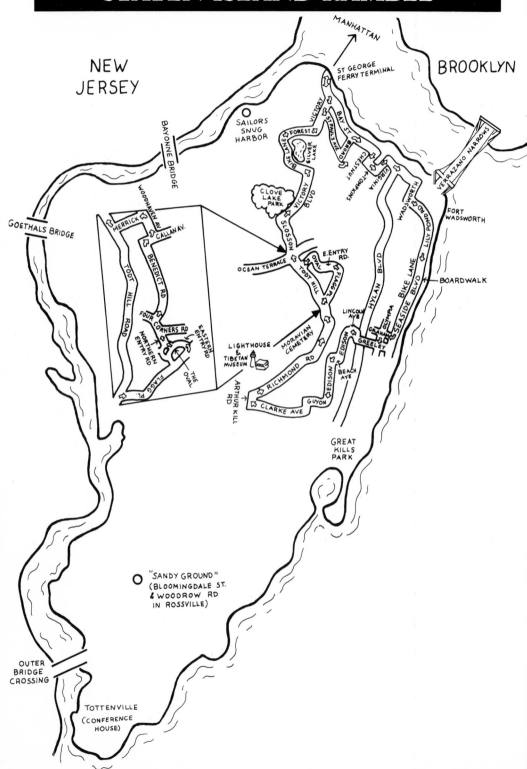

New York's least populated, most rural borough is one where the country seems very much alive. It is a borough of fine woods, swaying marshes, pounding surf, beautiful views, and occasionally steep hills. (Note: A detailed street map is a must for this tour because of the many unmarked streets on Todt Hill.) Start at the Staten Island Ferry Terminal by Battery Park. Buy your ticket at the kiosk where cars enter and follow cars onto the ferry. The ferry ride takes about 20 minutes. On weekends, the ferries run hourly until 8:30 A.M.; then they run every 30 minutes.

TOTAL DISTANCE: **22 miles.**

[0.0 miles] Follow cars off the ferry and up the exit ramp. Turn left on Bay St. and go to Victory Blvd. Turn right on Victory Blvd. and continue for about 200 yards. Turn left just past the Burger King onto Van Duzer St.; immediately bear right onto St. Paul's Ave. This is a pleasant, rolling street, lined with substantial wood-frame houses, which eventually turns into Van Duzer St.

[1.9] Turn left on Broad St. and continue back to Bay St.

[2.5] Turn right on Bay St.

[3.2] Turn left on Chestnut Ave. (by the U-Haul lot) and take it to the Garibaldi-Meucci House. (Call ahead if you want to visit.) Italian patriot Giuseppe Garibaldi lived in exile here for three years with his friend Antonio Meucci (whose claim to have invented the telephone before Alexander Graham Bell is bolstered by documents here).

Turn left on Tompkins Ave. and left on St. Mary's Ave. Turn right onto Bay St. (At 1134 Bay St. you can stop at Montalbano's, an excellent Italian delicatessen.) Turn left on Hylan Blvd. and ride to the end. Straight ahead is a view across the Narrows to Brooklyn. The Alice Austen House is now a museum (2 Hylan Blvd., Tel.: 718/816-4506; open Thursday–Sunday, May–September) that has revolving exhibitions of works by the path-breaking photographer. Return to Bay St. and turn left.

[5.1] Turn right on School St. just before the entrance gate to Fort Wadsworth. (In spite of the forbidding sentinel, you're encouraged to ride through the base. There are some lovely areas by the water almost underneath the Verrazano Narrows Bridge. Alternatively: You can go into Von Briesen park, on your left, for a nice view of the lower bay.)

Follow the bike lane on School St. It becomes Lily Pond Ave. where the road curves under the Verrazano Narrows Bridge toll plaza. As you descend to the beach, Basilio, one of the island's best Italian restaurants, is on your right. Look for an intersection where you can cross what is now Father Capodanno Blvd. and ride onto the boardwalk.

[6.3] Originally built as a New Deal project, the boardwalk has been rebuilt recently and you'll enjoy a lovely ride for nearly two miles. After the end of the boardwalk there's a paved path along the beach for some way. Follow this.

[8.2] Turn right just before a baseball field and cross Father Capodanno Blvd. to Graham Blvd. Ride on Graham Blvd. through a high, grassy marsh. It's a poorly paved swampy area that seems more like southern bayou country than New York City. The twin towers of the Verrazano Narrows Bridge glint through the reeds. The view is not to be missed!

[8.6] Turn left onto Olympia Blvd., which will take you through a neighborhood of beaten-down bungalows.

[9.1] Turn right on Lincoln Blvd. Cross Hylan Blvd. Turn left onto Edison St. Jog right at New Dorp Ave. and left onto 10th St. Continue to the end of 10th St. Turn right onto Peter Ave., then left on S. Railroad Ave. Turn right on Guyon Ave., then left onto Amboy Rd. Take the next right onto Clarke Ave. Continue along Clarke Ave. to Richmondtown Restoration.

[12.7] Richmondtown Restoration is a restored village, along the lines of Colonial Williamsburg, but on a much smaller scale. It has buildings from the early Dutch and English settlements on the island, including the oldest extant elementary school in America. The grounds are always open, but opening hours for the buildings are irregular. Call the Staten Island Historical Society (Tel.: 718/351-1611) for more information. (If you wish, you can cut through to Richmond Rd., on the far side, to continue the bike tour.)

[12.9] Turn right on Arthur Kill, at the end of Clarke St. Turn right on Richmond Rd., passing by the other side of Richmondtown.

For a difficult but rewarding side trip to the Jacques Marchais Museum of Tibetan Art and the Frank Lloyd Wright House, turn left on Lighthouse Ave. You'll see the Staten Island Lighthouse as you ascend this very steep hill (you may wish to walk your bike). The Tibetan Museum, which houses the largest privately owned collection of Tibetan art outside Tibet, is at 338 Lighthouse Ave. near Windsor Ave; the Frank Lloyd Wright House is at 48 Manor Court west of Lighthouse Ave. Return to Richmond Rd. Remain on Richmond Rd., which bears right at the intersection with Rockland Ave. (Watch out: The main road looks as though it goes left.)

[14.4] Richmond Rd. turns sharply left at the T-intersection with Amboy Rd.

[15.0] Turn left on Todt Hill Rd., marked by a traffic light at the far side of the Moravian Cemetery (on your left).

[15.2] Make the first right onto Flagg Ave.

[15.9] Turn left on Eastern Entry Rd., marked only by some partially hidden posts on the left. (It's shortly after a seminary.) Follow Eastern Entry Rd. through the Oval (there's a tennis club there) to Northern Entry Rd., which becomes Four Corners Rd. (These are all very short distances, no more than a couple of hundred yards each.) Turn right onto Benedict Rd. and follow it to the end. Take a short right onto Buttonwood Ave. and loop around to Whitwell Place, which will take you back to Todt Hill Rd. (It is essential that you have a map: Many of these roads are poorly marked.)

[17.4] Turn right onto Todt Hill Rd. and ascend the last bit to the top. If it's a nice day, the view is magnificent. Continue on Todt Hill Rd. as it descends a luscious hill to Victory Blvd.

[18.4] Turn right on Victory Blvd. As you are passing your third cemetery there is an entrance to Silver Lake Park (marked with a green sign) on your left.

[19.7] Turn left into the park and follow the marked bike path.

[20.5] Exit Silver Lake Park. Turn right onto Forest Ave. Turn left onto Victory Blvd. for a spectacular downhill ride with a tremendous view of Manhattan.

[20.9] Turn left onto Bay St. and return to the ferry.

Glossary

Ackee (Jamaica). Fruit cooked with cod in a traditional Jamaican breakfast (if not ripe can cause severe allergic reactions).

Adobo (Philippines). A common stew typically made with chicken or pork and spiced with soy sauce and vinegar.

Afali (Greece). Pistachio-studded pastry.

Ajiaco (Colombia). Chicken and potato soup.

Ajonjoli (Caribbean). Sweet sesame seed–based drink.

Amigdalota (Greece). Sugar and almond cookies flavored with rosewater.

Andrulis (Poland). Dry, Lithuanian-style white cheese.

Antipasto (Italy). Appetizers, typically vegetables and mushrooms that have been marinated in a vinaigrette sauce.

Arepa (Colombia). A flat, almost taste-less bread.

Arroz con pollo (Latin America). A rice and chicken dish.

Arroz zambito (Peru). Rice sweetened with caramelized sugar, cloves, and coconut.

Arvi (India). Gingerlike root, but more pungent.

Asopao (Latin America). Soup, typically thick with rice.

Asopao de mariscos (Peru). Seafood soup, liberally spiced with garlic and coriander.

Avgolemono (Greece). An egg-lemon soup.

Awaze (Ethiopia). Hot pepper sauce.

Babaganouj (Middle East). Eggplant and garlic spread or dip.

Baccalao (Caribbean). Dried, salted codfish.

Bagel (Jewish). Originally from Eastern Europe, it is in New York that this chewy, doughnut-shaped bread has been raised to the level of an art form; made with pumpernickel or white flour, plain or coated with poppy or sesame seeds, slathered with butter or cream cheese or draped with lox.

Baguette (France). Thin, long, crusty bread.

Baklava (Greece). The classic Greek pastry, made with layers of fillo dough and nuts bathed in syrup.

Bamy (Caribbean). Fish wrapped in a bread turnover, sold in many stand-up restaurants.

Barbuna (Greece). Red mullet.

Batido (Latin America). Sweet milkshake, often with a tropical fruit base (papaya, guava, pineapple, banana, etc.), trigo (wheat), or other flavors.

Bean threads (Asia). Thin, cellophane-like noodles.

Bialy (Jewish). An onion roll similar to a flattened bagel without the hole.

Biryani (India). A mild rice and (usually) meat dish.

Bistec a caballo (Colombia). Steak, cowboy-style; served with rice, salad, and fried eggs for hearty eaters.

Bistec criollo (Colombia). Steak in a spicy sauce.

Black pudding (Caribbean). Blood pudding.

Blintzes (Jewish). Crepes, typically filled with sweetened cheese or fruit.

Borscht (Eastern Europe). Thick soup; the classic is beet-based, served cold with a dollop of sour cream, although it may also be served hot and/or use a potato base.

Brazet (Middle East). Date cookies.

Brazo de mercedes (Philippines). Log cake.

Burec (Yugoslavia). Pastry filled with apple, cheese, or spicy ground beef.

Burrito (Mexico). Soft, rolled-up flour tortilla with filling.

Cachaca (Brazil). Sugarcane liquor used to make caipirinha.

Café con leche (Latin America). Espresso coffee with warm milk.

Caipirinha (Brazil). Alcoholic drink made with cachaca, sugar, ice, and pulverized lime.

Calabrese (Italy). "High" bread with soft dough.

Calaloo (Caribbean). Kale, crabmeat, and pork soup.

Calzone (Italy). Dough stuffed with cheese, sauce, and sometimes more; the calzone is Italy's answer to the empanada.

Cannelloni (Italy). Large tubular pasta, typically stuffed with cheese or meat and served in a cream or tomato sauce.

Cannoli (Italy). Dessert pastry, a deep-fried tubular cookie with ricotta cheese filling.

Capelletti (Italy). Tiny filled pasta, like tortellini.

Cappellini (Italy). A form of macaroni.

Caralla (Italy). Hard fennel-seed biscuit that is a staple of Bari, on Italy's southeastern coast.

Cassava (Caribbean, Latin America, Afro-American, and Brazil). Root similar to sweet potato and used in a variety of foods, including bread; also used to make tapioca.

Cavatelli (Italy). Shell-shaped pasta, good for soaking up sauces.

Cau cau (Peru). Tripe.

Cazuela de mariscos (Colombia). Seafood casserole.

Cebado (El Salvador). Bright-pink candylike flavoring used to make a cold drink (refresca).

Ceci (Italy). Garbanzos or chick-peas.

Ceviche (Latin America). Fish marinated in lemon or lime and served cold.

Challah (Jewish). Egg bread, traditionally braided.

Chalupas (Mexico). Indian word for tostadas, corn tortillas.

Cham cham (India). Fudgelike Indian sweet.

Changy root (Caribbean). West Indian cooking spice.

Chapati (India). Thin, crispy fried bread with spices.

Chicharrón (Puerto Rico). Fried pork rind.

Chicharrón de pollo sin huesos (Puerto Rico). Boneless chicken cracklings.

Chimichanga (Venezuela). Deep-fried flour tortilla stuffed with beef; served with guacamole.

Chruscik (Poland). A light pastry that is both crusty and crumbly; served with powdered sugar.

Cilantro (Latin America). Coriander, a remarkable, pungent herb used fresh as a spice and as a garnish.

Collard greens (Afro-American). Staple vegetable, usually boiled and served as a spicy side dish.

Congee (Cuban-Chinese). Thick, soupy stew.

Couscous (Morocco). A fine granular pasta that's steamed, not boiled; also gives its name to the classic Moroccan dish that includes meat (generally lamb) and a hearty vegetable sauce.

Cuban sandwich (Cuba). Toasted sandwich with pork, ham, cheese, and pickle.

Cuchifritos (Puerto Rico). Fried pork parts (ears, snout, etc.).

Dal (India). Yellow lentils, cooked and

served as a garnish that is a counterpoint to spicier dishes.

Dali-wada (India). Fried lentil balls in yogurt.

Debrecina (Czechoslovakia). Garlic-spiced pork and beef sausages.

Dim sum (China). Pastry buns, used more generally to refer to a variety of appetizers.

Doa (Sephardic Jewish). Bread spread made of ground sesame seed, walnuts, cumin, salt, and coriander.

Dokhla (India). Fried chick-pea cakes, often flavored with coriander.

Dolmades (Greece). Grape leaves, usually stuffed with rice and ground meat.

Dorowat (Ethiopia). Marinated chicken dish, garnished with hard-boiled egg.

Dulce (Argentina). A custardlike sweet, flavored with everything from chocolate to quince.

Egusi (West African). Cassava root used to make stews or ground as flour.

Empanada (Latin America). An envelope of deep-fried dough filled with meat and vegetables, sometimes spicy and sometimes not, according to the region, the whims of the chef, and what's on hand.

Empanada de leche (El Salvador). Empanada filled with ripe plantains that have been cooked with milk, cinnamon, and raisins.

Enchilada (Mexican). Soft, rolled-up corn tortilla with filling (usually meat).

Escabeche (Peru). Fish sautéed in oil and vinegar; served cold.

Fagioli (Italy). Kidney beans.

Farmer cheese (often made by kosher Eastern European Jews). A bland white curd cheese, similar to cottage cheese; often livened up with fruit, preserves, or even chocolate.

Felafel (Middle East and North Africa). Deep-fried garbanzo and spice balls; also refers to the pita bread sandwiches made with these balls.

Feojada (Brazil). The hearty national dish, a stew of black beans with sausage and other meats.

Feta (Greece). Salty white cheese, usually made with sheep's milk, that is common in Greece and (with variations) throughout the Balkans.

Filetillo (Venezuela). Chunks of steak in spicy tomato sauce.

Fillo (also spelled phyllo) (Greece). Paper-thin pastry dough used in many Greek sweets and in some other dishes, such as spanakopita.

Fitfit (Ethiopia). Tomato and onion stew, with pieces of injera bread cooked in.

Flaczki (Poland). Tripe soup.

Flan (Latin America). Custard bathed in a caramelized sugar sauce.

Flan con queso (Latin America). Flan with creamy white cheese on the side.

Flauta (Mexico). Deep-fried corn tortilla.

Flogera (Greece). Fillo-wrapped custard.

Frijoles (Latin America). Black, kidney, or pinto beans; often used to mean refried beans.

Garden egg (West African). Vegetable related to the green pepper.

Gefilte fish (Jewish). Traditional fish balls, made with various ground whitefishes.

Ghee (India). Clarified butter, used for cooking.

Ginseng (Asia). Pungent, gnarled root, used cooked or raw, as a spice or pharmaceutical.

Glabas (Middle East). Lamb and green pepper stew.

Gnocchi (Italy). Potato and flour dumplings.

Goraybe (Lebanon). Light, ring-shaped

cookies.

Gosh ka pakwhan (India). Lamb specialty.

Grits (Afro-American). Hominy grits, served with butter; a side dish at breakfast, lunch, and dinner.

Guanabana (Caribbean). Fruit, used in batidos and other drinks, also known as soursop.

Gumbo (Afro-American). Thick tomato-based soup, usually with shellfish, as in crab gumbo.

Gyoza (Japan). Fried dumplings.

Gypsy meat (Czechoslovakia). Heavily smoked and spiced bacon or steak.

Gyro (Greece). Lamb sandwich served in pita with tzatziki sauce.

Halawa be aljeban (Lebanon). Flaky, honey-sweetened cheese pastry.

Halo-halo (Philippines). Brightly colored ice drink with candied, canned, and fresh fruits and beans.

Haloumi (Greece). White Cypriot cheese.

Halvah (Middle East). Staple sesame-based sweet; large cakes of it, often flavored with pistachios, are in nearly every Middle Eastern food store.

Hawan samagi (India). Nonfood item: powder sprinkled on burning logs to create incense.

Hoisin (Korea). Fermented bean sauce.

Hummus (Middle East and North Africa). Cooked, mashed garbanzo beans, usually flavored with garlic, olive oil, and sesame paste. Served as a side dish.

Injera (Ethiopia). Millet bread, shaped like a pancake, used in lieu of utensils to scoop up food.

Jalowcowa (Poland). Salamilike sausage; no garlic.

Jaternice (Czechoslovakia). Pork sausage stuffed with rice or bread.

Jerk (Jamaica). Chicken or pork slowly barbecued with a strong, spicy sauce over a covered grill; a Jamaican favorite.

Kabanosy (Poland). Narrow, 2-foot-long dried sausage.

Kantaifi (Greece). Honey pastries, cooked in butter and covered with shredded dough.

Karela (India). Bitter melon/gourd.

Kasha (Jewish or Eastern Europe). Buckwheat groats, commonly served as a side dish with gravy.

Kasha varnishkas (Poland). Kasha and noodle dish.

Kebab (Middle East and Central Asia). Grilled meat, usually skewered.

Khanavi (India). Mixture of gram (chickpea) flour and buttermilk.

Kheer mohan (India). Milk-based sweet.

Kibbee (Middle East). Spicy ground lamb dish, often cooked with pine nuts.

Kielbasy (Poland). Finely ground pork sausage.

Kiszka (Poland). Sausage stuffed with blood, buckwheat, pork skin, fat, and liver.

Knish (Jewish). Eastern Europe's empanada: dough filled with a cheese, potato, cabbage, or kasha stuffing.

Koonafa be aljeban (Middle East). Honey-cheese pastry wrapped in a flaky dough.

Kopytka (Poland). Potato dumplings.

Kourabiedes (Greece). Cookies, topped with whole almonds and confectioner's sugar.

Krakowska (Poland). Sliced kielbasy.

Kugel (Eastern Europe and Germany). Potato or sweetened noodle pudding.

Kvas (Russia). Malt-barley drink.

Labneh (Middle East). Tangy yogurt spread.

Lahem jahne (Middle East). Flat bread, sometimes pita, covered with ground beef and mildly spicy tomato sauce—something like a pizza.

Lahmajun (Middle East). See Lahem jahne.

Latticini (Italy). Store selling primarily cheese and other dairy products.

Lavash (Lebanon). Paper-thin bread.

Legeplan (Philippines). Coconut custard.

Lomo saltado especial (Peru). Beef tenderloin fried with onions and tomatoes and served with rice and a fried egg.

Longaniza frita (Dominican Republic). Fried steak.

Lox (Jewish). Smoked salmon, best when sliced thin and piled on a bagel.

Ma'amul (Lebanon). Date pastries.

Malahi (Afghanistan). Curdled milk sweet.

Mamey (Caribbean). A kind of melon.

Mangu (Caribbean). Sweet plantains.

Manicotti (Italy). Tubular pasta; more generally refers to this pasta used in a creamy tomato-based dish.

Marcouk (Middle East). Thin, flat bread; often used to pick up food.

Maridas (Greece). Smelts.

Masa harina (Latin America). Fine corn meal, used to make tortillas.

Masala (India). General name for spice mixture; there are different masala combinations for different entrées (fish, meat, vegetarian, etc.).

Matambre (Argentina). Cold cut of rolled flank meat filled with eggs, parsley, spinach, carrots, and grated cheese.

Maté (Argentina). Green leaves used to make tea, which is traditionally brewed and served in a gourd.

Matzoh (Jewish). The unleavened bread that is a staple at Passover, the holiday celebrating the Jews' flight from Egypt.

Mauby (Jamaica). Drink made from bark that has a strong, medicinal flavor.

Mazamorra morada (Peru). Fruit compote.

Medianoche (Cuba). Sandwich, with a variety of meats.

Melizanosalata (Greece). Mashed roasted eggplant and garlic dip.

Melomakarouna (Greece). Orange-filled pastries covered with walnuts.

Mole poblano (Mexico). Sauce of unsweetened chocolate, chili, and spices; usually served on chicken or enchiladas.

Mondongo (Colombia). Tripe soup.

Mouloukhia (Sephardic Jewish). Egyptian green vegetable used in making soups and stews.

Moussaka (Greece). Meat and eggplant pie in cream sauce.

Mulligatawny (India). Pungent vegetable soup, usually with tomatoes and lentils, often flavored with coriander.

Mysliwska (Poland). Frankfurterlike sausage for barbecue.

Nopalitos (Mexico). Steamed cactus appetizer.

Nuoc nam (Vietnam). Ubiquitous condiment, made with fermented anchovies.

Orchata (El Salvador). Tan, nutty flavoring used in refrescas.

Orzapa (West Indies). Cane syrup.

Orzo (Greece). Pasta; uncooked, looks like thick grains of rice.

Ouzo (Greece). Aniseed liquor.

Paella (Spain and Latin America). Seafood and rice stew.

Pan caliendo (Puerto Rico). Hot bread.

Pan de casa (Italy). Round, crusty peasant bread.

Pan de queso (Colombia). Small, round bread made with cheese.

Pan de yucca (Colombia). Small, chewy bread made with yucca flour.

Pancit (Philippines). Noodle dish, typically including cooked meat or seafood, such as *pancit malabon*.

Paneer (India). Homemade cheese, similar to farmer or cottage cheese, used in cooking, as with spinach.

Panella (Italy). A round, flat, crispy bread.

Pappadam (India). Thin, crisp bread.

Paratha (India). Buttered and layered whole wheat bread.

Parrillada (Argentina). Mixed grill.

Pastele de carne (El Salvador). Similar to an empanada, stuffed with ground beef, and served with pickled cabbage on the side.

Pastellillo (Puerto Rico). Miniature patty stuffed with meat or fruit.

Pastilla (Puerto Rico). Patty with fruit or meat filling.

Patra (India). Leafy vegetable, like spinach.

Peas 'n' rice (Jamaica). A ubiquitous Jamaican dish, with rice and garbanzo beans (also called chick-peas, which is where the name comes from); the dish is seasoned according to the cook's whims, but includes everything from nutmeg to more pungent spices.

Pernil (Venezuela). Pork dish.

Picadillo (Cuba). Chopped meat.

Pirogen (Poland). Fried or boiled dumplings, filled with potato, cheese, meat, or sauerkraut.

Piselli (Italy). Pasta soup.

Pista burfi (India). Pistachio fudge.

Pita (Middle East). Round, flat bread with a pocket; often filled with felafel.

Placki (Poland). Potato pancakes.

Plantain (Latin America). Bananalike fruit, most commonly fried and served as a side dish.

Plato montañero (Colombia). Platter of ground beef, fried egg, fried pork, bread, and avocado.

Polenta (Italy). Cornmeal porridge.

Poori (India). Thin, pliable bread, best served fresh and puffy from the oven.

Pullao (India). Rice entrée.

Pulowrie (Jamaica). Mildly spiced cornmeal dumpling.

Pupusa (El Salvador). Similar to a small empanada stuffed with ground beef or cheese; served with pickled cabbage.

Queso frito (Caribbean). Fried white cheese.

Queso Oaxaca (Mexico). Melted cheese with sausage.

Ramen (Japan). Soup with noodles.

Ravioli (Italy). Pasta filled with cheese or ground meat; usually served with tomato sauce.

Refresca (Latin America). Iced drink.

Rice 'n' peas (Jamaica). Similar to peas 'n' rice, but coconut milk gives it a richer, creamier taste.

Ricotta (Italy). Creamy white cheese used in main dishes, such as lasagne, and in desserts.

Rigó jancsi (Hungary). Bittersweet chocolate cream pastry.

Roti (Jamaica). Large, thin crepelike bread stuffed with meat, seafood, or vegetable filling.

Salara (Guyana). Coconut bread.

Salep (Israel). Mediterranean orchid-petal drink, often served as a hot *digestif*.

Salumeria (Italy). Store selling primarily meat products, such as sausages.

Samosa (India). Fried dumpling, filled with spiced meat and vegetables.

Sancocho (Colombia). Thick soup with meat and vegetables, typically yucca and plantain.

Sans rival (Philippines). Layered napoleon cake.

Satay (Vietnam). Peanut-based curry sauce.

Schav (Eastern Europe). Cold "sour-grass" (sorrel) soup.

Schmalz herring (Jewish). Fatty herring from cold-water areas, such as the North Atlantic; typically pickled.

Sea moss (Jamaica). Drink made with a seaweed base and whipped into a frothy drink that looks something like a milkshake but has a unique, sweet taste.

Sfogliatelle (Italy). A seashell-shaped pastry of many layers, often filled with cheese.

Shashlik (Russia). Grilled, skewered meat.

Skordalia (Greece). Sauce of potato purée (or bread) flavored with garlic.

Smothered chicken (Afro-American). Broiled chicken drowned in gravy.

Sorrel (Jamaica). Carbonated drink with a fruity taste and an aftertaste like bubble gum.

Spaetzele (Hungary). Egg dumplings.

Spanakopita (Greece). Spinach pie.

Spanatirokopita (Greece). Cheese and spinach pie.

Spiedeni alla Romana (Italy). Deep-fried mozzarella sandwich.

Sushi (Japan). Raw or cooked seafood or vegetables wrapped in rice and rolled in seaweed.

Tabouli (Middle East). Salad made with cracked wheat; usually includes tomatoes and is spiced with a variety of herbs, such as oregano and thyme and sometimes mint.

Tahini (Middle East). Sesame paste.

Tamal (Latin America). A common and varied dish whose essentials usually include meat, rice, and cornmeal, wrapped in a plantain leaf or, in New York, aluminum foil.

Tamal de elote (El Salvador). Tamal filled with young, white corn cooked with milk, sugar, and sometimes raisins.

Tandoori (India). Marinated meat, poultry, or fish traditionally cooked in a clay pot in a charcoal oven.

Taramasalata (Greece). Caviar spread.

Taro (Japan). Root used in Oriental and Polynesian cuisine.

Teriyaki (Japan). Sauce marinade used to cook poultry, beef, or fish.

Tindora (India). Green vegetable resembling a small cucumber.

Tinola (Philippines). Chicken soup, with garlic, ginger, and onion.

Tofu (Japan). Soybean curd, cooked or eaten raw.

Tostone (Caribbean). Green plantain.

Touloubaki (Greece). Small oval-shaped fried semolina cakes dipped in honey syrup.

Tsoureki (Greece). Sweet, braided holiday bread.

Tzatziki (Greece). Cucumber, yogurt, and garlic dip, served on a gyro or as an appetizer.

Uthappam (India). South Indian–style pancake used as bread.

Vindaloo (India). A very spicy sauce, used on meat such as chicken and lamb.

Yetsom beyanetu (Ethiopia). Spicy combination of lentils and vegetables.

Yucca (Caribbean and Latin American). A starchy vegetable related to the yam, also called cassava.

Ziti (Italy). A tubular pasta, used in a baked dish of the same name.

Index

New York Notes

New York Notes